UNDERSTANDING VASCULAR PLANTS

UNDERSTANDING VASCULAR PLANTS

By
Dr. Pooja
Dept. of Botany
R.C.C. College
Ghaziabad (U.P.)
(India)

DPH

DISCOVERY PUBLISHING HOUSE PVT. LTD.
NEW DELHI-110 002

Published by:

Namit Wasan

DISCOVERY PUBLISHING HOUSE PVT. LTD.

4383/4B, Ansari Road, Darya Ganj

New Delhi-110 002 (India)

Phone : +91-11-23279245; 23253475; 43596065

E-mail : discoverybooksindia@gmail.com

discoverypublishinghouse@gmail.com

namitwasan9@gmail.com

web : www.discoverypublishinggroup.com

***First Edition:* 2010**

ISBN: 978-81-8356-547-9

Understanding Vascular Plants

Preface

The present title "Understanding Vascular Plants" has been written for those students interested in careers in diverse fields of biological sciences. It provides a structured approach to learning by covering all the important topics in a uniform, systematic format. The book has been comprehensively designed incorporating recent advances in this fast moving field. It also provides accessible information on molecular biology in compact form for undergraduate students in biology and related life sciences. It is intelligible to the educated layman, though it deals with some complex ideas. It is an adequate text for all the requirements of students in this area. In addition, busy lecturers who require a quick reference compendium will find it useful, particularly for tutional planning. Simple, yet hopefully clear figures and tables are provided throughout the book.

The over-riding goal of this book, and indeed of the whole *Understanding series,* is to present the essential information concering molecular biology in a compact, readily accessible form which leads itself to student learning and revision. The convergence of various approaches has generated a rich panorama of detail, the significance of which we are still attempting to unraval. The present text has been written as an introduction to this rapidly growing field.

To make the work more comprehensive and informative, the author has consulted many authoritative books, research journals, abstracts, monographs etc., so there can be no claim to originality except in the manner of treatment.

The author expresses his thanks to his friends and colleagues whose continue inspirations have initiated him to bring out this book.

The author expresses his gratitude to Mr. Wasan and staff of M/s Discovery Publishing House Pvt. Ltd. for their whole hearted cooperation in the publication of this book.

In the mean time, the author will remain sincerely responsible for any shortcomings of the book and be grateful to the readers for their suggestions and constructive criticism for the continuous betterment of the book. He takes this opportunity to appeal to the readers to send their suggestions straightaway to his Publisher.

Author

Contents

1

INTRODUCTION

It is generally agreed that life arose in an aquatic environment and then developed during more than 3 billion years. Terrestrial life, both plant and animal, is relatively recent in geologic time (inside front cover).

In the plant kingdom, *vascular plants* (having the conducting tissues *xylem* and *phloem*) evolved, colonized, and have come to dominate terrestrial habitats, so much so, in fact, that they are sometimes spoken of as "the *land plants*," a designation that quite overlooks many algae, fungi, liverworts, and mosses that share this same habitat.

Although the fossil record does not clarify for us the origin of vascular plants, it does reveal clearly that by Devonian times (inside front cover) considerable evolutionary diversification of these plants had already occurred, so that representatives of precursors of six or seven great lines of vascular plants are represented in the Devonian floras.

Their origin may have been monophyletic (forming a single evolutionary series) or polyphyletic (multiple or separate); in either case, a long prior period, during which diversification occurred (evidence for which is not yet available in paleobotanical data), must have preceded the Devonian floras.

Several evolutionary lines present in the Devonian floras are representatives of the divisions *Rhyniophyta*, *Zosterophyllophyta*, *Trimerophytophyta*, *Psilotophyta*, *Microphyllophyta*, *Arthrophyta*, *Pteridophyta*, and *Progymnospermophyta*; these will be discussed in the six chapters that follow.

Before beginning that discussion, some features of the classification and organization of vascular plants will be reviewed in the present chapter.

CLASSIFICATION OF VASCULAR PLANTS

Consideration of the modern period of plant classification may begin appropriately with the classification of Linnaeus, published in 1753 in his *Species Plantarum* and in 1767 in his *Systema Naturae*. In Linnaeus' summary, the vascular plants are dominant, since all but one of the 24 major categories of classification included vascular plants only.

The twentyfourth category, the Crypto gamia (Gr. *kryptos*, hidden, + Gr. *gamos*, marriage), Linnaeus characterized as plants having "flowers" scarcely visible to the naked eye, their sexual reproduction concealed.

In contrast, the remaining 23 divisions, often called "Phanerogams" (Gr. *phaneros*, apparent, + *gamos*, marriage), have flowers plainly visible and sexual reproduction (as manifested by stamens and pistils, according to Linnaeus) obvious or apparent.

In the period since Linnaeus, his group Cryptogamia (which included ferns and fernlike plants, mosses, liverworts, algae, and fungi) has been dismembered into a number of separate categories (inside back cover).

Furthermore, it has become clear that their sexual reproduction is not concealed or obscure. The terms "*Cryptogamia*" used by Linnaeus and "Phanerogamae" of earlier plant taxonomists' are no longer used as formal taxa in classification, nor do we use them in their original literal etymological sense.

Cryptogamic plants do not have "hidden" gametangia nor, conversely, are those of phanerogams exposed or obvious. In fact, quite the opposite is the case, because stamens and pistils are sporeproducing organs. The term cryptogam in current usage designates a plant lacking seeds.

All *phanerogams* are seedbearing and vascular; however, both nonvascular (algae, fungi, liverworts, and mosses) and vascular (*Psilotophyta*, *Microphyllophyta*, *Arthrophyta*, and *Pteridophyta*) *cryptogams* are known among the extant flora.

At present, there is a diversity of opinion regarding classification of vascular plants. According to one viewpoint, they are *monophyletic*, and vascular *tissuepostulated* to have evolved just ogceis the manifestation of their common origin. *Proponents* of this doctrine, accordingly, group all vascular plants in a single division, *Tracheophyta* (inside back cover).

However, that vascular tissue (i.e., *phloem*) evolved more than once is certainly evident from its presence in certain kelps.

Another group of botanists, impressed by:

(1) the evidence of the fossil record, which clearly indicates that there were at least six or seven distinct lines of vascular plants at the time (Devonian, inside front cover) they became prominent in the earth's land flora, and

(2) the fundamental diversities among the extant and extinct members of these lines (and later series), refuse to accept the unidivisional Tracheophyta concept. Alternatively, they have provisionally assigned divisional rank to the several classes of Tracheophyta (inside back cover) until such time as more compelling evidence of their relationship should become available.

This second alternative has been followed in classifying the vascular plants in the present text. Examination of the table on the inside back cover will reveal that, for the most part, the divisions of vascular plants as herein conceived correspond to classes and subclasses usually included under the single division Tracheophyta.

ORGANIZATION OF THE VASCULAR PLANT BODY

Most vascular plants are composed of welldifferentiated organs, both *vegetative* and *reproductive*. The former comprise the stem, root, and leaf; the latter include sporebearing organs, seeds, and fruits.

The Stem

Ontogeny of the Primary Stem

An'individual vascular plant may originate either sexually, as a zygote, or asexually, by growth of a fragment of the plant body. The fragment may be a totipotent single cell,' a group of cells (such as a callus or tissue culture), or a stem, leaf, or root cutting.

In the first alternative, the zygote develops initially into a seemingly undifferentiated' mass of cells, which subsequently differentiates both externally into organs (leaves, stems, roots) and internally with respect to component tissues.

These diverse tissues arise from localized groups of embryonic or *meristematic cells,* which are replicating themselves frequently. Such meristematic cells occur at the stem and root tips and in the young leaves. In a sense, the stem and root apices of vascular plants recapitulate continually the embryogenic development from the zygote, since these

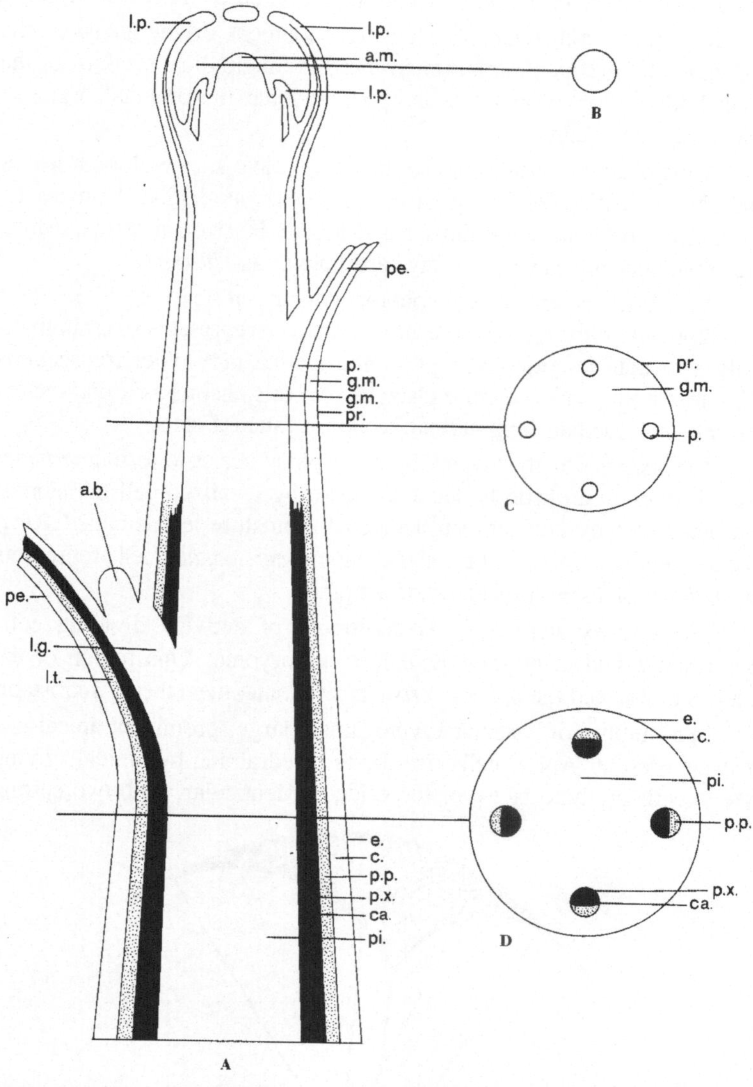

Figure 1.1: Stem ontogeny. A. Diagrammatic median longisection of a shoot apex. BD. Transections of same at levels indicated by lines. a.b., axillary bud; a.m., apical meristem; c., cortex; ca., cambium; e., epidermis; g.m., ground meristem; l.g., leaf gap; l.p., leaf primordium; Lt., leaf trace; p., procambium; pe., petiole; pi., pith; p.p., primary phloem; pr., protoderm; p.x., primary xylem.

apical groups of undifferentiated cells continue to reproduce themselves throughout the life of the plant, while some of their progeny differentiate.

It is most convenient to study development or ontogeny of the individual by means of serial transverse and longitudinal sections of the plant body. The axis or stem is apparently the fundamental organ in many vascular plants.

A majority of vascular plants, however, have axes with both leaves and roots. Leafy axes are often called shoots, as distinct from roots. Stems may be both subterranean and aerial. Horizontal stems, which are often, but not always, fleshy, are known as *rhizomes*.

Aerial stems are always photosynthetic, at least early in their development. Figure elsewhere in this chapter represents diagrammatically a median longitudinal section and increasingly older transections of a developing shoot; Figure elsewhere in this chapter is a *photomicrograph* of a median longitudinal section of such a stem.

The apex is usually covered by overlapping leaves to form a *terminal* bud. Leaves in an orderly sequence arise by localized cell division at various points on the stem surface. Each immature leaf is called a *leaf primordium,* and in its axil a small group of *meristematic* cells represents an *axillary bud*, the precursor of a branch.

The convex stem apex is composed of actively dividing cells accordingly said to be meristematic or embryonic. This region of the stem is designated the *apical meristem,* or, sometimes, the promeristem.

In a number of vascular cryptogams a large, prominent apical *cell* may be present. Apical cells may be tetrahedral and pyramidal, giving rise to cells on three faces, or threesided or lenticular, with two cutting

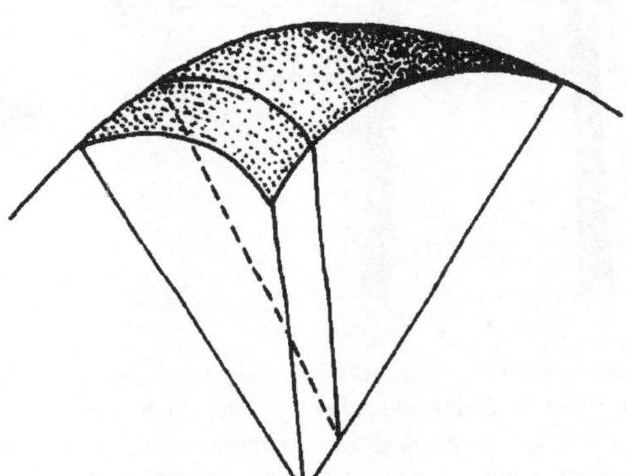

Figure 1.2: Tetrahedral type of apical cell from three faces of which derivative cells arise in stems (from all four sides in certain roots).

faces. In many Anthophyta (flowering plants) the apex is differentiated into a superficial layer, the *tunica* (in which most divisions are anticlinal), surrounding an internal *corpus;* the cell form and division patterns differ in these. At varying distances (in different species) from the apical meristem, the cells, although still meristematic, undergo divisions that result in their changing form.

Thus, there are organized at a level below the apical meristem the three primary *meristems,* namely, the *protoderm,* the *procambium* (sometimes called the provascular tissue), and the ground *meristem*. The procambium, depending on the species, may have the form of a central strand, a ring of strands, or a hollow cylinder.

From these three regions, as cell division abates, there differentiate the primary *mature tissues* of the stem. The protoderm becomes differentiated into the *epidermis*. This may produce various types of appendages such as glandular and nonglandular hairs and scales.

At maturity the living epidermal cells have their walls impregnated with the fatty substance cutin, and a common waxy layer, the cuticle, may cover the outer epidermal walls. The epidermis is interrupted periodically by intercellular fissuers surrounded by pairs of guard cells.

The opening and guard cells together form the *stoma (pl., stomata)* (Gr. *stoma*, mouth). Van Cotthem has summarized the organization, terminology, and classification of stomata. The stomatal complex includes the stoma (pore and guard cells) and those surrounding cells that participate in the mechanism of opening and closing the pore.

In some plants (e.g., *Equisetum*) these become modified as *subsidiary cells*. The ground meristem matures into the regions called the *cortex* and *pith*. The outermost cells of the cortex usually contain chloroplasts and, accordingly, are photosynthetic.

The inner layers of the cortex often function in storage. The cortex is composed mostly of thinwalled living cells, which together are called parenchyma *tissue*. Certain zones of the cortex may be composed of thickwalled cells, which provide support and rigidity to the stem.

The cell walls of the innermost layer of the cortex in certain cryptogams and in the rhizomes of other vascular plants may become specially thickened or otherwise modified to form an *endodermis*. The pith, when present, occurs in the center of the stem.

It is usually composed of relatively thinwalled parenchyma which functions in storage. The procambium or provascular tissue ultimately matures into vascular tissue, the primary xylem and primary *phloem,* the former lignified and functioning in the conduction of water and inorganic salts, and the latter cellulosic and functioning in the conduction of sugars and other complex compounds. At any given level, the primary phloem usually differentiates from the *procambium*, on the outer tangential surface of the latter.

The first phloem to mature, the *protophloem,* does so before elongation of the stem has ceased. Thus, much of the protophloem may be crushed and obliterated. The *metaphloem* matures from procambium after elongation of the stem has stopped. In the seedless vascular plants and in gymnospermous seed plants, the conducting agents of the phloem are *sieve cells*.

In the contiguous (lateral and/or terminal) walls of these, specialized *sieve areas* occur. These are places on the wall with fine pores through which delicate strands of protoplasm effect continuity of the cells.

In almost all flowering plants (angiosperms), the conducting elements of the phloem, *sieve tube members,* are joined in a series, the *sieve tube;* the individual members are separated terminally by *sieve plates*.

The latter may consist of single sieve areas (simple sieve plates) or of several sieve areas (complex sieve plates). In either case, the pores are usually larger than those in the sieve areas of nonangiosperms; they are lined with callose and transversed by relatively thick strands of protoplasm.

On the lateral walls of the sieve tube members are sieve areas similar to those of *nonangiosperms*. For a succinct and more comprehensive review of phloem. The sieve cells and sieve tube members, which are usually enucleate at maturity, are in some cases flanked by smaller, nucleate *companion cells*.

In addition, parenchyma cells (nonspecialized living cells, which here function in storage) and lignified fibers (supporting cells) may be present in phloem. With respect to the pattern or direction of differentiation of primary xylem from procambium, four relationships are common.

Their recognition depends on a distinction between two kinds of primary xylem, protoxylem and metaxylem. *Protoxylem* is the firstformed primary xylem, its elements usually smaller in diameter, differentiated before elongation of the organ has ceased, and lignified in annular or spiral fashion.

In contrast, the metaxylem differentiates after the protoxylem, its elements are larger in diameter, they mature only after elongation of the organ has ceased, and their secondary wall pattern is usually reticulate or pitted. The pits may be elongate (scalariform) or circular. However, there are transitions between protoxylem and metaxylem.

The four common patterns of primary xylem differentiation are exarch, *mesarch*, *endarch*, and *synchronous*. Three of these are illustrated in Figure elsewhere in this chapter and explained in its legend. The number of points at which protoxylem differentiates varies with the organ and the species.

An axis with only one group of protoxylem is said to be monarch; those with two are *diarch,* with three, triarch, and so on. The primary xylem may contain the waterconducting elements tracheids and/or vessels, parenchyma cells, and fibers.

One or another of these elements may be absent. *Tracheids* are elongate, with tapering, interlocking end walls, nonliving at maturity, their secondary walls occurring in various patterns of cellulose and lignin deposition.

These patterns of lignification, in order of increasing amounts of lignin deposited, are annular, spiral (helical), reticulate, and pitted (elongate to circular, often transitional). Intermediate patterns occur. Vessels are composed of series of tracheidlike members, the vessel members, between the walls of which perforations occur; these are thought to facilitate movement of liquids.

Vessel members or elements differentiate from a series of procambium cells, while each tracheid arises from only a single one. There is strong evidence that vessels have arisen phylogenetically by actual dissolution of the closing membranes of pit pairs in the sloping, contiguous terminal walls of adjacent tracheids.

Primitive vessels are composed of elongate tracheidlike segments, angular in transection, and are similar in pitting. The segments of the most specialized vessels are short, oval to circular in transection, have single large terminal perforations, and are quite unlike tracheids.

Vessels have arisen both from tracheids with circular and from those with elongate pits, as well as from elements with secondary thickenings characteristic of protoxylem and early metaxylem.

The changes in cellular organization during xylem differentiation have been summarized by Torrey, Fosket, and Hepler (1971). The rigidity of the primary stem depends on the amount of xylem and the degree of its lignification as well as on the presence of supporting tissue within the vascular tissue or elsewhere.

Fibers are elongate, heavily lignified cells, often with interlocking ends, which strengthen stems. Fibers and other lignified cells in the cortex (collectively termed sclerenchyma) also may contribute to support of the primary stem.

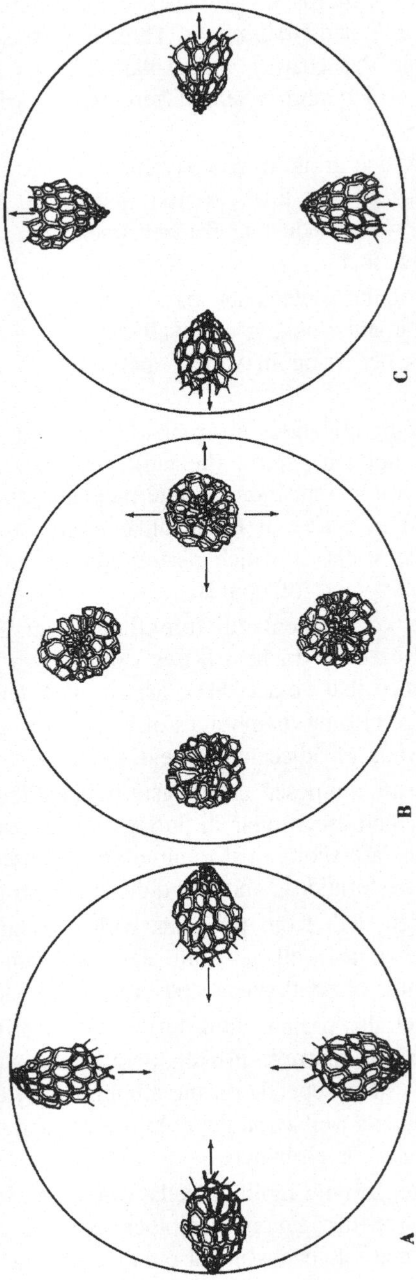

Figure 1.3: Diagrammatic illustrations indicating (by arrows) some common patterns of primary xylem differentiation from procambium. A. Exarch. B. Mesarch. C. Endarch.

Nodal Anatomy

The locus of leaf emergence on a stem is called the *node,* the portion of the stem that lacks leaves being the *internode*. In the preceding account of stem ontogeny, no consideration was given to the effect of the emergence of *leaf traces,* or vascular connections to the leaves, at or near the nodes, on the organization of the vascular tissue.

In some plants the traces are single and delicate, composed of only a few xylem and phloem cells, and their departure occasions little disturbance in the vascular tissue of the stem.

This is true of the incipient or vestigial traces of Psilotophyta and of the leaf traces of the Microphyllophyta. In the remaining vascular plants, a significantly large branch or several branches of vascular tissue pass out as leaf traces.

Although we speak of traces as "passing out," they, of course, do

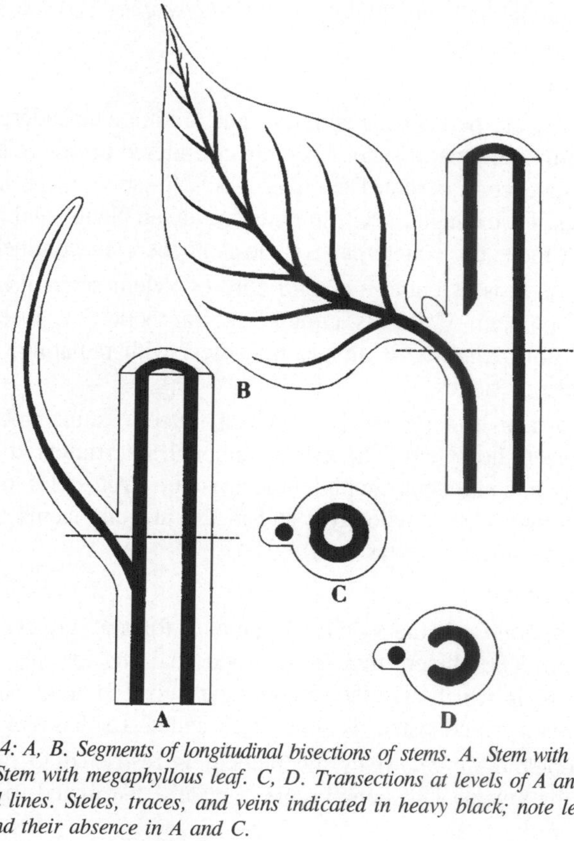

Figure 1.4: A, B. Segments of longitudinal bisections of stems. A. Stem with microphyllous leaf. B. Stem with megaphyllous leaf. C, D. Transections at levels of A and B indicated by dotted lines. Steles, traces, and veins indicated in heavy black; note leaf gaps on B and D and their absence in A and C.

not move but differentiate in position from precursor strands of procambium. Parenchyma cells may form a gap at and above the point of departure of the trace from the stele; this is a gap only in the sense that there is an interruption in the continuity of the xylem.

Steles

The xylem and phloem, the vascular tissue of the region of primary permanent tissues, together form the *stele* (L. *stela*, rod or column). Different arrangements of vascular tissue result in different stelar configurations among the vascular plants.

These different types will be summarized at this point because they are often useful attributes in discussions of classification and relationship of vascular plants.

The following types of stele occur: (A) the *protostele* (including the haplostele, the actinostele, and the plectostele), (B) the *siphonostele* (both amphiphloic and ectophloic), (C) the *dictyostele,* (D) the *eustele,* and (E) the *atactostele.*

Protosteles

Protosteles are perhaps the simplest, and are often considered to be the most primitive, type of stele. They are considered primitive because of their occurrence in certain Devonian fossils (in spite of the fact that siphonosteles, for example, occur in other Devonian plants) and because some see in them the counterpart of the Anthocerotan columella.

A *protostele* is essentially a solid core of xylem surrounded by a cylinder of phloem; if this is circular in transection, it is called a *haplostele*. An *actinostele* is simply protostele with radiating, coglike protuberances or ridges.

A *plectostele* is a protostele in which phloem is interspersed in masses between the xylem. The xylem, although interrupted at a given level, forms a continuous amphiphloic system. Protosteles occur in Psilotophyta and Microphyllophyta and in the juvenile stems of other groups (and in many roots as well).

The Siphonostele

In the *siphonostele* the xylem and phloem form a cylinder around a central pith. The phloem may be both external and internal, as it is in many ferns, in which case the siphonostele is said to be amphi*phloic*. An amphiphloic siphonostele is sometimes called a solenostele.

In ectophloic *siphonosteles* the phloem is restricted to the outer surface of the xylem. The siphonostele is widely distributed, occurring frequently in the ferns.

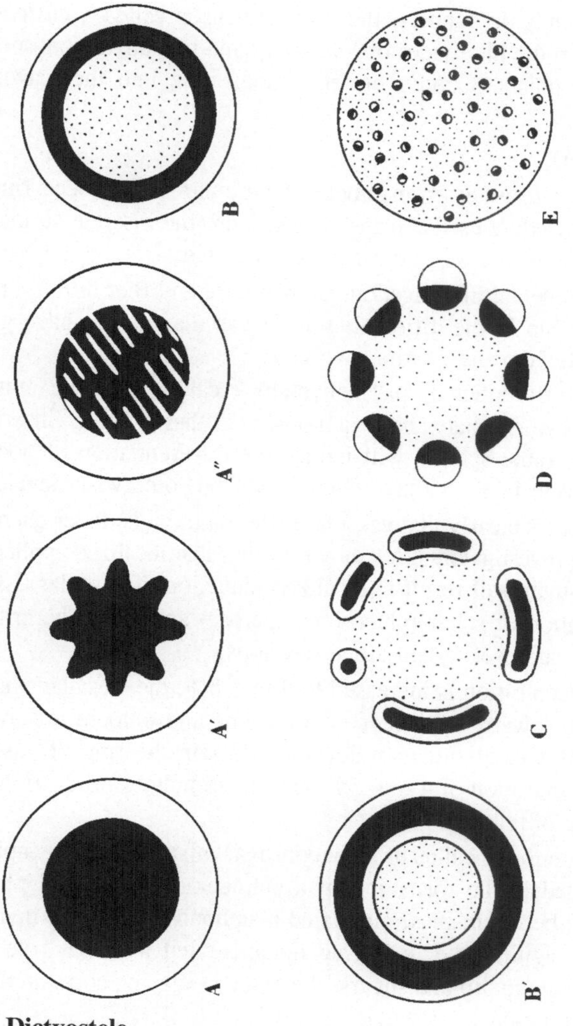

Figure 1.5: Types of stele, diagrammatic transections. AA". Protosteles. A. Haplostele. A'. Actinostele. A". Plectostele. B. Ectophloic siphonostele. B'. Amphiphloic siphonostele or solenostele. C. Dictyostele. D. Eustele. E. Atactostele. Xylem, black; phloem, white; pith, stippled.

The Dictyostele

In siphonostelic stems with short internodes, overlapping of the nodal leaf gaps results in dissection of the stele. As seen in transection, the stele appears as discrete strands or bundles, each surrounded by an endodermis and the phloem surrounding the xylem. A siphonostele thus dissected is called a *dictyostele*. This type of stele characterizes many ferns.

The Eustele

Where the xylem and phloem occur in discrete collateral or

bicollateral strands or bundles, the arrangement is called a *eustele*. A eustele occurs in the internodes of *Equisetum* and in many gymnosperms and flowering plants. Certain of the strands pass into the leaves as traces.

The Atactostele

An *atactostele* is an arrangement of vascular tissues occurring in many monocotyledonous flowering plants. Here the discrete strands of xylem and phloem are scattered through the stem.

The experimental investigations of Wetmore and Bier (1963) on the causal relationship in the differentiation of vascular tissues have given us some insight into the factors involved.

Using undifferentiated, parenchymatous callus in tissue culture, Wetmore and his associates have demonstrated that grafting (insertion) of buds of the same species will induce the differentiation of nodules of vascular tissue in the callus which would not otherwise develop.

This indicates clearly that vascular differentiation is under chemical control. These investigators have shown further that localized application of auxin and sugar will result in localized induction of vascular tissues. The concentration of sugar (glucose or sucrose) appears to be critical. At 1.5 to 2% sucrose, xylem alone develops.

If the concentration is increased to 3 to 3.5%, the vascular nodules develop xylem toward the center of the callus and phloem toward the periphery, and a cambium may develop and join the ring of vascular nodules. Concentration of 4 to 4.5% sucrose stimulates production of a preponderance of phloem.

Application to the callus of the auxinsugar mixture through capillary pipettes resulted in the formation of a cylinder of xylem and phloem with *cambium* between; these simulated a siphonostele. These investigations are of significance in having demonstrated a causal role of a growth hormone (auxin) and sugars, the latter in varying concentrations, in the differentiation of vascular tissues.

What is the evolutionary relationship among these various types of stele? It has been hypothesized that siphonosteles developed by progressive replacement of xylem elements by parenchyma cells in the center of protosteles.

This hypothesis is supported by the occasion of persistence of xylem elements (tracheids) in pith. This process may be designated *medullation,* a reference to the pith as "*medulla*." The dissection of siphonosteles in plants with short internodes by emergent leaf traces and associated gaps in many ferns suggested to some botanists that eusteles and atactosteles represent phylogenetic end results of the process of dissection. An alternate scheme proposes that *eusteles*, especially those of gymnosperms, arose by *fragmentation* of lobed prosteles into discrete *vascular* strands.

Secondary Growth

In most vascular cryptogams and in many flowering plants the axis is entirely primary in ontogenythat is, the component tissues differentiate entirely from the promeristem and primary meristems. In a few vascular cryptogams and in many seed plants, however, the primary tissues are augmented by the formation and differentiation of additional cells throughout the life of the individual.

This is called secondary growth because the added cells are derived from the cambium and cork cambium, which are secondary meristems. The *cambium* is a zone of meristematic cells between the primary xylem and phloem.

At least that part of the cambium that lies between the primary xylem and phloem originates from procambium. In axes with siphonosteles, the entire cambium would have such an origin. In eusteles and other dissected steles, the parenchyma cells between the vascular strands become meristematic at the inception of cambial activity within the strand so that a complete cylinder of cambium arises.

A preponderance of cells formed by tangential divisions of the cambium differentiate into the secondary *xylem*, which lies between the cambium and the primary xylem. Fewer of the outer derivatives of the cambium differentiate into secondary *phloem;* this lies between the cambium and the primary phloem.

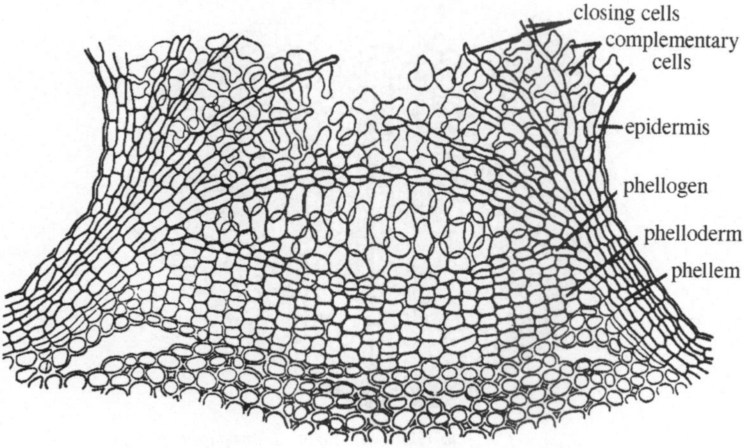

Figure 1.6: Transection of a lenticel of Prunus avium stem.

Accordingly, the vascular tissues increase radially in thickness as long as secondary growth continues. Where this is of long duration, stresses arise that rupture the epidermis and cortical tissue.

This or other factors stimulate the organization of the peripheral zone of meristematic cells, the *cork cambium,* or *phellogen,* either as a continuous cylinder or as localized strips. The outer derivatives of the phellogen are *cork cells,* or *phellem,* the impervious walls of which are thickened with suberin.

The internal derivatives are parenchyma cells, which may augment the cortex of the stem. As the corky layers replace the epidermis, there are organized *lenticels*, which apparently replace the stomata in function. Longcontinued cambial activity results in extremely woody stems as in trees and shrubs, or, if the cambium adds more parenchyma than secondary xylem cells, the stem, although augmented in diameter, may become fleshy rather than woody.

THE ROOT

The stems of all vascular plants except the Psilotophyta and *Salvinia* and a few exotic ferns bear roots. Roots differ externally from stems in not bearing leaves and in lacking nodes and internodes. Some of the epidermal cells of most roots, furthermore, produce absorptive protuberances called *root hairs*.

The apical meristem of the root is covered by a mantle of cells, the *root cap*. Branch roots, in contrast to stem branches, originate

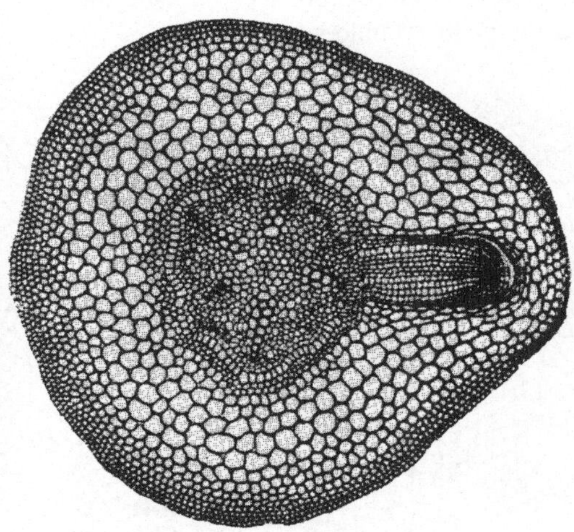

Figure 1.7: Phaseolus sp., bean. Transection of root showing origin of branch roots.

endogenously from the pericycle, a zone surrounding the vascular tissue of the stele and just within the endodermis; in some species they arise from the endodermis.

They grow through the cortex and epidermis into the soil. The procambium and primary vascular system in many roots are organized with a solid, central strand of xylem, which is exarch in ontogeny. Roots may be monarch to polyarch.

Between the protoxylem points in roots occur groups of primary phloem cells, so that primary xylem and phloem are radially alternate in roots rather than collateral or bicollateral as they are in stems.

The roots of some plants have a central pith. In all woody plants and in many herbaceous types, cambial activity in the root also results in secondary growth and increase in diameter and woodiness of that organ. Here the outer tissues (cortex and epidermis) may be sloughed off during secondary growth and replaced by corky layers, which originate from a phellogen organized in the pericycle.

THE LEAF

Leaves arise ontogenetically as meristematic emergences or primordia at the surface of young stems. Several layers near the stem surface may undergo active division to initiate the leaf. The primoridum at first consists largely of axis, but later marginal meristems, from which the bulk of the leaf blade develops, are organized on opposite sides of the axis.

In some leaves—those of many ferns, for example—a prominent apical cell functions in leaf ontogeny. At maturity, leaves vary widely

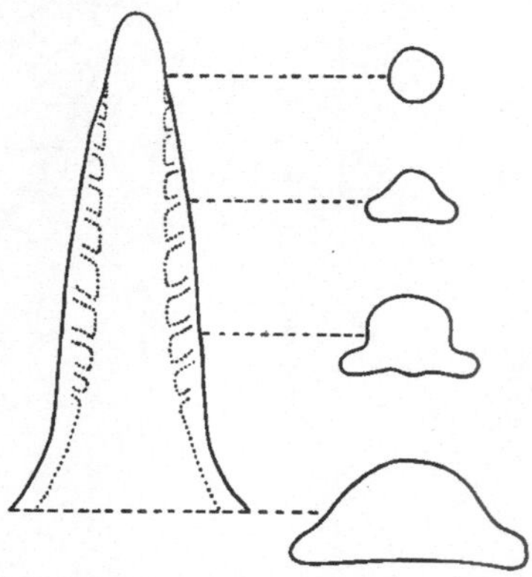

Figure 1.8: Tobacco: leaf ontogeny. Diagrams of leaf primordium and transections at four levels from apex to base; note midrib and marginal meristem in three lower transections.

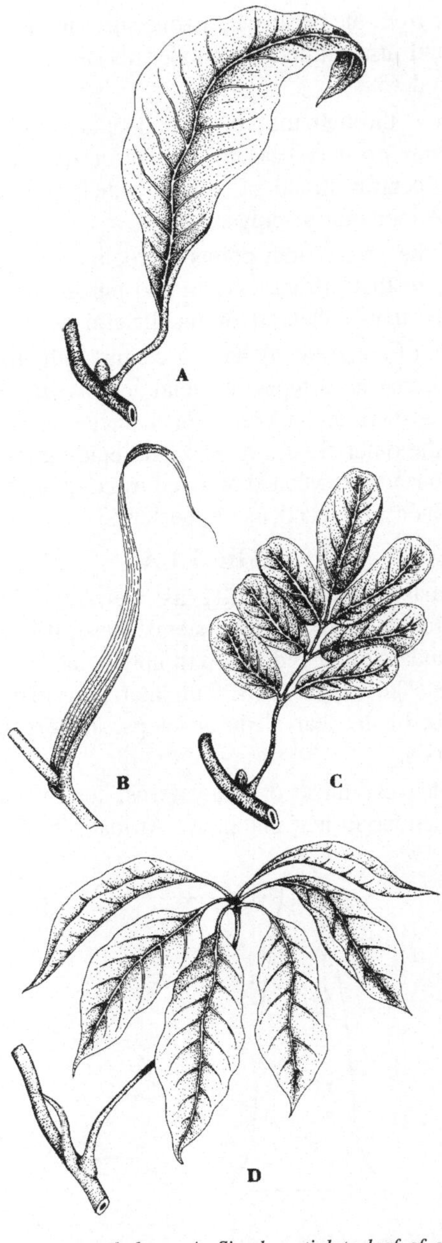

Figure 1.9: Leaves; gross morphology. A. Simple petiolate leaf of croton. B. Sessile, simple leaf of a grass. C. Pinnately compound leaf of a legume, Sophora. D. Palmately compound leaf of Schefflera sp.

in both external and internal organization. They may be *simple leaves,* with undivided blades, or variously *compound,* with divided blades.

They may be *petiolate* or *sessile* in their attachment to the axis. The vascular tissue of the leaf, the veins, may be unbranched (Microphyllophyta, *Equisetum*) or variously branched. Open *dichotomous* venation occurs in many ferns and *Ginkgo*.

In many monocotyledonous flowering plants, the venation is striate, the main veins being elongate and connected at intervals by deli cate, transverse, ladderlike veins. In certain ferns and in many dicotyledonous flowering plants, venation is *reticulate,* the veins being abundantly branched and anastomosing.

Intermediate types of venation also occur. Histologically, most leaves are relatively simple, being covered by a more or less heavily cutinized epidermis (with stomata on the lower, upper, or both epidermal layers); veins and photosynthetic cells, the *mesophyll*, lie within. In some species the latter is differentiated into palisade and spongy zones.

Comparative morphology distinguishes between two categories of leaves in vascular plants, *microphylls* (in the Microphyllophyta and Arthrophyta) and *megaphylls (megaphyllous*), which occur in all other groups. Microphyllous leaves are usually of small size (although there are exceptions, such as those of *Isoetes*, and certain fossil Microphyllophyta) and have single, unbranched veins, traces to which leave no gap in the stem stele.

By contrast megaphylls are usually large and have richly branching veins, and their leaf traces leave gaps in the stem stele. Microphylls and megaphylls may be of quite different phylogenetic origin. The scalelike emergences on the stems of certain Psilotophyta, which lack veins, may well represent precursors of microphyllous leaves.

In some species and for some of the scales, traces leave the stem stele but end in the cortex short of the leaf base. Microphyllous leaves differ from these only in that the trace continues into the leaf to form its single vein.

Microphylls then, if this view is correct, would be simple enations or emergences from the stem surface, which ultimately became vascularized. Megaphylls, on the other hand, since the late nineteenth century, have usually been considered to represent modified stems that originated in evolution from the more distal branches of axes.

In this development, it has been suggested, the first step was a change from dichotomous to monopodial branching by dominance and *overtopping* of one dichotomy. The second modification was restriction

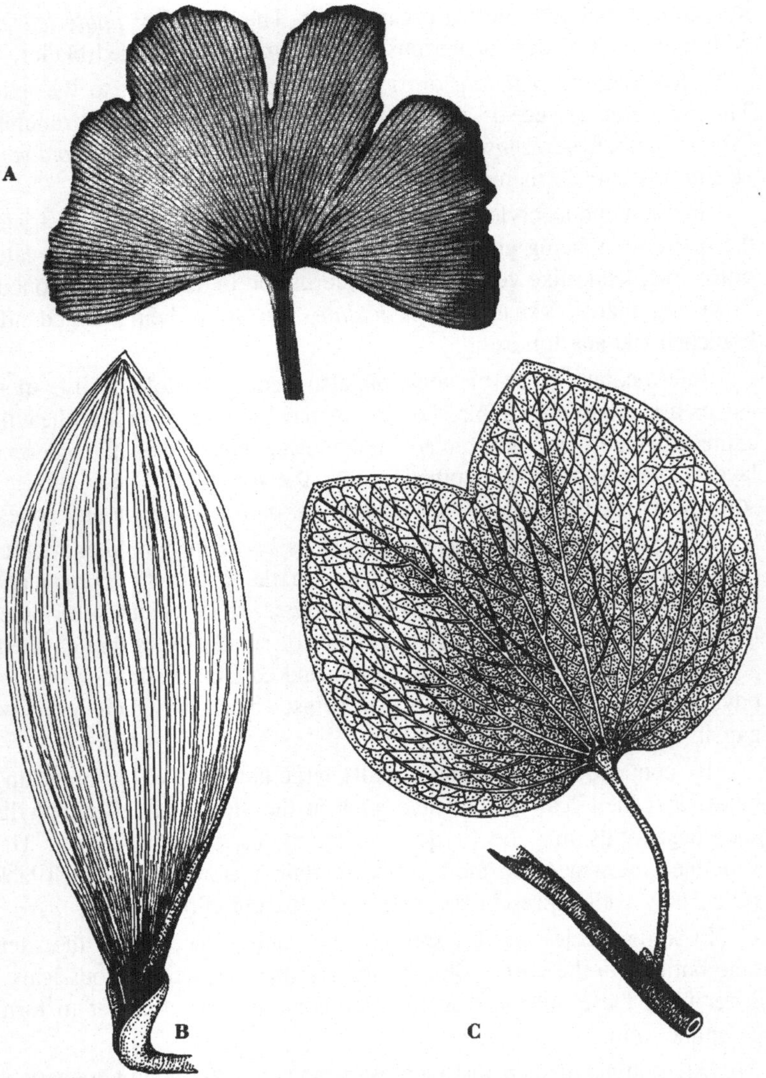

Figure 1.10: Types of venation. A. Opendichotomous, Ginkgo biloba. B. Striate venation in Clintonia. C. Reticulate or netted venation in Bauhinia leaf.

of the remaining dichotomies to one plane, planation. Finally, there occurred lateral fusion and *webbing* to form the leaf blade.

These did not all necessarily occur in the same plant or in that order. (The presence of open dichotomous venation in the leaves of many ferns and the prolonged apical growth in development of fern leaves are cited as evidence for this interpretation. Although it was stated above that the supposed phylogenetic origin of the microphyll was quite different from that of megaphylls, there is an alternative interpretation, namely, their origin by reduction.

The phenomena of overtopping, planation, webbing, and reduction are discussed further in other chatper of this book. The preceding paragraphs have presented a brief summary of some fundamental concepts regarding the organization of the vegetative body of the vascular plants.

The organization and functioning of the reproductive structures of the vascular plants are discussed with the representative types where these are described in the remaining chapters of this text. More detailed and comprehensive discussion of the material briefly referred to in this chapter will be found in the texts by Esau (1965), Cutter (1969, 1971), and Fahn (1974).

2

VASCULAR CRYPTOGAMS I: DIVISION PSILOTOPHYTA

This chapter and in other chapters of this book will discuss the seedless vascular plants, often called *vascular cryptogams*. In this book they are classified in eight divisions, some of which contain only extant, some only extinct, and some both types of organisms.

In the earlier editions of this book, and in a number of others, there were included in the division Psilotophyta[1] two genera of living plants (*Psilotum* and *Tmesipteris*) and a rather heterogeneous assemblage of extinct genera, including *Psilophyton*, *Rhynia*, and *Asteroxylon*, mostly Devonian (inside front cover) plants.

New information obtained by paleobotanists about the latter has resulted in their reclassification into other groups. Furthermore, it has recently been proposed that the two living genera (*Psilotum* and *Tmesipteris*) have affinities with the ferns (Pteridophyta).

However, for the present, in this text, they are retained in the division Psilotophyta as its sole representatives. Of the vascular plants, the members of the Psilotophyta have the least complex organization.

The plants consist of sparsely, or profusely, dichotomously branched axes arising from subterranean, rootless rhizomes. Their synangia are borne on short lateral branches and hence are cauline.

Their gametophytes are cylindrical, subterranean, and saprophytic, and their sperms are multiflagellate. A single order, Psilotales, and family, Psilotaceae, including two genera, *Psilotum* and *Tmesipteris*, constitute the division as herein conceived.

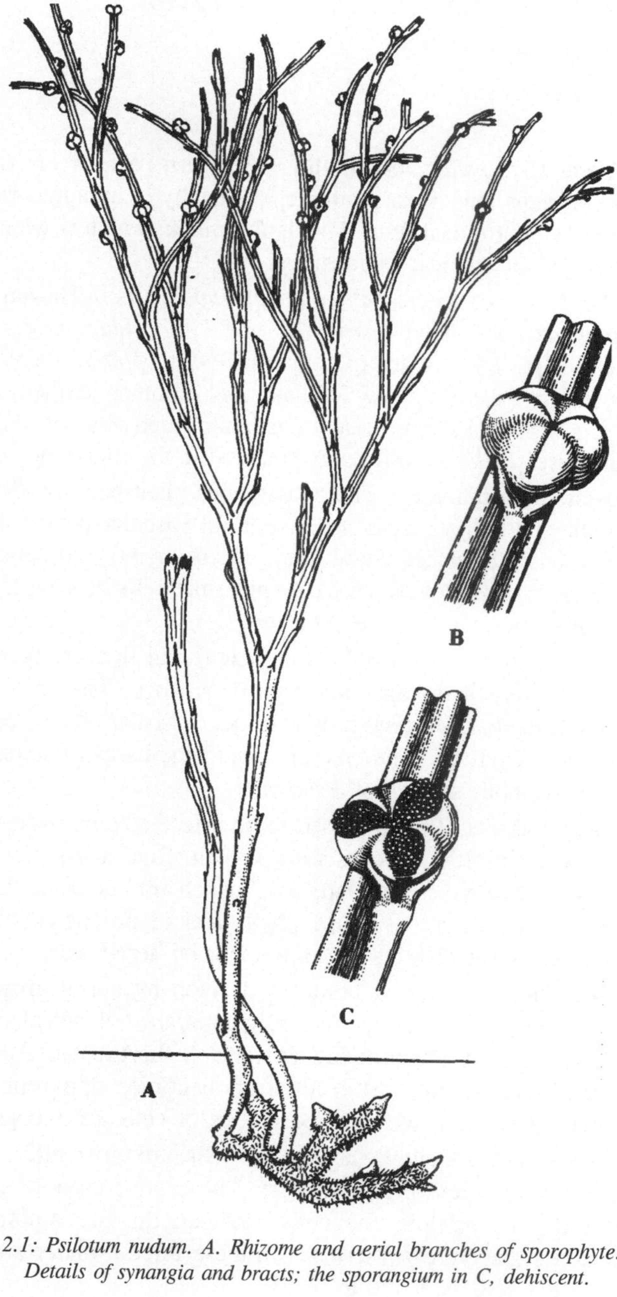

Figure 2.1: Psilotum nudum. A. Rhizome and aerial branches of sporophyte. B, C. Details of synangia and bracts; the sporangium in C, dehiscent.

CLASS I. PSILOTOPSIDA

Order 1. Psilotales

Family 1. Psilotaceae

Psilotum

Psilotum (Gr. *psilos*, bare), the whisk fern, occurs in Arizona, Florida, Louisiana, and Texas, either epiphytically or in humus-rich soil and also grows in tropical Asia. This is *P. nudum*, which is widespread in tropical and subtropical regions.

Of the two other species, *P. complanatum* occurs in Hawaii and is erect, abundant, and widely distributed, and *P. flaccidum* is pendulous. *Tmesipteris* (Gr. *tmesis*, act of cutting, + Gr. *pteris*, fern) grows natively only in Australia, New Zealand, and on other southern Pacific islands. Because of its more ready availability and ease of culture in the greenhouse, *Psilotum* will be emphasized in the following account.

Vegetative morphology. The conspicuous plant body of *Psilotum*, which is the sporophyte, as is the case in all vascular plants, consists of dichotomously branched aerial axes, 30 cm or more in height, and of subterranean rhizomes which have epidermal cells bearing rhizoids; the latter may be one to three cells long.

The aerial stems are ridged, often pentagonal in cross sections of the lower portions of the axis and triangular above. They bear small, scalelike appendages, *prophylls*, which lack vascular tissue, although vascular traces from the stele emerge toward the bases of some of the scale leaves in both species of *Psilotum.*

Roots are absent. *Psilotum* used to be prized as a cultivated plant, in Japan and about 100 varieties were known. Rouffa has described a variety, called *Bunryu-zan* in Japanese, which differs from the usual *P. nudum* in lacking scales or prophylls and in producing multiple, terminal synangia at the tips of some elongate aerial axes.

Both rhizome and aerial branches develop by apical growth that may be traced to the activity of a single tetrahedral apical cell and its derivatives, all of which divide actively. A short distance posterior to the apical meristem, differentiation becomes apparent in the meristematic tissues, in which three groups of cells are recognizable.

In the outermost single layer, the cells are prismatic, radially elongate, and constitute the *protoderm*. The central mass of elongate cells is the *procambium*; the cells between the procambium and protoderm are the *ground meristem*. In these three *primary meristems* the component cells continue to divide.

The organization of the aerial axes and rhizomes of *Psilotum* upon completion of differentiation is somewhat variable, according to the level between apex and base and the diameter of the axes. The erect stems may be almost circular in transection as they emerge from the soil, but toward the lowermost (first) dichotomy they are often pentagonal and between the more distal dichotomies, triangular.

The stele also changes at different levels and in different individuals. Thus, it may be triarch or tetrarch at soil level; of much greater diameter and pentarch to octarch approaching the first dichotomy; and tetrarch, triarch, or diarch in the most distal dichotomies.

Furthermore, the stele is mesarch at the base of the aerial shoot, and this condition may extend beyond the first dichotomy. More distal portions of the axes are exarch. The stele of *Psilotum* has been interpreted as a protostele (actinostele) by some and as a siphonostele by others.

This is because the stem center is composed of lignified, sclerenchymatous cells that may belong either to the xylem (protostelic interpretation) or represent a sclerotic pith (siphonostelic interpretation).

It should be noted that the stele always develops from a solid core of procambium. The phloem of *Psilotum* has recently been investigated. The mature phloem cells are devoid of nuclei and have oblique or transverse terminal walls.

The latter are organized as a large sieve area. Single, prominent pores occur in the lateral walls common to the sieve elements and parenchyma cells. Sieve cells, with sieve areas in their oblique terminal walls, are present.

Their nuclei disintegrate as the cells mature. A prominent endodermis surrounds the stele. The cortex is massive as compared with the stele and consists of a parenchymatous storage region adjacent to the endodermis.

This is surrounded successively by a zone of scierenchyma and by several layers of photosynthetic parenchyma cells. The latter represent the major photosynthetic region of the plant, and the increase of the internal surface of the cells by lobing suggests the chlorenchyma in the leaves of certain conifers.

The cortical cells of rhizomes frequently contain fungi. The fungi regularly associated internally and externally with roots and rhizomes are called mycorrhizal fungi and the association is termed *mycorrhiza*. Went and Stark (1968) have rather comprehensively discussed mycorrhizae.

The epidermis is heavily cutinized and interrupted here and there, between the ridges of the stem, by stomata and guard cells, the latter slightly sunken, as in many xerophytes. A small substomatal chamber is present beneath each stoma.

The scalelike appendages of the stem lack vascular tissue and are made up entirely of photosynthetic tissues covered by an epidermis. As noted previously, vascular traces may extend from the stem stele to the bases of some of the prophylls.

Reproduction: the sporophyte. Spores are produced in complex, trilobed structures called synangia, which are borne on the enlarged apices of short lateral branches. The synangia are, therefore, *cauline*. It has been suggested that the synangium represents three phylogenetically united sporangia.

Two basal emergences curve about the synangium and its stalk. The latter is transversed centrally by a trace, which is connected with the stele of the main axis. The trace extends into the base of the synangial partition and divides into three branches.

As noted earlier, the synangia usually arise on branches on limited growth, the earliest stages being at the growing apices of the aerial stems. Rouffa has reported that in an appendageless Japanese variety, as well as in certain appendaged (with prophylls) races of *P. nudum*, the synangia are terminal on the main axes, sometimes exclusively so.

In development, three superficial groups of cells just below the apex of the immature branches divide *periclinally* (parallel to the surface) into two layers. The outer, by subsequent anticlinal and periclinal divisions, forms the several-layered sporangial wall, while the inner cells divide repeatedly to form the sporogenous tissue and *tapetum*.

The latter is several layers of cells thick, but their walls disintegrate during sporogenesis to form a *tapetal plasmodium*, a multinucleate mass of nutritive protoplasm. Later the cells of the sporogenous tissue function as sporocytes. The latter undergo the meiotic process, forming tetrads of spores that ultimately separate.

The mature spores are colorless and kidney-shaped and have transparent walls. During sporogenesis, the synangial wall undergoes thickening by additional deposition of wall material. However, three vertical layers remain thin-walled and, upon drying, serve as the sites of dehiscence.

The pattern of synangial development just described, which characterizes the development of the sporangia in a number of other vascular cryptogams, is said to be *eusporangiate*.

In such a process, as noted, the synangium (or sporangium) arises from superficial cells that divide periclinally. By further divisions, the outer cellular products of the division form a several-layered, sterile enclosure or wall around the sporogenous tissue; the latter develops by further division of the inner (subsuperficial) cell layer.

The dichotomy into wall and tapetal development from the outer (more superficial) layer and of sporogenous tissue from the inner, is not absolute in all cases. Some sporogenous cells may arise from cells derived from descendants of the superficial layer and, in plants with a two-layered tapetum, the outer layer may differentiate from the sporangial wall and the inner from the sporogenous tissue.

This type of sporangial development is in contrast to that of many, but not all, ferns, in which sporangial origin may be traced to a single superficial embryonic cell. The cell undergoes more or less of a periclinal division or a series of transverse divisions in what is often designated as *leptosporangiate development*.

While in general eusporangiate sporangia (and synangia) differ in method of development, often in wall thickness, are larger than typical leptosporangiate sporangia, and, in contrast to the latter, have an indefinitely large number of spores, there have evolved variations in sporangial development that give some evidence of intergradation.

Reproduction: the Gametophyte

The spores of *Psilotum* are slow to germinate; they have so far not been grown into mature gametophytes under laboratory conditions. Whittier succeeded in germinating the spores of *P. nudum* in axenic culture in defined media. Germination occurred only in darkness, although less than 0.1% germination occurred.

So far, Whittier has not succeeded in growing the gametophytes to sexual maturity (personal communication). The gametophytes found in nature are cylindrical, rarely more than 2 mm in diameter, are sometimes forked, and are covered with numerous rhizoids.

They lack chlorophyll and are saprophytic, possibly because of their association with an endophytic fungus. They have little internal differentiation. Their *cylindrical* form, *dichotomous* branching, and subterranean habitat render them difficult to distinguish from young rhizomes without *microscopic* examination.

The occasional presence of tracheids, phloem, and endodermis in the center of gametophytes, along with their cylindrical form and rhizoids, have been interpreted as an incipient or reduced stele and as support for the homologous theory of alternation of generations, according to which sporophytes and gametophytes are merely different manifestations of a single ancestral plant body. It should be noted that the gametophytes in which vascular tissues have been observed have been shown to be diploid; apparently most greenhouse specimens of *Psilotum* are tetraploid.

The sex organs develop from surface cells of the monoecious gametophytes. The antheridia are hemispherical and slightly protuberant, the single layer of jacket cells enclosing a small number of coiled, multiflagellate sperms.

The *archegonia* are partially sunken with the gametophyte and have necks that are much shorter than those in the Hepatophyta and Bryophyta. The necks are composed of only four rows of neck cells.

Reproduction: Embryogeny

Following fertilization, the zygote undergoes transverse division. The outer product of the division gives rise to the embryonic stem; the derivatives of the inner one are organized as an enlarged foot.

The primary stem is a branched rhizome, which develops rhizoids and becomes infected with a fungus as it emerges from the gametophyte.

Some of the branch tips become negatively geotropic and produce aerial axes when they are exposed at the soil surface. By this time the embryonic stem usually has separated from the foot, which remains within the gametophyte.

Tmesipteris

Tmesipteris is a pendulous epiphyte on the trunks of tropical tree ferns, or it may be terrestrial and erect. Both flattened and radially symmetrical species are known.

The plant consists of branching, rhizoid-bearing rhizomes, which anchor it, and aerial branches, which may be unbranched or undergo one or several dichotomies, depending on the species.

From base to apex, the scalelike, nonvascular appendages are succeeded by small flattened leaves, each of which is transversed by a single, central unbranched vein connected to the stele by a trace.

The fact that the stem apex itself is modified as a leaf has suggested that the "leaves" of *Tmesipteris* may represent flattened branchlets.

The synangia of *Tmesipteris* also are subtended by a pair of bracts and are bilobed. The gametophytes are similar to those of *Psilotum*.

3

Vascular Cryptogams II: Division Microphyllophyta

Members of the division Microphyllophyta (*Gr. mikros*, small, + Gr. *phyllon*, leaf, + Gr. *phyton*, plant), a group accorded only subdivisional rank under the name Lycopsida in many schemes of classification (inside back cover), are readily distinguishable from the Psilotophyta by having vascularized leaves and roots and by the intimate association of their sporangia with fertile leaves known as *sporophylls* (Gr. *spora*, spore, + Gr. *phyllon*, leaf).

Some of these plants are commonly known as club and spike mosses,' because their small size and their mosslike leaves, closely arranged on the stems, suggest mosses; furthermore, the aggregation of the sporophylls of certain species into terminal groups has suggested the terms "club" and "spike."

Whether they are given class or divisional rank, two series are usually distinguished in the classification of these plants. In one series, exemplified in this chapter by the extant *Selaginella* and *Isoetes* and by the extinct *Selaginellites* and the Lepidodendrales, each leaf produces a small, basal protuberance, the *ligule* (*L. ligula*, little tongue).

These genera are grouped in the class Glossopsida (Gr. *glossa*, tongue, + Gr. *opsis*, appearance of), sometimes called the Ligulatae; in the other series, the Aglossopsida, the ligule is absent. The extant *Lycopodium* and, *Phylloglossum* and the extinct *Protolepidodendron* belong in the latter category.

CLASS 1. AGLOSSOPSIDA

The *Aglossopsida* include the single order Lycopodiales, family Lycopodiaceae with extant species.

Lycopodium

Introduction and vegetative morphology. *Lycopodium* (Gr. *lykos*, wolf, + Gr. *pous*, foot) and *Phylloglossum* (Gr. *phyllos*, leaf, + Gr. *glossum*, tongue), the only living genera included in this class, comprise 200 to 400 species. *Phylloglossum*, of which only a single species is known, occurs only in Australasia. Species of *Lycopodium* are widely distributed and are familiarly known as "ground pines," "trailing evergreens," and "club mosses."

Most species are perennials, living on the forest floor in temperate climates, but some tropical species are pendulous epiphytes. The plants are rather firm herbs with dichotomously or pseudomonopodially branched stems. In the latter case the branch system consists of a main axis that supports minor branches.

The latter represent members of dichotomies that failed to develop to as great an extent as their counterparts. The genus *Lycopodium is* a large one and it has not infrequently been suggested that it be divided into several genera.

Wilce (1972) has discussed this but recommends retention of the diverse species within the single genus *Lydopodium* in three subgenera—*Urostachya*, *Lepidotis*, and *Lycopodium.* Bruce (1976b) has tabulated the sporophytic and gametophytic characteristics of these three subgenera.

The leaves are small, sessile, and spiral or whorled in arrangement. Chu described the anatomy of the leaves of 31 species. The stomata may be adaxial, abaxial, or both, depending on the species. In *L. complanatum*, the leaves are much reduced and almost scalelike.

All species have branching rhizomes from which aerial branches develop. The roots are delicate and dichotomously branched and are scattered along the underground portions of the stem. The roots of some species of *Lycopodium* arise deep within the stems, not superficially like those of most vascular plants.

They grow through the cortex and emerge into the soil at points somewhat removed from the level of their origin. Stevenson described the phyllotaxis, stelar morphology, and gemmae of *L. lucidulum.*

The pattern of stem and leaf development has been investigated by Freeberg and Wetmore, who emphasized that it is difficult to analyze. Development of both the stem and root of *Lycopodium* may be traced

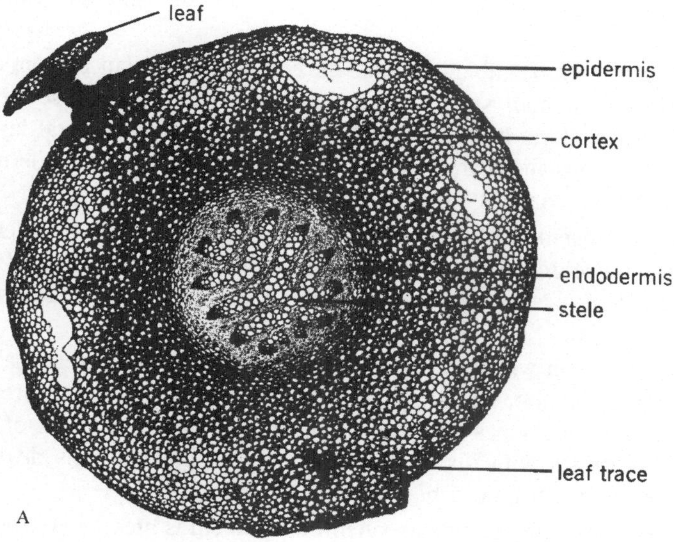

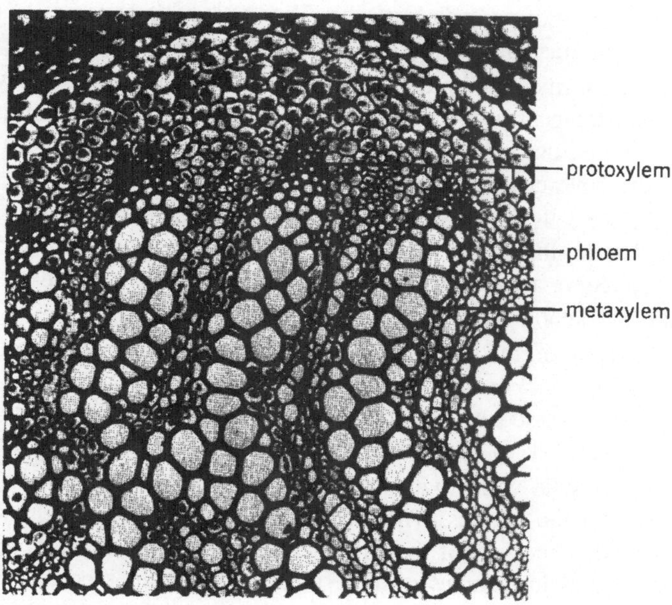

Figure 3.1: Lycopodium clavatum. A. Transection of stem showing protostele (plectostelar type). B. Portion of stele more highly magnified.

to an apical group of meristematic cells, no one of which is specially differentiated.

A central procambium strand develops some distance from the promeristem in both stem and root and ultimately gives rise to an exarch protostele in both. The stem stele is bounded by several layers of pericycle cells and sharply delimited by a well-developed endodermis. The epidermis contains stomata and guard cells.

The arrangement of xylem and phloem in the stem varies in different species, in accordance with the degree of ridging or dissection of the central xylem mass. It also varies within a species in accordance with stem diameter.

In species in which the xylem seems to consist of discrete masses in transverse section, serial transverse sections reveal that the apparently discrete units are lobes that join each other at different levels of the stem. In species with dissected xylem masses, phloem cells develop between them, forming a *plectostele.*

In species with continuous xylem, the phloem is present external to the xylem. Functional phloem is, however, always separated from the xylem by a layer of parenchyma cells. The conducting elements of the xylem are all tracheids.

The first formed are lignified in annular fashion; these are followed later in development by tracheids with circular bordered pits, and last, by those with elongate (scalariform) bordered pits. The sieve cells of the phloem have tapered ends.

The sieve cells may have thickened walls early in development, but in those that do, the wall is eroded, seemingly by the protoplast, during maturation. Sieve areas with plasmodesmata and pores occur in both the terminal and lateral walls of the sieve cells in *L. lucidulum.*

Two types of mucilaginous canals are present in some species (subgenus *Lepidotis*) or only one in the subgenus *Lycopodium.* They are *veinal,* that is, associated with the leaf vein, or *basal,* the latter a cylindrical network in the cortex of the strobilar axis.

The root stele varies with the size of the root in a given species and also with the species. The exarch stele may be crescentic with phloem in the concavity of the xylem crescent, as in *L. lucidulum*, or a plectostele, as in *L. complanatum*; other configurations occur.

The tip of the root is covered by a root cap. The root hairs are anomalous in that they develop in pairs from the epidermal cells. Roots of *Lycopodium* usually branch dichotomously; the branches originate through the reorganization of the apical meristematic cells into two groups. The leaves of *Lycopodium* arise by localized growth of groups of superficial cells near the stem apex.

As they grow, each develops a central procambium strand, which finally differentiates into a vascular strand of tracheids surrounded by scattered sieve elements and parenchyma. The chlorenchyma of the leaf is rather uniform in structure, small intercellular spaces being present.

Depending on the species, the stomata occur either on the epidermis of both leaf surfaces or only on the lower epidermis. The vascular supply of the leaf is connected to the stem stele by a leaf trace, which is connected with the protoxylem of the stem stele.

Leaves with a single unbranched vein, the traces of which leave no parenchymatous gap in the stele above its point of departure, are said to be *microphyllous*.

It should be emphasized at this point that small size is merely a secondary attribute of some microphylls; their single, unbranched veins and the absence of leaf gaps near the point of departure of their traces from the stem stele are their distinguishing features.

Reproduction: the sporophyte. Species of *Lycopodium*, such as *L. lucidulum*, in which the sporophylls are not localized in compact aggregations, in many instances produce special mechanisms for vegetative propagation, namely, gemmae or *bulbils*.

These consist of a proximal, enlarged base and a distal, short axis with several pairs of leaves. The distal portion is abscised and may develop into a young sporophyte under favorable conditions. The sporophyte of *Lycopodium* at maturity produces spores in rather massive, kidneyshaped sporangia which are often borne on short,stalks either on the leaf base or in the axil of the leaf and stem.

In some species, *L. lucidulum*, for example, the fertile, sporangium-bearing leaves, the *sporophylls,* are entirely similar to sterile leaves and occur in zones among them; such species are considered to be primitive.

In species such as *L. complanatum*, on the other hand, localization of the sporophylls into a terminal conelike structure, the *strobilus*, is accompanied by their modification into nonphotosynthetic, scalelike structures that are reduced in size. This condition is interpreted as the most advanced in the genus.

A *strobilus* is a stem having short internodes and fertile appendages. In the Microphyllophyta these are fertile leaves or *sporophylls*. Some morphologists regard the *lucidulum* type as a strobilus constituting an entire plant. According to this view, the sterile leaves represent

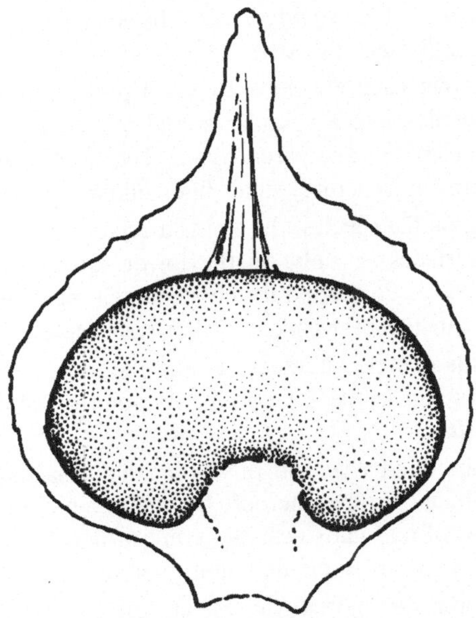

Figure 3.2: Lycopodium complanatum. Adaxial view of sporophyll.

secondarily sterilized sporophylls. The strobilus develops from an apical meristem, and its vascular structure is similar to that of the vegetative axis.

Each sporophyll is supplied from the stele by a single trace, as are the vegetative leaves of the plant. The individual sporangium arises by periclinal division of a group of surface (protodermal) cells near the base of an embryonic leaf.

In further development it may become shifted to the stem, depending on the species. The outer cells resulting from original periclinal cleavage, as a result of continuing anticlinal and periclinal divisions, form a several-layered sporangial wall and tapetum, while the inner divide to form a mass of sporogenous tissue.

The tapetum completely encloses the latter in young sporangia but disintegrates, serving a nutritive function during sporogenesis. The sporangia in some species are stalked. As the sporangium develops, the sporogenous cells become isolated and spherical and ultimately produce a tetrad of spores each.

These finally separate and secrete a wall with ornamentation, which varies with the species. The spore wall consists of two layers: an inner *intine* and the outer *exine*. Pettit reported that the developing exine of *L. gnidioides* has channels through which substances move into the spore from the locular fluid. The spores are yellow at maturity. Dehiscence of the sporangium occurs along a line of cells running across the upper surface of the reniform sporangium and hence transverse to the long axis of the sporophyll.

In species with compact strobili, this is preceded by slight elongation of the internodes and by drying and spreading of the sporophylls, which are facilitated by the shrinkage of a cavity in the lower side of each *sporophyll*.

Reproduction: The Gametophyte

The gametophytes of only relatively few species of *Lycopodium* have been found in nature and fewer still have been grown in laboratory culture. Late in the nineteenth century, the German botanist Bruchmann (1898) described the gametophytes of a number of species. Several American botanists have described the gametophytes of American species of *Lycopodium.*, largely on the basis of laboratory cultures.

The spores of some species, for example, *L. cernuum*, germinate readily in laboratory cultures and produce chlorophyllose gametophytes similar to those found in nature on the surface of soil. These are tuberous with photosynthetic lobes.

Whittier succeeded in obtaining spore germination (only 0.01%, however) and development to sexual maturity, in axenic culture, of the gametophytes of *L. obscurum.* Spore germination occurred only in darkness, according to Whittier, although Freeberg and Wetmore (1957) had reported germination in both light and darkness.

The gametophytes remained colorless but became green upon illumination. The morphology of the gametophytes grown in the laboratory, in the absence of a mycorrhizal fungus, was identical to that of those growing in nature and infected with a fungus. This last is in contrast to the report of Freeberg.

The gametophytes are abbreviated conical and appear disclike when viewed from above. A meristematic zone is present in a groove and rhizoids emerge from the portion of the gametophyte below the groove. The gametophytes of *L. obscurum*, both in culture and in nature, are differentiated into an epidermis, cortex, palisade region, and inner "*storage*" region.

The sex organs arise on the upper surface of the gametophytes of *L. obscurum*. Whittier (1977b) also has grown the gametophytes of *L. complanatum* var. *flabelliforme* to sexual maturity in axenic culture in darkness. The oldest, mature gametophytes were carrot-shaped. In addition to the *L. cernuum* and *L. obscurum* types, *L. complanatum* exhibits a third type of gametophyte, the subterranean, saprophytic, carrot-shaped type. Bruce (1976b) has compared these three types of gametophytes as well as the gametophytes of the *L. phlegmaria* group (mostly epiphytic species) and the *L. selago* group (terrestrial species similar to the epiphytic group).

He found the gametophytes of *L. cernuum* to be characteristic of the subgenus *Lepidotis;* those of *L. obscurum* and *L. complanatum* to be characteristic of subgenus *Lycopodium;* and the gametophytes of *L. selago* and *L. phlegmaria* to be characteristic of subgenus *Urostachya.*

Both antheridia and archegonia occur on the crowns of individual mature gametophytes. The development of both antheridia and archegonia may be traced to single superficial cells. In each case, these undergo periclinal division; by further division, the inner of the two cells gives

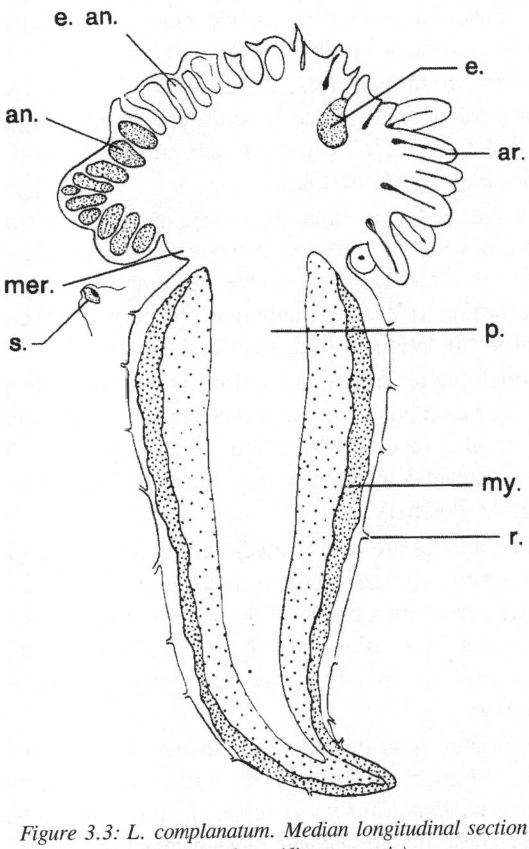

Figure 3.3: L. complanatum. Median longitudinal section of gametophyte (diagrammatic).

rise to the major portion of the antheridium and archegonium.

The sex organs, therefore, are partially embedded. The antheridia are massive and produce large numbers of flagellate sperms, which are liberated through the ruptured superficial wall cells. Robbins and Carothers (1975, 1978) and Carothers, Robbins, and Haas (1975) have investigated spermatogenesis electromicroscopically.

Centrosomes arise *de novo* in the spermatid mother cells, according to the latter authors. The archegonial necks vary, among the several species, in length and degree of emergence. The necks are composed of four or five rows of neck cells.

Reproduction: embryogeny

The occurrence of *Lycopodium* gametophytes, each with several attached sporophytes in various stages of development, indicates not only that the gametophytes are long-lived and active in the nutrition of the embryonic sporophyte, but also that the sex organs may function over long periods.

The zygote divides by a transverse wall into an outer, *suspensor* cell, and an inner, embryoforming cell. The latter develops the embryo itself; the former may divide once or twice. The embryo-forming cell gives rise to a massive foot, stem, and leaf.

The root develops adventitiously at the base of the first leaf. The

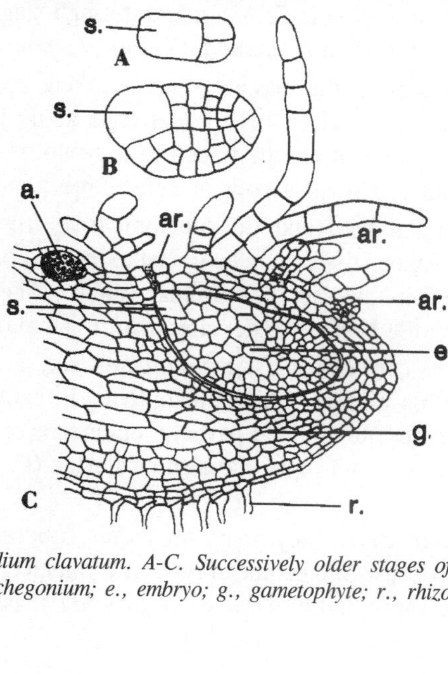

Figure 3.4: Lycopodium clavatum. A-C. Successively older stages of embryogeny. a., antheridium; ar., archegonium; e., embryo; g., gametophyte; r., rhizoid; S., suspensor. A, B. ×120.

primary axis grows out of the gametophyte and up into the light. Axes and leaves of sporophytes borne on subterranean gametophytes remain colorless until they emerge above the substratum.

The gametophyte may persist for a long time attached to the sporophyte, but it ultimately disintegrates as the latter becomes established. The first leaves in some species differ from those on the mature plant in their scalelike habit as well as in the absence of vascular tissue and chlorophyll.

The sporophytes of *Lycopodium* may develop apogamously in laboratory cultures; whether or not this occurs also in nature has not been ascertained.

Summary

The axis of the sporophyte in many *Lycopodium* species is fundamentally protostelic. Its branching may be dichotomous or pseudomonopodial. Although the mature sporophytehas microphyllous leaves and roots, organs that are absent in *Psilotum*, there is evidence that these organs are secondary additions to the axis of *Lycopodium.*

This is suggested by the absence of vascular tissue in the early leaves of the embryonic plant and the lack of a specially differentiated rootforming region in the embryo. The several species show variation in the distribution of sporogenous tissue, apparently progressing from a scattered zonate condition in *L. lucidulum* through stages in localization at the stem apex found in *L. innundatum* and *L. complanatum.*

For the most part, the massive, short-stalked, reniform sporangia occur on the adaxial surface of the leaf base at its junction with the stem. Their development can be traced to a group of surface cells that divide periclinally to form a row of cells three tiers deep.

The sporangial wall and the tapetum arise from the uppermost layer; the sporogenous tissue may be traced to the eusporangiate condition characteristic of a majority of vascular plants. The spores of most species require long periods to develop mature gametophytes in nature.

Lycopodium cernuum, *L. carolinianum*, and *L. innundatum* are exceptional in this respect. The gametophytes in nature are of several kinds, either photosynthetic and partially epiterranean (*L. cernuum*), or completely devoid of chlorophyll and subterranean (*L. complanatum* and *L. obscurum*).

In the latter case, they may be either tuberous or branching cylindrical structures. Subterranean types are infected with mycorrhizal fungus and are saprophytic. The sex organs are massive and partially embedded; the sperms are biflagellate.

Each gametophyte may produce several sporophytes at intervals as long as a year apart. The gametophytes persist during the slow development of the embryonic sporophyte.

CLASS 2. GLOSSOPSIDA

The Glossopsida include the order *Selaginellales*, family *Selaginellaceae*, and *Isoetales*, family Isoetaceae with living members.

Selaginella

Introduction and vegetative *morphology. Selaginella* (dim. of *L. selago*, name of plant resembling the savin, a juniper, + *L. ella*, dimunitive) is one of three extant genera of the class Glossopsida, all the members of which have ligulate leaves.

Although it has such *Lycopodium-like* attributes as small, microphyllous leaves, the *herbaceous* habit, and strobili composed of sporophylls bearing a single sporangium on the adaxial surface, *Selaginella* also has features that distinguish it from *Lycopodium.*

The most significant of these is the production of two kinds of spores, a condition known as *heterospory,* which is associated with profound changes in the morphology and physiology of the gametophyte generation. Furthermore, both the vegetative leaves and the sporophylls of *Selaginella* have small, tonguelike ligules.

The genus *Selaginella*, sometimes called the spike moss, is a large one, including approximately 700 species, which are developed most abundantly in tropical regions with heavy rainfall. In the United States, *S. apoda*, an inhabitant of moist soils, is widely distributed, as is the xerophytic *S. rupestris*, an inhabitant of exposed rocks.

The so-called resurrection plant, often sold as a novelty, is the xerophytic *S. lepidophylla*, which is native to the southwestern United States. A number of tropical species are cultivated in conservatories and in Wardian cases because of the beauty of their branches and foliage; *S. kraussiana* and *S. uncinata* are encountered frequently as a ground cover in greenhouses.

Most species of *Selaginella* exhibit abundant branching, often in a single plane. The branches are arranged dichotomously or in pseudomonopodial or sympodial fashion, depending on the species.

Branching and planation in some species result in the production of frondlike growths, which may arise from a common center, simulating a fern. Other species are climbers, still others prostrate and creeping.

Development of the stem may be traced either to a single apical cell and its derivatives or to a group of apical meristematic cells, depending on the species. In some species the apical cell is later replaced by a group of meristematic initials. *Selaginella kraussiana* is typical of those with a single apical cell.

Some distance back from the apical meristem, the central region of the stem differentiates as procambium, from which the vascular tissues arise. In older regions of the axis in species such as *S. caulescens*, the central portion is separated from the cortex by a cylindrical cavity.

The cortex and central tissues are connected by elongate endodermal cells and in some species by one to four cortical cells called *trabeculae* (*L. trabecula*, little beam).

Casparian thickenings are apparent on the walls of these endodermal cells. The stele may be circular or ribbon-shaped in transection, depending on the species. The stele in *S. kraussiana* is a dual structure for part of the distance between successive branches. This duality results from a forking of the stele in precocious preparation for departure of the trace to a more distal branch.

In other species there may be one or several steles, the polystelic condition. Each stele in *S. kraussiana* is surrounded by a single layer of pericycle cells, immediately within which the phloem is located. According to Burr and Evert, the size of the sieve pores in the lateral and terminal walls of the sieve elements falls in the same size range, so they may be called "*sieve cells.*"

The pores occur singly, not in groups, in the terminal and lateral walls. The central portion of each stele contains the xylem, which is exarch and monarch. The xylem of the stem stele is mesarch in some species-in *S. martensii*, *S. uncinata*, *S. emmeliana*, and *S. caulescens*, among others.

The cortex is composed of thin-walled, photosynthetic parenchyma cells, bounded externally by an epidermis without stomata. It should be noted that in some species of *Selaginella* (*S. rupestris*, for example), series of procambium cells differentiate into vessels rather than into tracheids.

Vessels, it will be recalled, are composed of cell segments in which the common terminal walls have become perforated; they are multicellular in origin, and lacking in all but a few genera of vascular cryptogams. The vessels of *Selaginella* have single terminal perforations. The protoxylem tracheids are lignified in a helical pattern, while those in the later-formed metaxylem have scalariform pits.

Some species (e. g., *S - apoda* and *S. ludoviciana*) lack vessels in their xylem. In many species of *Selaginella*, prominent, leafless axes originate near the points of branch origin and grow toward the substratum. Until recently, these were interpreted as specialized, root-bearing stem branches and termed *rhizophores*.

Recent, intensive studies of several species, including *S. kraussiana*, indicate that these are adventitious roots that fork repeatedly and dichotomously near their apices.

These roots arise exogenously and at first lack root caps and root hairs. *As* the roots enter the soil, they organize root caps and later produce root hairs. Wochok and Sussex reported that cultured roots apices of *S. wildenovii* could develop as leafy shoots.

Webster and Jagels have investigated the morphology of the roots as they develop in moist chambers. Growth of the main root and }ts smaller branches may be traced to a prominent apical cell in some species (e.g., *S. apoda* and *S. ludoviciana*) according to Buck and Lucansky.

In these species the noncutinized epidermis is shed as the root ages, and the next cellular layer centripetally functions as a thick-walled epidermis. The cortex, endodermis, and a two- to fourlayered pericycle surrounded the exarch protostele.

The ligulate leaves of *Selaginella* may be arranged either spirally, a primitive attribute, as in *S. rupestris*, *S. riddellii*, and *S. sheldonii*, or spirally and com pressed in four rows, as in *S. kraussiana* and *S. apoda*.

In species such as the latter, which are dorsiventral, the two dorsal rows of leaves are smaller than the two rows with ventral or lateral insertion. This condition is known as anisophylly. Other species of *Selaginella—S. riddellii*, for example—are isophyllous, like most species of *Lycopodium*.

Such species are radially symmetrical. The leaves are sessile on the stem and alternately inserted, and each is traversed longitudinally by a single unbranched vein that is connected to the stele by a leaf trace.

The leaves, therefore, are microphyllous. Mention has already been made of the basal ligule on the adaxial surface of each leaf. Kollenbach and Geier, Horner, Beltz, Jagels, and Boudreau, and Sigee have investigated the organization and possible function of the ligule.

The ligule consists of an enlarged basal region, a neck, and a tip and is covered over its entire surface by a cuticle. The cells of the ligule have few chloroplasts and become inactive early in development. The function of the ligule has not been clearly elucidated.

It may be a vestigial structure. Transverse sections of the leaf reveal lower and upper epidermal cells containing chloroplasts, and between them the mesophyll composed of photosynthetic parenchyma cells with intercellular spaces.

The leaf cells of different species vary in number of chloroplasts from one to several. In some species-*S. apoda* and *S. uncinata*, for example-the cells of the adaxial leaf epidermis each contain a single, cuplike chloroplast, while the other cells have several (ca. four) lenslike ones.

The plastids are usually larger than those of other vascular plants. Stomata are present on the abaxial surface of the leaf and are localized near the midrib in some species (*S. kraussiana* and *S. ludoviciana*), but in others they occur in both surfaces of the dorsal leaves. In *S. apoda* stomata are scattered over the abaxial leaf surface.

Reproduction: the sporophyte

All species of *Selaginella* produce their eusporangiate sporangia in strobili. The sporophylls are scarcely different from vegetative leaves, and in some species they are arranged so loosely as to render the strobili inconspicuous. The sporophylls, like the vegetative leaves, are ligulate. Each bears a single stalked sporangium adaxially near its base.

Growth of the strobilus is apical; hence, median sections of a young strobilus show various stages in the eusporangiate development of the sporangia. The sporangium wall is twolayered and separated from the sporogenous tissue by a tapetum.

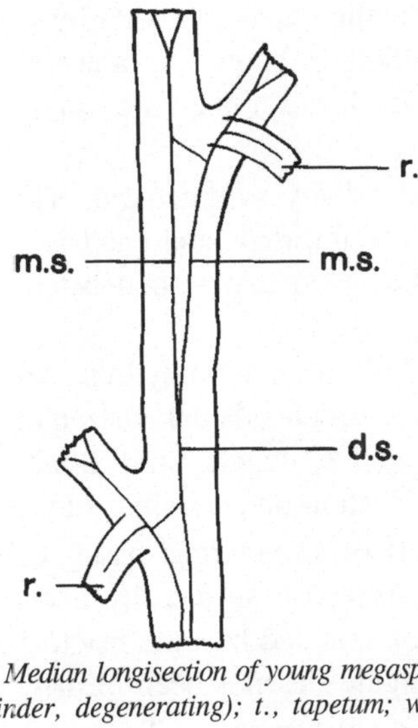

Figure 3.5: Selaginella sp. Median longisection of young megasporangium. f. m., functional megasporocyte (the remainder, degenerating); t., tapetum; w., sporangial wall.

The latter develops from the innermost layer of the sporangial wall. The sporogenous tissue is segregated into individual cells, which function as sporocytes as development proceeds. It subsequently becomes apparent that there are two types of sporangia.

In some, a small percentage of sporocytes may degenerate, the remainder undergoing meiosis and cytokinesis to produce many tetrads of spores. While still in tetrads and before their exines have formed, the microspores have been shown to take in substances from the material that surrounds them. In other sporangia, usually all except one of the sporocytes degenerate.

The survivor undergoes meiosis and cytokinesis, producing a single spore tetrad, the members of which gradually enlarge, apparently by appropriating the materials made available by the degeneration of the other sporocytes. They become filled with lipids and protein granules. Ultimately, the four spores in these *sporangia* grow large enough to cause bulging of the sporangial wall.

This account of the ontogeny of the two types of sporangia indicates that they are fundamentally similar during the early stages of development. However, by the sporocyte stage divergence in development begins. The greatly enlarged spores are called *megaspores* (sometimes, macrospores), and sporangia in which they develop and the sporophylls that subtend the sporangia are known as *megasporangia* and *megaspor-*

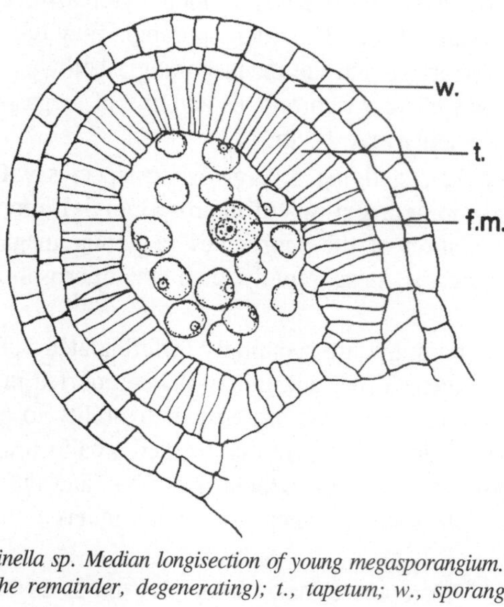

Figure 3.6: Salaginella sp. Median longisection of young megasporangium. f.m., functional megasporocyte (the remainder, degenerating); t., tapetum; w., sporangial wall.

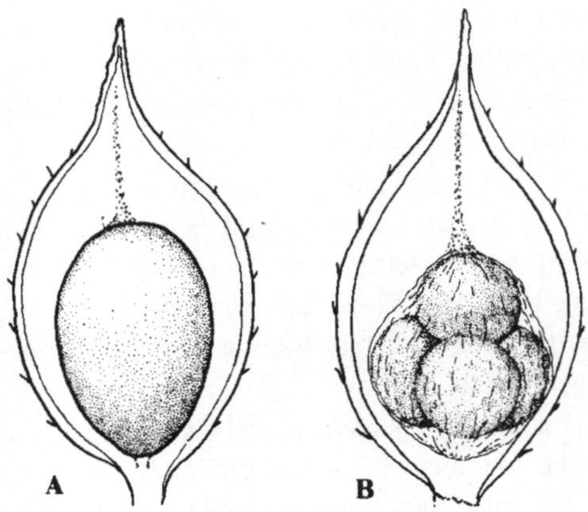

Figure 3.7: Selaginella pallescens. A. Microsporophyll and microsporangium. B. Megasporophyll and megasporangium. Both in adaxial view.

ophylls, respectively.

The smaller spores are called *microspores,* their sporangia are *microsporangia,* and their sporophylls are *microsporophylls*. The sporocytes that give rise to megaspores are called *megasporocytes,* while those that form microspores are known as *microsporocytes*. This dimorphic condition of the spores is known as *heterospory*.

Both the surviving megasporocyte and the microsporocytes that undergo meiosis have much RNA in their cytoplasm, and their walls are thickened with callose. The microsporangia may occur in the apical portion of the strobilus and the megasporangia below, or there may be two vertical rows of microsporophylls and two of megasporophylls; less regular arrangements may occur.

French (1972), studying *S. bigelovii* (a species with two vertical rows of megasporangia and two of microsporangia), reported that prior to the differentiation of the sporocytes, a young megasporangium is larger and elongates more rapidly than the microsporangium at the same node.

Thus, the sporangia are seemingly differentiated before they reach the sporocyte stage. Horner and Beltz (1970) reported in the megasporangium all the sporocytes but one lost their ability to stain for RNA; this, too, was the only sporocyte that formed a callose wall. According to these authors, retention of cytoplasmic RNA and the ability to form callose walls demonstrate which cells will undergo meiosis to form spores.

Pettitt (1977a) reported that, frequently, the megasporangia mature megaspores of different sizes. The smaller are abortive and do not develop gametophytes. The difference in fertility of the members of these megaspore tetrads, he reported, was foreshadowed in the differential distribution of the cytoplasm in the megasporocyte that produced them.

Of the living vascular plants discussed so far, *Selaginella* is the first to exhibit heterospory. While the ontogenetic cause of heterospory in *Selaginella* obviously is degeneration of a majority of sporocytes in certain sporangia and increase in size of the survivors, the factors that evoke this condition are obscure.

That the number of degenerating megasporocytes is not absolutely fixed is indicated by the presence of as many as 42 and as few as one megaspore in megasporangia of the individuals. As the microspores and megaspores mature, their walls thicken.

Those of the microspores are red in certain species and those of the megaspores are cream-colored. The tapetum of the megasporangium seems to play a role in the thickening of the megaspore walls. Both microspores and megaspores have prominent *triradiate ridges,* which mark the lines of cytokinesis of the spores within the spore mother cell walls.

At dehiscence the spores are ejected through a vertical cleft in a sporangial wall. Ingold (1974) described dehiscence of the sporangia in *Selaginella* and ejection of the spores (microspores to a distance of 1 cm or more, megaspores 10 to 20 times farther because of their size).

Reproduction: the gametophyte

The development of dioecious gametophytes is an invariable results of heterospory. Microspores develop into male gametophytes, and megaspores into female gametophytes. Unlike spore germination in *Psilotum* and *Lycopodium*, that of *Selaginella* often is *precocious,* so that at the time of their ejection the spores are in various stages of gametophyte development.

These intrasporangial stages are sometimes said to represent *primary germination.* Under certain conditions, the gametophytes may reach maturity, as manifested by their production of sex organs, by the time of their dissemination from the sporangia.

In two extreme cases, which, however, require confirmation, fertilization and embryo development have been reported to occur while the megaspores and their contained gametophytes are still within the megasporangia. Ruf (1975) reported that it is probable that Lyon actually saw young lichen thalli growing out of the apices of *S. rupestris.* Apomictic sporelings were observed by Geiger (1934) growing out of undisturbed strobili of

S. anocardia; he stated that Goebel had also observed this. Recently, however, Ruf (personal communication) found sexually initiated sporelings emerging from megaspores in undisturbed strobili of *S. intacta*. In this species the single large megasporangium is surrounded by two sterile sporophylls, in addition to the megasporophyll; these form an interesting cup-shaped structure into which the microspores can sift to effect fertilization.

He inferred that the sporophytes resulted from fertilization because he observed microspores within the megasporangium and also because megaspores, isolated by him in culture, formed gametophytes but no embryos. Further comparative study of a number of species of *Selaginella* is desirable to establish the factors that effect the liberation of the spores in relation to the degree of maturity of their enclosed gametophytes.

The mature microspore is uninucleate at first. Its development of the male gametophyte is initiated by an internal mitosis and cytokinesis that result in the formation of a small, peripheral *prothallial cell,* or *sterile cell,* and a large cell, the *antheridial cell.*

The prothallial cell has been interpreted as the sole remnant of the vegetative tissue of a free-living gametophyte, although it undergoes no further divisions. The basis for this interpretation is by no means convincing. It has also been suggested that the prothallial cell represents a rhizoid precursor.

The antheridial cell, by anticlinal and periclinal divisions, forms a single-layered jacket enclosing 128 or 256 spermatogenous cells, each of which gives rise to a single biflagellate sperm. The microspore of *S. kraussiana* is shed from the microsporangium before the antheridium is fully formed.

The latter matures in the microspores that fall into environments that favor further development. The prothallial cell and wall cells of the antheridium ultimately disintegrate, and the sperms are liberated by rupture of the microspore wall. Chlorophyll is absent from the male gametophyte. Robert (1974, 1977) has investigated spermatogenesis in *S. kraussiana* with the electron microscope. He found that in the mature sperm one flagellum is apical and one median.

The megaspores also begin their development into female gametophytes while still grouped together in the tetrad and before they have attained their maximum size. The young megaspore contains a large central vacuole surrounded by a thin peripheral layer of cytoplasm. The

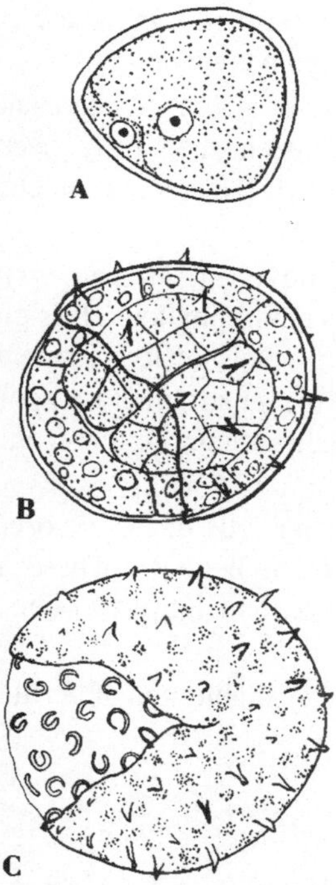

Figure 3.8: Selaginella pallescens. Development of microspore into d gametophyte. A. Section of microspore; note small prothallial cell. B. Partially exposed d gametophyte; note jacket cells and two antheridia. C. Microspore with mature d gametophyte ready to liberate sperm.

megaspore wall at maturity is composed of two layers, a thick, outer cream-colored *exospore* and a more delicate inner layer, the *endospore*. A *mesospore* may also be present in some species.

The single nucleus undergoes mitosis that is not followed by cytokinesis. This process continues, and the cytoplasm, which gradually increases in amount, becomes multinucleate.

The occurrence of successive mitoses without ensuing cytokineses is known as *free nuclear division*. With continued increase in number of nuclei and amount of cytoplasm, the nuclei lying in the portion of the megaspore near the triradiate ridge are gradually separated by cell walls.

This process may continue until much of the megaspore lumen is filled with cellular tissue. The apical tissue of the gametophyte may be separated incompletely from the deeper tissue by a diaphragm. This may not occur, however, until after fertilization. The megaspore is finally ruptured in the region of the triradiate ridge by the protrusion of the developing female gametophyte.

It is in this region that the several archegonia develop. Gametophytes in megaspores that have been shed have been reported to develop chloroplasts and rhizoids if they come in contact with soil in the presence of light.

Although rhizoids develop, in the writers' experience the gametophytes are always achlorophyllous. It is probable, moreover, that the gametophyte derives the bulk of its nutriment from the metabolites freed by degeneration of the supernumerary sporocytes, by the activity of the tapetum of the megasporangium, and from the food stored within the megaspores.

A number of superficial cells of the exposed portion of the female gametophyte develop into archegonia. These are largely embedded, except for their short necks, which are two tiers high and composed of four rows of neck cells.

If carbohydrates are available and if fertilization is inhibited, the

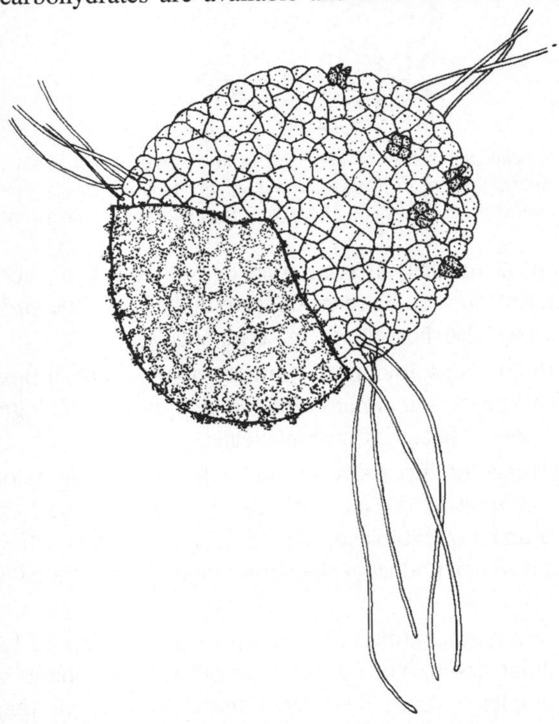

Figure 3.9: Selaginella pallescenes.A. Megaspore with mature gametophyte.

female gametophyte continues to grow and produce more archegonia and rhizoids.

Union of the sperm and egg may occur either after the spores containing the gametophytes have been shed from the strobilus or, in two species, according to an old, unverified report, while the megaspores and their female gametophytes are still within the megasporangia. If, indeed, this does occur, such a transfer of microspores and/or sperms would suggest pollination in seed plants.

Reproduction: embryogeny

As in *Lycopodium*, the first division of the zygote in *Selaginella* gives rise to a *suspensor* initially near the neck of the archegonium; the lower cell and its derivatives form the embryo proper. In some species the suspensor remains relatively inactive as it does in *Lycopodium*, whereas in others it undergoes cell division with subsequent elongation, so that the developing embryos are thrust into the nutrient-filled vegetative tissue of the female gametophyte.

The portion of the embryo opposite the suspensor becomes organized as a foot, and the remainder develops into an axis consisting largely of primary root (*radicle*) and stem bearing two embryonic leaves. As development continues, the embryo, except for the foot, emerges from the female gametophyte and megaspore, and the young plant is soon established independently.

This embryonic sporophyte, attached to the female gametophyte within the megaspore, looks strikingly like a minute seedling at this stage.

Summary

Although *Selaginella* is similar to *Lycopodium* in a number of respects, it differs in having ligulate leaves, frequently polystelic stems, and vessels in its xylem, and especially in its heterospory. As a result of the latter, the gametophytes are strictly dioecious. The ontogeny of the spores of *Selaginella is* instructive in providing a clue as to a possible origin of heterospory.

In view of the great similarity in development of both microsporangia and megasporangia through the sporocyte stage, along with the variation in megaspore number in certain individuals and species, it seems probable that heterospory here is occasioned in part by differences that are initiated prior to sporogenesis.

Four significant differences become apparent in mega- and microsporangia even before meiosis occurs: (1) The megasporangia are slightly larger than the microsporangia; (2) cytoplasmic RNA disappears from all but one of the megasporocytes; (3) abortion of most megasporocytes occurs in every megasporangium; and (4) callose walls form only around the sporocytes (mega- and micro-) with the potentiality of undergoing meiosis.

The ultimate causes of heterospory are not clear. The precocious germination, and, in reported instances, of maturation, of the spores into gametophytes before they are shed from the sporangia is a noteworthy departure from the reproductive cycle of *Lycopodium* and *Psilotum*. Spore dimorphism in *Selaginella* is correlated with gametophyte dimorphism.

Both male and female gametophytes are much reduced in size, duration of existence, and complexity of structure as compared with free-living gametophytes, the male gametophyte especially so. It should be noted that single spores of a homosporous plant (e.g., *Polytrichum*, *Sphaerocarpos*, and *Marchantia*) may develop into dioecious gametophytes.

In such homosporous plants, meiosis results in two members of every spore tetrad growing into male and the other two into female gametophytes. In *Selaginella* and other heterosporous plants, however, all the products of meiosis of a single sporocyte form either male or female gametophytes.

The major source of food for the female gametophyte, as well as for the developing embryo, is the material stored in the megaspore during its long period of enlargement.

The food is sporophytic in origin. While the reported transfer of sperms, or of microspores containing male gametophytes, to the opened megasporangia containing megaspores with female gametophytes would suggest pollination in the seed plants, as the occurrence of fertilization and embryo development within the megasporangium likewise do, there are significant differences.

Furthermore, the frequency of occurrence of these phenomena in *Selaginella* requires confirmation.

Isoetes

Isoetes is a member of the order Isoetales, family Isoetaceae.

Introduction and vegetative morphology

Although morphologists differ in their opinion regarding the relation of *Isoetes* to other plants, there is considerable evidence that its affinities may be with the Microphyllophyta, in which division it is included in the present text, although some botanists do not consider that *Isoetes*

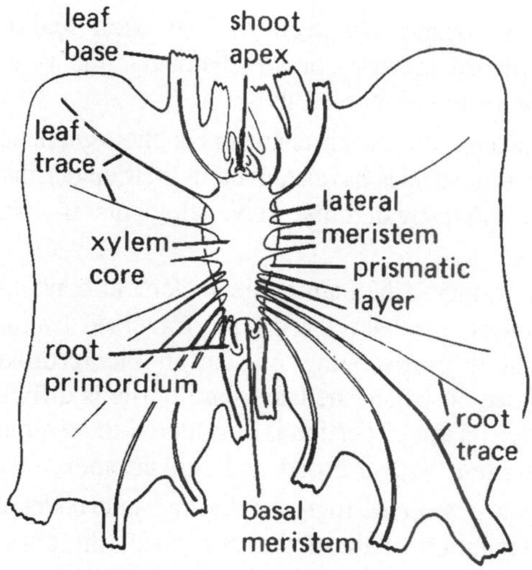

Figure 3.10: Isoetes outleri.
Diagrammatic median longisection.

belongs there.

A related South American genus, *Stylites*, with two species, from a lake in the high Andes of Peru, was described in 1954 and has been studied intensively by Rau and Falk (1959). *Stylites* is sometimes considered not to be distinct from *Isoetes* (Kubitzki and Borchert, 1964).

Isoetes (*L. houseleek*; Gr. *isos*, equal, + Gr. *etos*, year, = evergreen plant) is a genus containing 40 (Bierhorst, 1971a) to 70 (Sporne, 1970) species familiarly known as "*quillworts*" because of their narrow, elongate leaves, the bases of which are rather spoonlike.

Most species are either partially submerged aquatics (*I. engelmannii*) or amphibious; a few, such as *I. butleri*, are terrestrial. *Isoetes butleri* is perennial, but active growth occurs only during the early spring and late autumn rains. *Isoetes lithophila* is an inhabitant of shallow granitic pools and is subject periodically to desiccation; *I. butleri* occurs on moist soils.

A comprehensive summary of the anatomy and development of *Isoetes* has been prepared by Paolillo (*1963*). The quill-like leaves are attached in spiral fashion to a subterranean cormlike structure.

Their spiral arrangement is readily apparent in transverse sections through the overlapping leaf bases. Although the leaves in some species, as in *I. engelmannii*, attain a length as great as 65 cm, they are considered to be microphyllous, inasmuch as they have single, unbranched veins and the traces leave no gap in the vascular tissues of the stem.

It is evident, in transverse section, that each leaf contains four longitudinally placed lacunae, or air chambers; the vein is located in the solid tissue in the center of these.

The tissue external to the air chambers is photosynthetic parenchyma. Leaves of terrestrial species have stomata in their epidermis. Kruatrachue and Evert have investigated the sieve elements in the leaves of *I. muricata.*

According to them, the mature sieve element contains an elongate, degenerate nucleus, the lateral walls are traversed by plasmodesmata, the latter or sieve pores being present in the terminal walls. The cormlike structure on which the leaves are borne is difficult to interpret morphologically. Its upper portion is considered to be a much shortened, fleshy, vertical stem with a broad and sunken apex.

The nodes are so close together that the internodes are practically obliterated. Elongation of the upper portion of the axis is very slow, most of the *derivatives* of the apical meristem cells becoming involved in the formation of leaves and the portions of the stems immediately subtending the leaves.

The vascular tissue is arranged as a central protostele, the xylem of which consists of a large number of parenchyma cells and relatively few tracheids, a characteristic of aquatic plants in general. The xylem is surrounded by phloem. Outside the phloem there is a meristematic layer, the exact nature of which is somewhat in dispute.

It functions as a *cambium* in that its divisions add to the tissues of the stem. Apparently, the cambium derivatives develop as sieve elements, occasionally as tracheids, or as parenchyma cells adjacent to the phloem. The secondary sieve elements are similar at maturity to the sieve elements of the leaf except that pores occur in all their walls.

Most of the cells produced by the cambium augment the cortex, the outer portion of which, with the older leaf bases, is sloughed off each growing season. No endodermis is present. The surface of the corm is covered by the remains of the leaves of previous seasons.

The surface layers of the corm become suberized. The lower portion of the corm is a bilobed or trilobed organ. It may branch more frequently in some species and in *I. tegitiformans* it may be elongate and rhizomatous. Its structure and homologies have received various interpretations.

It often is referred to as the *rhizophore,* inasmuch as the delicate roots are borne in orderly series only on this region of the plant. The rhizophore end of the plant develops from its own meristem, which is sunken in a groove.

This is scarcely distinguishable from the cambium. The youngest roots, therefore, occur near the deepest portion of the groove, and the older ones arise from the sides of the rhizophore lobes.

The roots are endogenous in origin; each is connected to the central vascular tissue of the rhizophore by a trace. Karrfalt and Eggert (1977) and Karrfalt (1977) have investigated the comparative morphology and development of *I. nuttallii* and *I. tuckermanii*.

The corms of young plants are usually two-lobed at their bases but may become three- and four-lobed as new furrows appear. The bases may branch dichotomously. The delicate roots are protected by root caps, beneath which a group of apical cells is present; these add to both the root cap and the root itself.

The roots branch dichotomously as a result of the organization of two groups of apical initials below the root caps. Karrfalt (1977) reported that the developing roots of *Isoetes* displace substrate from under the corm and that tension on the roots pulls the corms down into the substrate.

Mature roots contain delicate protosteles that are excentric in position because of the disintegration of the inner cortical cells on one side of the stele to form a lacuna. The stele is bounded by a well-differentiated endodermal layer.

Kruatrachue and Evert (1978) have investigated the ontogeny of the sieve elements in the roots of *I. muricata*. These lack nuclei at maturity. The cortex is surrounded by an epidermis. This unusual type of root, with its excentric stele and air chamber, is very similar in organization to the roots of fossil *Lepidodendrales*, also borne on *rhizophores*.

Reproduction: the sporophyte

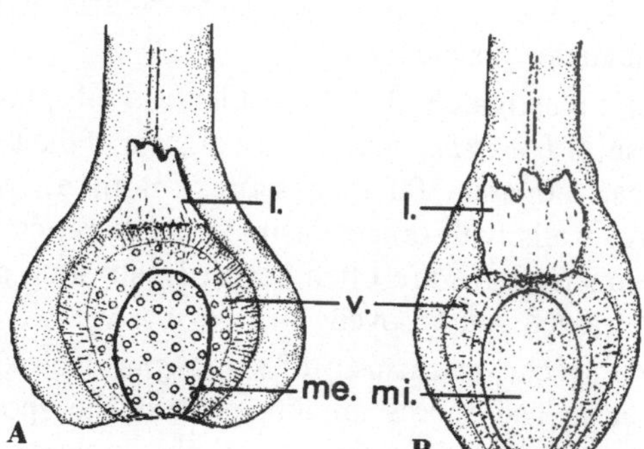

Figure 3.11: Isoetes sp. Adaxial views of A. megasporophyll, and B. microsporophyll. l. , ligule; me., megasporangium; mi., microsporangium; v., velum.

Every leaf of *Isoetes* is potentially a sporophyll, and the plants are heterosporous. The firstformed leaves of any season, the outermost, are frequently sterile, however. The next older leaves mature as megasporophylls and are followed by microsporophylls within.

The last-formed leaves of the season frequently bear abortive sporangia. Microsporophylls and megasporophylls are indistinguishable at first. In each case the single sporangium arises from superficial cells near the adaxial surface of the spoon-shaped leaf base; the cells undergo a series of periclinal divisions.

These periclinal divisions give rise externally to a severallayered wall and internally to sporogenous tissue. Development of the sporangium is eusporangiate. The sporangium is massive and larger than those in *Lycopodium* and *Selaginella;* it may attain a length of up to 7 mm.

A small ligule arises just above the apex of the sporangium, and other superficial cells in that region grow down to form an indusiumlike covering, the *velum* (*L. velum*, veil).

The sporangia are incompletely chambered by strands of sterile tissue, the *trabeculae,* which extend from the walls partially across the sporangial lumen. The innermost layer of the sporangial wall differentiates as a twolayered tapetum.

The trabeculae and the portion of the tapetum that covers them are derived from potentially sporogenous tissue. As in *Selaginella*, development of both microsporangia and megasporangia is largely similar through the sporocyte stage.

Practically all the microsporocytes undergo meiosis and form tetrads of microspores; hence, tremendous numbers of spores, estimated to be between 150,000 and 1 million, develop in each microsporangium. Certain of the megasporocytes enlarge, but only a small number divide and form tetrads; the remainder disintegrate.

Pettitt has investigated the multiplication of plastids during megasporogenesis in *I. engelmannii*. Megasporangia of the several species produce between 50 and 300 megaspores. Both microspores and megaspores have walls with ornamentation, which varies from species to species; the microspores are often covered with long spines, while megaspores are ridged and grooved.

There is no special mechanism of sporangial dehiscence, at least in aquatic species. The spores are liberated as the sporophylls and sporangia walls disintegrate at the end of the growing season. The sporophylls may be abscised and float to the surface. The spiny microspores are often found attached by their spines to the megaspores, an important adaptation in dioecious gametophytes.

Reproduction: the gametophyte

Unlike *Selaginella*, the spores of *Isoetes* do not begin their development into gametophytes until they have been set free from their sporangia. The spores of *I. lithophila* require light and variable temperatures (to near freezing) for germination.

The male gametophyte, as in *Selaginella*, *is* entirely enclosed within the microspore wall. It arises by internal divisions of the microspore protoplast to form a single prothallial cell (sterile cell) and a single antheridial cell.

The latter develops into an antheridium consisting of a single-layered wall enclosing four spermatogenous cells. Each of these gives rise to a single multiflagellate sperm at maturity. Development of the female gametophyte of *Isoetes*, as of *Selaginella*, involves a series of free-nuclear divisions of the megaspore nucleus and its descendants.

Cell-wall formation occurs first in the region of the triradiate ridge and gradually extends through the remainder of the female gametophyte. It may still be incomplete in the basal portion of the gametophyte for some time after fertilization.

The megaspore wall cracks open, exposing the cellular apex of the developing gametophyte, which develops unicellular rhizoids. Certain superficial cells undergo division to form archegonia, which are largely embedded. Their necks, composed of three or four tiers of four cells, are longer than those of *Selaginella*.

Reproduction: embryogeny

Usually only one zygote in each female gametophyte develops into a sporophyte. Nuclear and cell division by the zygote and its derivatives produce a spherical mass of tissue, which later differentiates into the embryonic regions of the sporophyte.

These include a rather massive foot in contact with the starch-filled cells of the female gametophyte, an embryonic root, and a leaf. The stem develops secondarily in the region between the leaf and the root.

Although the young sporophyte soon becomes established as an independent plant, it remains attached to the female gametophyte and megaspore for a considerable period. It should be noted that no suspensor is present in the embryo of *Isoetes*.

Summary

Although the leaves of *Isoetes* are markedly larger than those of

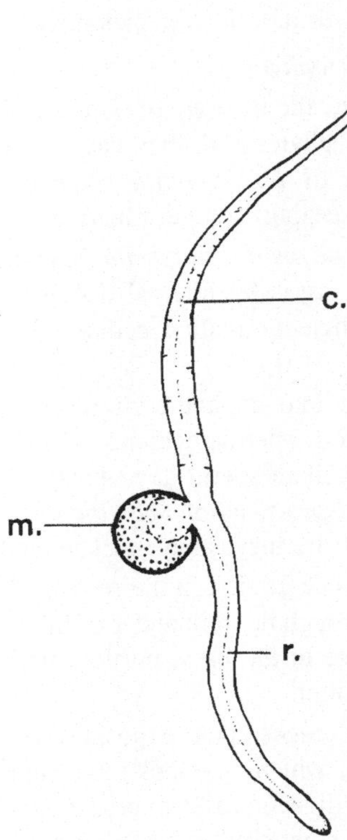

Figure 3.12: Isoetes sp. Young sporophyte attached to 4 gametophyte within megaspore. c., cotyledon; m., megaspore; r., root.

Selaginella and *Lycopodium*, they are microphyllous, as indicated by their single unbranched veins and the absence of gaps in the stele.

All organs of the plant show evidences in their anatomical structure of adaptation to an aquatic habitat. Among these are air lacunae and the paucity of lignified xylem tissue. The leaves of *Isoetes* are ligulate and spirally inserted on a short, underground, cormlike structure.

Each leaf is potentially a sporophyll. Although growth in length of the corm is very limited, the presence of a cambiumlike layer contributes to its increase in girth.

The cortex of the corm is composed of starch-filled cells, an indication that the perennial corm is primarily a storage organ. The stem is protostelic with few tracheids, most of the xylem cells maturing as parenchyma.

The lower portion of the corm is called a rhizophore. This is a lobed structure on which the delicate roots are borne in orderly fashion.

Both stem and root develop from a group of apical meristematic cells rather than one. Root branching is dichotomous.

The roots are characterized by excentric steles and a central air chamber. The sporangia are massive and heteromorphic. A variable number of megaspores mature in the megasporangium. The number is always larger than in *Selaginella*, and unlike the latter, the spores do not initiate development into gametophytes until they have been shed from their sporangia.

Evidences of further reduction of the gametophytes, as compared with those of *Selaginella*, are present in *Isoetes*. Among these, the reduction of spermatogenous cells to four and the failure of the female gametophyte to project from the megaspore wall are noteworthy.

The gametophytes of *Isoetes* are colorless and saprophytic, depending on reserves stored within the spores. Unlike both *Selaginella* and *Lycopodium*, the sperms of *Isoetes* are multiflagellate. The development of the embryo differs from these genera in the complete absence of a suspensor and in the long-delayed development of the stem.

In spite of the differences just cited, there are many evidences of similarity in morphology between *Isoetes* and *Selaginella* and *Lycopodium*. The roots and rhizophore suggest the fossil Lepidodendrales. Some morphologists, however, on the basis of the multiflagellate sperms and anatomical considerations, are of the opinion that *Isoetes* is more closely related to certain ferns.

This view seems to ignore such a fundamental attribute as the microphylly of *Isoetes* as contrasted with the macrophylly of ferns.

4

Vascular Cryptogams III: Division Arthrophyta

The division Arthrophyta (Gr. *arthros,* jointed, + Gr. *phyton*, plant) is the third group of vascular cryptogams known from Devonian (inside front cover) strata. Arthrophytan plants were abundant and dominant during the Paleozoic, but only a single genus, *Equisetum*, has survived in our present flora.

CLASS 1. ARTHROPSIDA

Order 1. Equisetales

Family 1. Equisetaceae Equisetum

Equisetum (*L. equus*, horse, + L. *saeta*, bristle), with 10 to 25 species, the only living member of the family Equisetaceae and order Equisetales, is widely distributed; the various species are familiarly known as "horsetails" (the branching species) and "*pipes*" and "*scouring rushes*" (the *unbranched species*).

Some, such as the common *E. arvense*, grow both on moist and in somewhat xeric habitats, whereas others, such as *E. sylvaticum*, frequently flourish only in marshy situations. Temperate-zone species are relatively small in stature, rarely exceeding 4 ft in height.

The tropical *E. giganteum* may exceed 5 m in height and have stems up to 2.4 cm in diameter. This large species and a related hybrid are used medicinally in *Costa Rica* as the basis of an infusion that is said to cure kidney ailments. Some species of *Equisetum* have been reported to be poisonous to livestock. The stem is the dominant organ of the plant body in the genus *Equisetum;* the minute leaves, although photosynthetic for a short period after their formation, soon become dry and scalelike.

In *E. arvense* and other species, the plant consists of a subterranean, deep-growing rhizome and an erect aerial stem. Rhizome systems of *E. arvense* have been observed growing horizontally 6 to 7 ft below the surface of the soil and covering areas of many hundreds of square feet.

The rhizomes of some species produce tuberous storage structures at their nodes. The aerial stem may be richly branched, as in *E. arvense*, or branching may be rare, as in *E. hyemale* and *E. kansanum*.

The fact that unbranched species (e.g., *E. hyemale*), under such stimulation as injury to the apex, develop branches at the nodes is often cited as evidence that branching is a primitive attribute in the genus, the branch primordia being present at the nodes.

After the strobili of main axes have shed their spores, they often become detached, whereupon branching is initiated at some of the lower nodes of the aerial stems. These branches arise from dormant buds which are present from the time of early development of the stem.

Associated with each of the buds is a root meristem, from which all the roots of adult plants arise at the lower, subterranean nodes. Both the aerial stems and rhizomes have well-defined nodes and internodes.

The surface of the stem is ribbed or ridged, the ribs of successive internodes being arranged in an alternating pattern. The bases of the leaves are fused into a deep collar, which ensheaths the node and gives the appearance of a scalloped collar.

Both rhizomes and aerial stems bear the scalelike leaves, each of which has an unbranched vascular bundle. A few rudimentary stomata are present near the tips of the adaxial surface of the leaves of *E. arvense*. Stomata are present in two or three rows on both sides of the projecting midrib on the adaxial leaf surface.

The central region of each leaf is photosynthetic when the leaves first appear. The individual leaf tips may be united into groups of varying number. The relation between the branches and leaves in *Equisetum* differs from that in all other vascular plants.

In those of the latter that branch at the nodes, stem branches originate from the axils of the leaves, and thus opposite them, whereas in *Equisetum* they emerge from the region of the node between the leaves, and thus alternatively with them.

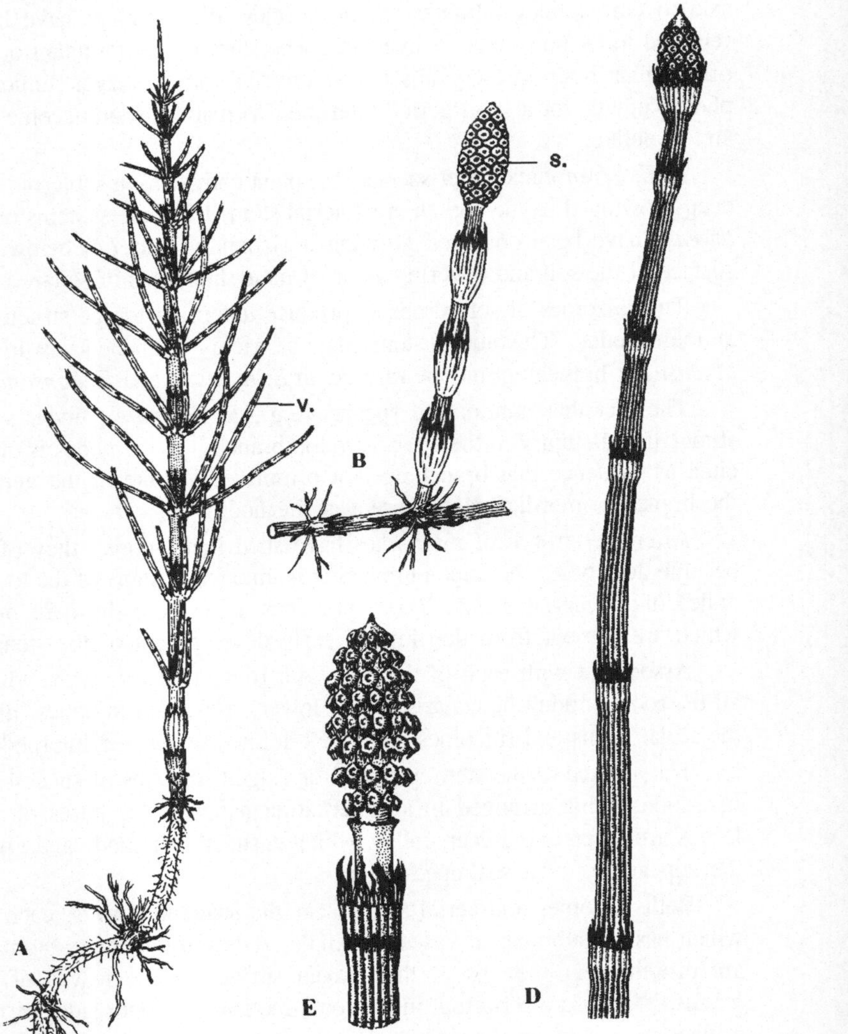

Figure 4.1: A-C. Equisetum arvense. Segments of rhizome with vegetative (v.) (in C, left and right) and fertile shoots with strobili (s.) (s. in center in C.). D-E. E. hyemale. Vegetative shoot with terminal strobilus, the latter enlarged and dehiscent in E.

As the branches elongate, they pierce the nodal leaf sheath. Development of the stem originates in a single pyramidal apical cell, which divides -regularly in three directions.

The derivatives of the apical cell divide in an anticlinal direction soon after they are delimited. One of the cells thus formed in each case contributes by further division to the internodal, and the other to the nodal, portion of the axis. In the development of the stem, certain cells at each node remain meristematic; these constitute the intercalary meristem, which adds to the length of the internodes.

The leaves originate as superficial, ringlike outgrowths of the nodal cells. A short distance back from the apical region, tissue differentiation is initiated in the axis. The surface cells form an epidermis with silicified cells.

The distribution of the siliceous material has been investigated by Kaufman, Bigelow, Schmid, and Ghosheh (1971) and by Dayanandan and Kaufman (1973). It is deposited mostly as knots and rosettes on the inner walls of the epidermal cells. Certain of the latter undergo two successive divisions to form guard cells and their more superficial accessary cells. The latter are thickened with siliceous ribs.

In *E. arvense* the stomata are superficial, but in *E. hyemale* they are sunken. Stomata are present most abundantly on the slopes of the ridges of the fluted stem surface. Page (1972) has demonstrated with scanning electron microscopy that the stomata are useful criteria in establishing possible phylogenetic relationships among species.

Associated with the stoma and guard cells are a pair of subsidiary cells, which have radiating bands composed in part of siliceous material. Figure elsewhere in this chapter shows a transverse section of the erect vegetative stem of *E. arvense* taken from an internode where differentiation has been completed.

The central region of the stem is hollow at maturity and is surrounded by the remains of the parenchymatous pith. This cavity is called the *central* canal. Outside the pith there is a ring of circular canals, the position of which is directly internal to the surface ridges of the stem.

These, therefore, are known as carinal (*L. carina*, keel) canals, and they mark the position of discrete strands of xylem and phloem. Experiments with dyes indicate that these canals have a role in conduction. The first-formed annular and helical protoxylem cells arise near the inner limit of each procambium strand.

This xylem associated with the carinal canal is sometimes called the carinal xylem. With the formation of the carinal canals, after differentiation of protoxylem, the position of the protoxylem elements is disturbed. The phloem, which lies directly outside each carinal canal, is bordered laterally by two groups of xylem cells; these differentiate from cells of the intercalary meristem.

Vessels, with not more than two component elements, occur in the near-nodal xylem; their perforations connect with the carinal canal, which is a water-conducting channel.

A second type of vessel with reticulate perforations occurs in the lateral xylem of the internodal vascular strands of the rhizomes of five species. Dute and Evert (1978) reported that sieve elements of the mid-internodal regions are organized as sieve-tube members.

The end walls of the sieve elements in the internodal phloem are oblique, and the sieve areas are transversed by plasmodesmata. The pericycle is represented by a single layer of cells just within a rather prominent endodermis. In some species of *Equisetum*, each vascular strand is completely surrounded by the endodermis.

In others, there are both outer and inner common, continuing, endodermal layers; and in still others, as in the aerial stems of *E. arvense*, only a continuous outer endodermal layer is present. The cortex consists internally of parenchyma cells interrupted by large vallecular or cortical canals, which have a position corresponding with that of the depressions of the stem surface.

Groups of other cortical cells contain abundant chloroplasts. The walls of the cortical cells beneath the surface ridges are markedly thickened sclerenchyma and contribute to the support and rigidity of the stem.

The epidermal cells are heavily silicified and provided with stomata; the complex organization of their guard cells, overlaid by subsidiary cells with radiating siliceous thickenings, has already been described. The guard cells and subsidiary cells may be at, or sunken below, the surface of the plant.

Chen and Lewin (1969) have demonstrated that silicon is required in the normal growth of *Equisetum.* Although the xylem and phloem are present as discrete strands (eustele) in the internodes of *Equisetum*, serial sections through the nodes reveal that they join there to form a short siphonostele.

A diaphragm of tissue at the nodes interrupts the internodal canal. The vascular strands above and below the nodal region are joined to the siphonostele in alternating fashion. A ring of small protoxylem leaf traces leaves the stele at each node; branch traces originate between the leaf traces.

The absence of leaf gaps indicates that the leaves are probably to be interpreted as microphyllous. The internodal stele is known as a eustele; here the parenchymatous gaps between the internodal bundles are neither leaf nor branch gaps. It is worthy of note that the internodes of the axis of the embryonic sporophyte at first contain a protostele; the eustele differentiates in later development.

Roots of mature plants are nodal, endogenous, and adventitious in origin and arise at the bases of lateral branches or their bud primordia. The root grows as a result of the activity of a single apical cell and its derivatives and is protostelic and exarch.

Specially differentiated cubical cells of the root epidermis give rise to root hairs. The occasional branch roots develop endogenously from the pericycle. Dute and Evert (1977a) have described sieve-element ontogeny in the roots of *E. hyemale* var. *affine*.

The roots are characterized by a central metaxylem tracheid and three protoxylem poles. Some vessels occur in the roots. The mature sieve element is enucleate, its protoplast bounded by a plasmalemma, and contains plastids, mitochondria, endoplasmic reticulum, and refractive spherules.

Reproduction: the sporophyte

It is well known that various species of *Equisetum*, such as *E. arvense* and E. *hyemale*, may propagate new individuals from segments of their rhizomes. It has also been reported that floating segments of the aerial axes of *E. hyemale* in aquatic habitats can regenerate new individuals, which may be dispersed by water as propagules.

Equisetum is homosporous. The sporogenous tissue in all species of *Equisetum* is localized in a strobilus, but the relation of the strobilus to the vegetative branches varies. In some species—*E. hyemale* and *E. kansanum*, for example—the strobili develop at the tips of vegetative axes. In *E. arvense* and *E. telmateia*, however, the strobilus is usually borne on a nonchlorophyllous fertile branch that develops from the rhizome.

The rhizome produces green vegetative branches later, as the strobilate branches wither away. *Equisetum sylvaticum* is intermediate between these two extremes in that the unbranched axis that bears the strobilus lacks chlorophyll at first.

It becomes green and branched after the spores have been discharged. In *E. arvense*, the strobilus-bearing branch is formed in the autumn preceding the spring in which it is to appear above the soil. As in the vegetative stem, growth of the strobilus is apical.

In some species its axis continues to grow slightly beyond the apex of the strobilus. The axis of the strobilus produces a series of surface enlargements, each of which grows into a spore-producing appendage called a *sporangiophore*. Hauke (1970), on the basis of unusual material of *E. littorale* in which there were strobili with whorls of appendages transitional between leaf sheaths and typical sporangiophores, concluded that the appendages of the strobilus have dual potentialities.

Accordingly, he considered the fertile appendages to be sporophylls. The term "*sporangiophore*" is used by those who are impressed with evidence from certain fossil Arthrophyta in which both branchlike sporangiophores and leaflike whorls occur in the strobilus.

Page (1973) discussed hypotheses regarding the organization of the strobilus and its homologies with the vegetative axes. Mature sporangiophores typically are hexagonal in surface view because of mutual pressure. In young strobili the sporangiophores are moundlike.

Between five and ten equidistant single cells on their surface function in initiating sporangia. As they function, expansion of the central tissue of the sporangiophores pushes the sporangial initials and their cellular progeny over the margin to the adaxial surface of the sporangiophore.

The walls of immature sporangia are several cells thick but become unistratose at maturity by disintegration of the inner layers. In their origin from single cells, the sporangia of *Equisetum* differ from the synangia of *Psilotum* and the sporangia of *Lycopodium*, *Selaginella*, and *Isoetes*.

Each sporangiophore is served by a trace that branches distally and dichotomizes so that one trace reaches the base of each sporangium. The mature sporangia are elongate and fingerlike. The sporogenous tissue of the young sporangium is surrounded by a *tapetum* and a wall

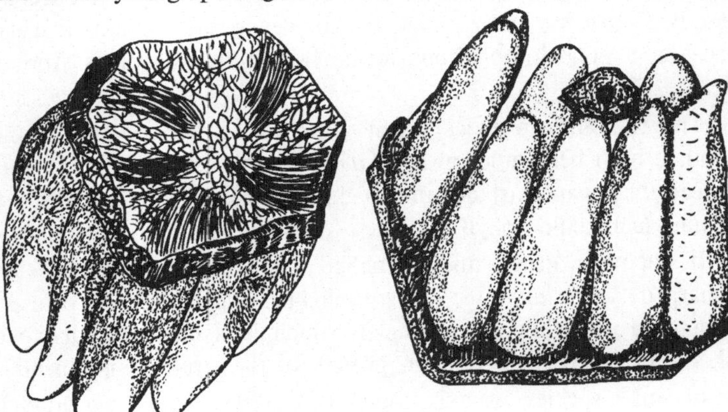

Figure 4.2: Equisetum arvense. Enlarged views of sporangiophore and sporangia.

several cells in thickness. As development progresses, the walls of the tapetum disintegrate.

There is thus formed a *tapetal plasmodium*, which contributes to the nutrition of the sporogenous tissue and formation of the outermost layer of the spore wall. A number of the sporocytes abort, but those that remain undergo meiotic division, each producing a tetrad of spores.

The haploid chromosome number is approximately $n = 108$ in *E. arvense* and *E. hyemale*. The outermost layer of sporangial wall cells thickens spirally and the cells beneath disintegrate. Dehiscence of the sporangium is longitudinal along a vertical line in that portion of the sporangial wall adjacent to the sporangiophore stalk.

The wall structure of the mature spores is complex, the outermost wall layer consisting of four spirally arranged portions. These separate at the time of sporangial dehiscence, so that each spore bears four somewhat spoonlike appendages sometimes called *elaters*

The latter are hygroscopic and quickly affected by slight changes in humidity. When the spores are ready for dissemination, the internodes of the strobilus elongate slightly, thus separating the sporangiophores.

The stalk of each now increases in length on its lower side, so that the sporangia are approximately perpendicular to the soil surface when the spores have been shed.

Reproduction: the gametophyte

The green spores of *Equisetum* germinate rapidly after their dissemination, provided that they are carried to suitable substrates. Lloyd and Klekowski (1970) determined that green spores, such as those of *Equisetum*, *Osmunda*, and certain other ferns, germinate in less than 3 days, the mean being 1.46 days.

They remain viable, however, for a year or less (mean 48 days). By contrast, nongreen spores require 4 to 210 days (mean 9.5) for germination but retain their viability for a mean period of 1045 days.

In the case of *E. arvense*, which frequently is found in rather xeric situations, it is doubtful that any considerable number of spores produce mature gametophytes in such habitats. Vegetative multiplication by means of the rhizome fragments probably accounts for the formation of extensive colonies.

Germinating spores and mature gametophytes of several species have been found on moist soil in nature. Mesler and Lu (1977) found gametophytes of *E. hyem.ale* 3 cm in diameter in nature in northern California. Naturally occurring gametophytes of *E. arvense* varied in size from that of a pinhead to *8* mm in diameter. The spores of *E. arvense* and *E. hyemale*, among others, germinate rapidly in laboratory cultures on suitable media and on moist *Sphagnum*.

The developing gametophytes are extremely sensitive to such unfavorable environmental conditions as crowding, and their form is modified accordingly. However, well-isolated spores form disclike or cushionlike green gametophytes several millimeters in diameter.

They are anchored to the substrate by numerous unicellular rhizoids that arise from the lower side of the cushion. The superficial cells of the gametophyte develop lamellar lobes of photosynthetic cells, which densely cover the moundor cushionlike basal portion.

This basal portion has a marginal meristem. In the writers' cultures the gametophytes of *E. arvense* sometimes produced antheridia, archegonia, and emergent sporophytes within 21 days after the spores had been planted.

Considerable dimorphism of the gametophytes was apparent at this time. Hauke has investigated the gametophytes of *Equisetum* in the field and in laboratory cultures. He reported that the gametophytes of *E. arvense* and *E. bogotense* (of Central and South America) are strictly male or female and somewhat dimorphic.

Hauke also reported that light intensity had an effect on the numbers of male gametophytes produced in cultures of *E. arvense* (greater number of males with increasing light intensity); intensity had no effect on the sex ratios in *E. hyemale*, but light quality did (higher number of males in red light), whereas the gametophytes of *E. fluviatile* were unaffected by either light quality or intensity.

Duckett has made an incisive and comprehensive study of sexuality and spore size in five branched species of *Equisetum* (subgenus *Equisetum*). There is no morphological evidence of heterospory. Under laboratory conditions, the antheridia may be produced on gametophytes only 25 days old (*E. arvense*), but most developed between 40 and 60 days after the spores had been sown.

The male gametophytes were covered with antheridium-bearing lobes and had few sterile lamellae. A majority of the spores developed this type of male gametophyte, which continued to produce antheridia for 300 days in laboratory culture.

By contrast, fewer of the spores grew into gametophytes with sterile lamellae, the archegonia being embedded in the moundlike gametophyte. The archegonial necks protruded between the bases of the sterile photosynthetic lamellae.

Such gametophytes produced archegonia for between 35 and 80 days. Ultimately, however, they developed meristematic antheridial lobes, which continued to produce antheridia, while archegonial development ceased.

All the initially female gametophytes ultimately produced antheridia. Duckett has found that the gametophytes of nine species of *Equisetum* are of two kindsnamely, entirely male gametophytes and monoecious ones which are *protogynous* (*i.e.*, they produce archegonia before the antheridia).

A similar distribution of sex organs occurs in the fern *Platyzoma* and in a number of other species of ferns. It has been demonstrated that (homozygous) sporophytes can develop as a result of self-fertilization of the bisexual gametophytes. Environmental factors have a marked effect on the ratio of male to bisexual gametophytes produced.

At 32°C, the spores of five species produced only male gametophytes, but at 15°C over 50% of the gametophytes of three of the species were bisexual. High light intensities, which favor vegetative development, evoke the formation of bisexual gametophytes, while high temperatures seem to influence the development of male gametophytes.

In another report it is stated that not only light intensity but also light quality may affect the expression of sexuality in *E. arvense* and *E. hyemale*, while *E. fluviatile* seems not to be markedly affected by these.

Hauke, however, has reported that the gametophytes of *E. bogotense* of Central and South America are strictly male or female and somewhat

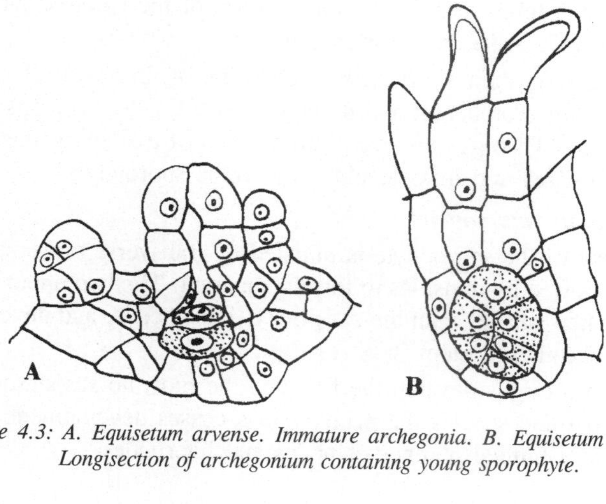

Figure 4.3: A. Equisetum arvense. Immature archegonia. B. Equisetum hyemale. Longisection of archegonium containing young sporophyte.

dimorphic. In 1972 Duckett reported that in the subgenus *Hippochaete* of *Equisetum*, also, the gametophytes were initially male or female and that the males produced only antheridia, but the females finally produced antheridia as well as archegonia.

The male gametophytes were smaller and less longlived than the female. Duckett suggested that Hauke's report of dioecious gametophytes in *E. bogotense* may have been based on cultures grown for too short a time. The discrepancy between Hauke's and Duckett's investigations has yet to be resolved.

Each antheridium originates from a single superficial cell, which undergoes division into an outer cell and an inner cell. The outer forms the wall of the upper portion of the antheridium; the inner, by successive divisions, forms the spermatogenous tissue.

The antheridium produces a large number of multiflagellate sperms, which are liberated explosively when the mature antheridia are moistened. Duckett has investigated spermatogenesis at the ultrastructural level.

According to Bilderback, Bilderback, John, and Fonseca (1973), as the antheridia are immersed in water, their two cover cells separate and the sperms emerge in the passageway thus created.

The sperms are released within the spermatid cells, which have 6 to 12 processes. The spermatid cells split open and the sperms escape. They may swim at the rate of 300μm/sec, or 15 times their own length! The sperms of *Equisetum* are relatively large.

Duckett and Bell (1977) have studied the mature sperms electron microscopically. The archegonia always occur near the bases of the photosynthetic lobes on the prostrate portion of the gametophyte. The archegonia also arise from superficial cells.

At maturity, their short necks, consisting of four vertical rows of neck cells, are protuberant and divergent distally; the venter is buried in the thallus. The eggs of several archegonia of a single gametophyte may be fertilized and may develop embryonic sporophytes.

Reproduction: embryogeny

Growth of the sporophyte is initiated by transverse division of the zygote, followed by divisions to form a quadrant. The two upper (outer) cells are often smaller than the two lower (inner) cells, and develop the first leaf sheath and stem in *E. arvense*.

The lower cells develop the foot and the root, no suspensor being present. In some species the primary axis ceases development after it has formed a limited number of nodes and internodes.

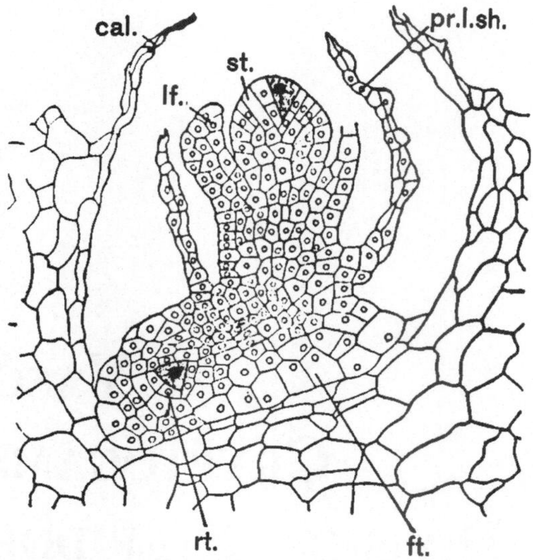

Figure 4.4: Equisetum arvense. Median section of older embryo. cal., calyptra; e., embryo; ft., foot; lf., leaf; pr. l. sh., primary leaf sheath; rt., root; st., stem.

In such forms, secondary axes are successively formed, one of which ultimately gives rise to the mature axis. The embryonic root grows through the gametophyte into the soil, thus establishing the independence of the young sporophyte.

Each gametophyte may produce many sporophytes, 27 having been reported on one gametophyte of *E. hyemale*. The gametophytes persist for some time in laboratory culture after sporophyte development has been initiated. In the authors' cultures of *E. arvense*, young emergent sporophytes 0.4 cm long became visible 30 days after the spores had been sown.

5

Vascular Cryptogams IV: Division Pteridophyta

Because of their number and diversity, the final group of vascular cryptogams, the Pteridophyta, are discussed in this and the following two chapters. The Pteridophyta, broadly speaking the ferns, include approximately 10,000 species.

Probably precursors of the Pteridophyta flourished during the Middle Devonian (inside front cover). Consideration of these and of the remainder of the fossil record will be deferred to other chapter in this book. Of the four divisions of vascular cryptogams with extant members-*Psilotophyta*, *Microphyllophyta*, *Arthrophyta*, and *Pteridophyta*—only the members of the last are clearly megaphyllous, although it is possible that the seemingly microphyllous leaves of *Equisetum* have been reduced from megaphyllous precursors.

The leaves in a number of genera are the largest and most complex in the plant kingdom. In many ferns the leaves appear to be the dominant organs of the sporophyte, the stems being smaller and less prominent. All have branching veins, and the traces of all mature fern leaves are associated with gaps in the stem steles, unless the stele is a protostele, in which case a groove is sometimes visible.

They share the attribute of megaphylly with the phanerogams or seed plants. Those who classify all vascular plants in the single division Tracheophyta group ferns and seed plants together in the class Pteropsida.

Survey of the Pteridophyta indicates that the group may be divided into two, albeit unequally, with respect to the type of sporangium produced.

The first series has a type of sporangium similar in development and organization to that of the *Psilotophyta*, *Microphyllophyta*, and, probably, the seed plants, that is, *eusporangiate*. These sporangia are relatively large, sessile or with massive stalks, and contain a large number of spores enclosed by a severallayered sporangial wall, at least during early sporogenesis.

In the second series, comprising many times the number of species, the sporangial origin may be traced to single cells that undergo more or less periclinal divisions. After this division the outer cell, by its further divisions and those of its cellular products, forms the bulk of the protuberant *sporangium* and its delicate *sporangial stalk*, which is a few cells, or even one cell, thick.

Here the number of spores per sporangium is usually definite, a multiple of *2* (varying between *16* and *512* in homosporous species). Such sporangia are said to be *leptosporangiate*. The vast majority of familiar cultivated and wild ferns are leptosporangiate, or show slight modifications thereof.

Some botanists are of the opinion that it is not always possible to distinguish absolutely between some varieties of eusporangiate and leptosporangiate sporangia. Although the classification of ferns is controversial and in a state of flux, disagreement is most often expressed at the familial level.

There is rather unified agreement that living ferns may be grouped in five ordersnamely, the *Ophioglossales*, *Marattiales*, *Filicales*, *Marsileales*, and *Salviniales*—and representatives of these orders are included in this book. The writers follow Bierhorst in grouping the *extant* ferns in three classes, as follows:

Class 1. Ophioglossopsida (order Ophio glossales)

Class 2. Marattiopsida (Order Marattiales)

Class 3. Filicopsida (Orders Filicales, Marsileales, Salviniales)

The Filicales, a very large order of fundamentally leptosporangiate and homosporous' ferns, are discussed in other chapter of this book and the leptosporangiate, heterosporbus Marsileales and Salviniales in other chapter.

CLASS 1. OPHIOGLOSSOPSIDA

The Ophioglossopsida contain but a single order and family, the *Ophioglossales* and *Ophioglossaceae*.

Ophioglossum and Botrychium

Introduction and vegetative morphology

The genera *Ophioglossum* (Gr. *ophis,* serpent, + Gr. *glossa,* tongue), the adder'stongue fern, and *Botrychium* (Gr. *botrychos,* grape), the grape fern, with between 20 and 30 species each, are rather widely distributed in temperate North America.

The former occurs in old fields, meadows, and cedar glades, and the latter is frequently an inhabitant of the forest floor, where it thrives in partial shade. *Ophioglossum engelmannii is* often quite abundant after spring and fall rains in partial shade, near and under cedar trees (*Juniperus virginiana*). The leaves in both genera arise from a rather short, fleshy subterranean stem, which bears fleshy, adventitious roots.

The roots of some species of *Ophioglossum* produce adventitious buds, which may develop new plantlets, a phenomenon that results in the formation of rather extensive colonies. Both *Botrychium* and *Ophiogl-*

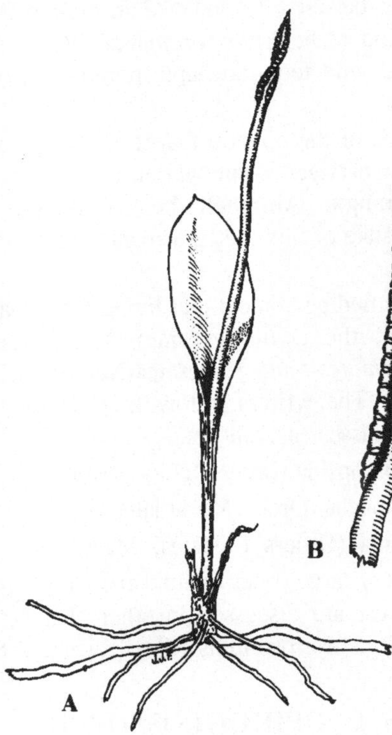

Figure 5.1: Ophioglossum engelmannii.
A. Single fertile plant. B. Dehiscent fertile spike.

ossum usually elevate only a single leaf from the perennial stems each growing season.

The leaves are annual in activity. Serial transverse sections of the axis of O. *engelmannii* reveal that the leaves arise in spiral order in five vertical rows, although usually only one leaf is present at a time. In *B. virginianum*, the leaf blade is large and dissected, but in other species of the genus the leaves are smaller and simpler.

The leaf of *O. engelmannii* is simple and entire. It has been suggested that simple leaves are reduced rather than primitive in these ferns. Inasmuch as the leaf is the dominant and most conspicuous organ of these, plants, its structure will be described first.

The young leaves are rolled up along their longitudinal axes and protected by the remains of the ensheathing stipular sheath of the preceding leaf as they emerge from the soil. The leaflets of *Botrychium* are characterized by open dichotomous venation; the leaf blade in *Ophioglossum* is traversed by a reticulate system of veins, which are mostly united at the leaf margins.

The leaves appear as primordia near the slow-growing stem tip several years before they are raised above the ground, and their development is extremely slow. The vascular tissue of the leaf is connected to that in the stem through the petiole.

In *O. engelmannii* the double leaf trace branches into four or more strands soon after it enters the petiole. The single trace in *Botrychium* divides into two as it enters the petiole. Evert investigated the sieve elements of the petioles and rachises of *B. virginianum.*

They are of the *nacreous* types-that is, early in ontogeny the walls thicken with a pearly-looking substance, but the thickening gradually disappears as the sieve elements mature and lose their nuclei. Pores occur in both the lateral and terminal walls of mature sieve elements.

The leaf blade in *Ophioglossum* is covered by epidermal cells above and below; the central portion is composed of photosynthetic parenchyma cells, which are not differentiated into palisade and spongy layers. Stomata occur abundantly on both surfaces of the leaf.

The guard cells, alone among the epidermal cells, contain chloroplasts. The underground stems of both *Ophioglossum* and *Botrychium* are erect, slowgrowing, and fleshy. They are covered with the remains of previous seasons' leaves at their summits, and with rather closely arranged, fleshy roots below, one of the latter associated with each old leaf base.

Development of the stem in both genera is localized in the division of a single apical cell and its derivatives. These differentiate in older portions of the stem into stelar, cortical, and epidermal regions. The vascular tissue in the primary (*embryonic*) stems of some species is protostelic, but as the stem grows older, the vascular tissue formed later is arranged as an ectophloic siphonostele.

The latter is much dissected into discrete strands in *Ophioglossum* because of the close proximity to each other of the departure of leaf traces, which, in these megaphyllous plants, leave *parenchymatous* gaps in the stele above the point of their departure.

The shortness of the internodes and the overlapping of leaf gaps result in the dissection of the stele, which has endarch maturation of the xylem. The phloem is external to the xylem. *Endodermis* and pericycle are absent in mature stems of *O. engelmannii*.

In the stems of *Botrychium, a* cambium adds secondary vascular tissues to the primary ones. The cortex is parenchymatous and starch-filled. The stem surface is suberized in older portions by the formation of a periderm layer. *Botrychium is* the only extant fern genus with secondary vascular tissue and a periderm.

Evert has investigated the sieve elements of the petioles and rachises of *Botrychium virginianum.* The roots in both genera also develop through the activity of single apical cells. They arise endogenously in the rhizome near the phloem in association with the leaves and below them.

In *Ophioglossum* the root may be monarch, diarch, or tetrarch; it is most often tetrarch in *B. virginianum.* The phloem alternates with the xylem, and both are surrounded by one or more layers of pericycle cells. The stele is delimited from the cortex by a well-differentiated endodermis.

The cortex is extensive and serves as a storage region. The epidermis is devoid of root hairs; in older regions of the root, the surface is suberized. Endophytic fungi usually are present in these genera. Petersen and Brisson (1977) have studied the structure of the root cap of *O. petiolatum.*

Reproduction: the sporophyte

Both *Ophioglossum* and *Botrychium* are at once distinguishable from other Pteridophyta by the arrangement of their sporogenous tissue, which is localized in a branched or unbranched *fertile spike*. The latter emerges at the junction of the leaf blade and petiole. Anatomical evidence has been interpreted as indicating that this structure represents a pair of fertile, lateral pinnae (leaflets).

The fertile axis is unbranched in *O. engelmannii* but compound in

B. virginianum. In the former, it has two longitudinal rows of massive sporangia. Their walls are composed of several layers of cells.

A branch of vascular tissue runs to the base of each sporangium. There is one- or two-layered tapetumlike zone between the central sporogenous tissue and the wall. As the sporangium develops, the walls of the tapetal cells disintegrate and give rise to a tapetal plasmodium.

A few of the sporogenous cells also disintegrate, but the remainder undergo meiosis and give rise to tetrads of spores. The haploid number of chromosomes in *O . vulgatum is* approximately 258.

The cells of the sporophyte, therefore, contain more than 500 chromosomes; a tropical species, O. *reticulatum,* with 1260 chromosomes, has the largest number yet observed in a naturally occurring vascular plant.

The sporangia dehisce at maturity along a line perpendicular to the long axis of the fertile spike, the line of dehiscence predetermined by the formation of several rows of thin-walled cells. Each sporangium may contain as many as 15,000 spores in some species.

Reproduction: the gametophyte. Development of the gametophyte from the spores has until recently not been followed completely in

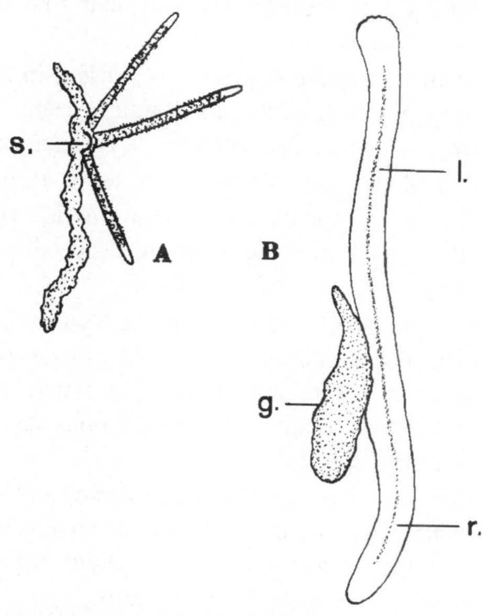

Figure 5.2: A. Ophioglossum vulgatum. Gametophyte showing roots and minute stem (s.) of young sporophyte. B. O. moluccanum. Embryonic sporophyte attached to gametophyte. g., gametophyte; 1., primary leaf or cotyledon; r., primary root or radicle.

laboratory cultures; hence, our knowledge of it is based largely on specimens collected in the field.

In both *Ophioglossum* and *Botrychium* the gametophyte is fleshy, subterranean, and nongreen and always is infected with the hyphae of an endophytic fungus. *Ophioglossum* gametophytes are cylindrical, up to 5 cm in length, and branched in some individuals. The diameter of the largest is about 0.65 cm.

Whittier, however, has succeeded in growing gametophytes of *B. dissectum* and of *O. engelmannii* to sexual maturity in axenic culture. In 11-month-old cultures tracheids develop in the gametophytes, and that of *Botrychium* formed haploid apogamous sporophytes.

Gifford and Brandon (1978) reported that gametophytes of *B. multifidum* grown in axenic culture developed only antheridia on a dorsal ridge. Mesler has described the gametophytes of *O. palmatum*, a southern Florida epiphytic species, and those of *O. crotalophoroides*.

The gametophytes of the former are cylindrical and branched, while those of the latter are globose to hemispherical. Mesler reported that the spores of *O. crotalophoroides* germinate immediately after their release in the spring; fertilization occurs about one year later, and gametophytes with young sporophytes with their first leaf develop 30 months after spore release.

A fungus with nonseptate hyphae was present in the monoecious gametophytes most of which were 2 to 20 mm beneath the soil surface. A few which were at the surface because of erosion were pale green.

The nutrition of the gametophyte here, as in *Psilotum* and some species of *Lycopodium,* apparently is saprophytic. However, small amounts of chlorophyll may develop in exposed portions of the gametophyte, the growth of which is apical.

The gametophyte of *O. vulgatum* in the Ryukyu Islands contains mycorrhizal fungi. The authors have searched in vain for gametophytes of O. *engelmannii* in nature but never have found any, in or near colonies of that species, in spite of the enormous numbers of spores shed from their fertile spikes.

Ophioglossum is monoecious, the antheridia and archegonia occurring together in various stages of development. Both kinds of sex organs arise from cells on the surface of the gametophyte, but at maturity they are largely sunken within it, as in *Anthoceros*.

The antheridia are massive and contain large numbers of multiflagellate sperms. Only the tips of the archegonial necks (with four rows of neck cells) protrude above the gametophytic surface. Fertilization has been observed to occur in the summer months in the northern hemisphere.

Reproduction: embryogeny

Development of the zygote into an embryonic sporophyte progresses slowly in various species of *Ophioglossum. A* small spherical mass of tissue is formed within the archegonial venter. This becomes differentiated into foot, root, and leaf primordium.

The apical initial of the stem appears later, and this perhaps foreshadows the inconspicuous state of that organ in the mature sporophyte. Several years are required in most species for the production f of a leaf with a fertile spike. Figures elsewhere in this chapter, H illustrate gametophytes with an attached juvenile sporophyte.

CLASS 2. MARATTIOPSIDA

The Marattiopsida contains only a single order, Marattiales, and family, Marattiaceae.

Marattia and Angiopteris

Introduction and Vegetative Morphology

The members of the Marattiales are exclusively tropical. Two of the seven genera, *Marattia,* with about 60 species, and *Angiopteris*, with about 100 species, are here chosen to illustrate the order. *Marattia* and *Angiopteris* are sometimes available in university and other Conservatories and as specimens in herbaria.

Species of these genera have the largest and most complex fronds in the family; the fronds are several times pinnately compound. The young leaves are circinately *vernate,* that is, curled in the bud. *Angiopteris is* native to Hawaii, the Philippines, and the western Pacific area, while *Marattia is* more widely distributed in the tropics.

The fronds of a New Zealand species are 6 to 9 m long and up to 4.5 m wide. The ultimate leaf divisions (pinnules) have dichotomous venation. Mucilage chambers occur throughout the rather fleshy plants.

Reproduction: the gametophyte. The gametophytes are massive and liverwortlike (suggestive of *Pellia*), up to several centimeters long. A mycorrhizal fungus is usually present within the gametophytic cells. The gametophytes are long-lived and many cells thick, except at the margins.

Antheridia, which produce multiflagellate sperms, may develop on both surfaces of the protandrous gametophytes; the archegonia occur only on the ventral surface. Both types of sex organs are immersed in the thallus as in the Ophioglossales and *Anthoceros.*

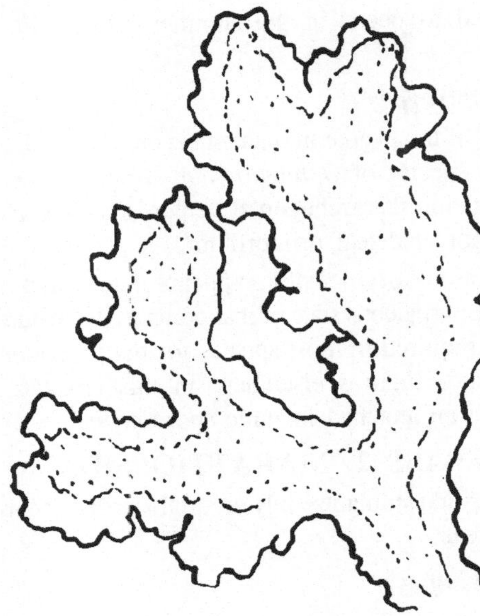

Figure 5.3: Marattia sambricina. Gametophyte 27 months after spore germination.

Reproduction: embryogeny

Usually only one zygote on each gametophyte develops into a juvenile sporophyte. The Marattiales differ in their embryogeny from the leptosporangiate ferns in that the primary leaf emerges from the dorsal surface of the gametophytes, rather than from the ventral.

The stems are fleshy, tuberous, and erect or trunklike and covered by the persistent paired stipules at each leaf base, from among which the fleshy roots emerge. The roots contain polyarch actinosteles with as many as 12 protoxylem groups (*M. alata*), many more than occur in most ferns.

The young stems develop from single apical cells and in their mature regions contain a single cylinder of vascular bundles. In older stems, however, the vascular tissue is present as a polycyclic dictyostele with two or more concentric vascular cylinders. Some of the strands are leaf traces.

Reproduction: the sporophyte

The eusporangiate sporangia of *Angiopteris* are massive and closely appressed laterally. They are borne near the leaf mar= gins along the veinlets in compressed rings of 10 to 20. Approximately 512 sporocytes are differentiated within each sporangium. The latter is thick-walled and provided with a tapetum.

The sporangia of *Angiopteris,* although crowded together, retain their individuality and dehisce into two valves by vertical splitting. The sporangia of *Marattia* are united into a compound unit called a *synangium.* The latter opens as a unit, exposing the vertically split, contiguous sporangia. Sometimes the bivalvular structure is called a *sporocarp.*

6

Vascular Cryptogams IV: Division Pteridophyta II

CLASS 3. FILICOPSIDA

As stated at the beginning of other chapter in this book, the division Pteridophyta contains both eusporangiate and leptosporangiate ferns. The former were described in the preceding chapter, and the latter will be discussed in this and in the other chapter of this book.

In leptosporangiate sporangium development, it will be recalled, the sporangium arises from a single cell, derivatives of which protrude from the fertile receptacle. Leptosporangiate sporangia are small, produce a definite number of spores (frequently 48 to 64, but up to 512), and usually have a wall one layer of cells in thickness.

Other attributes, in addition to sporangial characters, serve to distinguish the eusporangiate from the leptosporangiate ferns. These will be cited in the following account. In number of genera, species, and individuals, the leptosporangiate ferns far outnumber the eusporangiate.

Some 300 genera and 9000 species have been described. These are most abundant and diverse in the tropics, but they are also well represented in the temperate zone. Two species, *Onoclea sensibilis* and *Pteridium aquilinum*, have been reported to be poisonous to livestock.

Some ferns are edible by human beings, including the young leaves or "*fiddleheads*" of *Osmunda* and those of *Athyrium esculentum*, which reach a length of a decimeter. The latter are cooked and eaten in

Malaysia, as is a species of *Ceratopteris*. In habit, they vary from small, delicate, filmy plants to large tropical tree ferns with upright stems and enormous leaves; several are climbers.

The leptosporangiate ferns include a number of families, of which many species are inhabitants of the tropics, and, therefore, not readily available for study except in collections in herbaria and occasionally in conservatories.

For this reason, the treatment of the group in this text will be restricted to a brief discussion of representatives that are readily available; specialized treatises listed in the Bibliography give a more extensive treatment of the ferns.

The books of Bower (1923, 1926, 1928), Bierhorst (1971a), and Foster and Gifford (1974) provide more comprehensive discussions of ferns than does the present volume. The classification of leptosporangiate ferns with respect to orders and families has been in a state of flux during the past 25 years.

The most conservative classification grouped them in a single order, Filicales, which included 19 families. At the other extreme is their classification in 18 orders and 38 families! Most recently, Bierhorst has recognized three orders (*Filicales*, *Marsileales*, and *Salviniales*) and 27 families. Various schemes of phylogenetic relationships of ferns have been proposed (Jermy, Crabbe, and Thomas, 1973).

In the cited reference, however, Holttum writes: "As regards the great majority of ferns, their probable phylogeny can be inferred only from their classification; there is no other evidence available."

Members of the order Filicales will be discussed in this chapter and those of the Marsileales and Salviniales in other chapter of this book.

Order 1. Filicales

With the exception of the five genera of "water ferns" classified in the Marsileales and Salviniales, the majority of leptosporangiate ferns are often included in the very large heterogeneous order Filicales, which contains numerous families of homosporous genera and one genus seemingly with incipient heterospory.

A number of these are known only through tropical representatives from remote places; material of these ferns is not readily available. The present discussion, accordingly, will emphasize certain widely distributed and generally available genera of the family Polypodiaceae and will be followed by briefer treatment of representatives of some of the other families.

Family 1. Polypodiaceae

Introduction and Vegetative Morphology

A majority of the most familiar, naturally occurring, and widespread ferns of the temperate zone and tropics, as well as many cultivated varieties, are members of a vast assemblage of polypodiaceous ferns, so named from the genus *Polypodium* (Gr. *polys*, many, + Gr. *pous*, foot).

Among these are *Thelypteris* (Gr. *thelys*, female, + Gr. *pteris*), *Adiantum* (Gr. *adiantos*, maidenhair), *Polystichum* (Gr. *polys*, many, + Gr. *stichos*, row), *Woodsia* (after Joseph Wood, an English botanist), *Pteris* (Gr. *pteris*, fern), *Pteridium* (Gr. *pteris*), and *Nephrolepis* (Gr. *nephros*, kidney, + Gr. *lepis*, scale).

Most of these genera are plants of moist, mesic woodlands. *Adiantum capillus-veneris*, the Venus maidenhair, however, is an example of a rather hydrophytic species and is widely distributed on wet limestone cliffs; A. *pedatum* grows in moist, shady woods.

Pellaea atropurpurea, the cliff brake, and *Polypodium polypodioides*, the "resur= rection fern," on the other hand, are xerophytes. All temperate-zone members of this alliance are perennial, and a few (*Polystichum*, *Cyrtomium*) are evergreen; a number of ferns have mycorrhizal associations.

Adiantum capillus-veneris and *Thelypteris dentata* will be emphasized

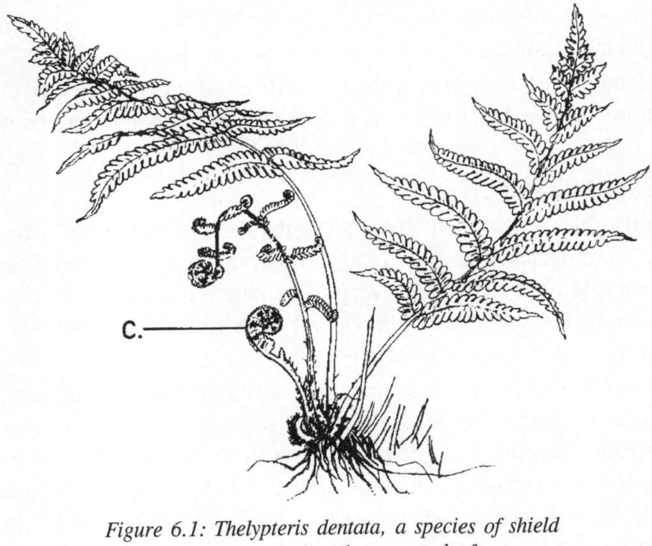

Figure 6.1: Thelypteris dentata, a species of shield fern. c., circinately vernate leaf.

as illustrative types in the following account, because they are widespread and readily cultivated in greenhouses or out-ofdoors in sufficiently mild climates. In both of them the stem is subterranean, although in the former it may be exposed.

The bases of the preceding season's leaves persist indefinitely and form a sort of jagged armor about the stems. The stem in *T. dentata is* ascending and relatively slow growing, but in *Adiantum* it is a horizontal, rapidly elongating rhizome.

Branching of the rhizome is abundant in *Adiantum* and results in colonization of the area around the original plant. The stems of both genera are clothed with a dense mass of adventitious roots, which emerge between the leaf bases.

Growth of the stem in each case may be traced to the activity of a single apical cell and its derivatives. In investigations of stem apices of many ferns, Bierhorst (1977) and Hebant, Hebant-Mauri, and Barthonet (1978) found few whose development did not originate in an apical cell.

This apical cell occurs at the stem tip, often concealed by a dense growth of superficial, multicellular, scalelike organs known as *paleae.* The apical cell of the stem of leptosporangiate ferns gives rise to three ranks of derivative cells.

Although the vascular tissues in the embryonic stems of all leptosporangiate ferns are reported to be protostelic, there is a gradual transition in older stems to a siphonostelic, solenostelic, or dictyostelic condition, depending on the species.

In *Adiantum*, the vascular tissue is completely surrounded by a well-differentiated endodermis that separates it from the parenchymatous pith and cortex; in *Thelypteris*, the endodermis surrounds each segment of the dictyostele. Portions of both of these may become sclerotic. *Adiantum is* solenostelic, while *Thelypteris* is dictyostelic.

The xylem is mesarch in development and composed chiefly of elongate tracheids with tapered ends with abundant, transversely elongate (scalariform), bordered pits. In a few genera (*Pteridium*), the closing membranes of the pits of the sloping terminal tracheid walls are dissolved at maturity, resulting in direct continuity between adjoining elements.

Thus, primitive vessels, previously noted in *Selaginella* and *Equisetum* and characteristic of the xylem of many flowering plants, are present in several ferns. The sieve elements are elongate, lack companion cells, and have numerous sieve areas in their vertical walls.

The sieve elements in some ferns have walls thicker than those of the associated parenchyma cells. These thickenings may be transitory.

All fern roots, with the exception of the embryonic radicle, are adventitious and arise endogenously from the stem. They develop between the leaf bases.

Development of the root originates in a single apical cell; in this case, however, the latter, in addition to the usual series, cuts off derivatives in a direction perpendicular to the long axis of the root, thus adding cells to the root cap.

The cells of the central procambium differentiate into an exarch protostele, the arrangement characteristic of the roots of most vascular plants. The roots of *Dryopteris dentata* are diarch. The stele is surrounded by a narrow pericycle, a prominent endodermis, cortex, and epidermis, the latter with root hairs.

The inner portion of the cortex is often sclerotic. Branch roots originate from endodermal cells opposite the protoxylem groups. Secondary growth is absent in both stems and roots of leptosporangiate ferns. As in the eusporangiate ferns, the leaves of *Thelypteris* and *Adiantum* and many other species are the dominant organs of the sporophyte.

The large compound leaves, *circinately vernate* in the bud, may be highly elaborate when mature. Complex, finely divided fern leaves are considered to represent the primitive condition. Simple leaves in ferns are probably reduced. The primary divisions (leaflets) of a compound fern leaf are called *pinnae*.

The ultimate divisions are called *pinnules*. The continuation of the petioles among the leaflets is the *rachis*. The fern leaf is often referred to as a *frond*. The petiole of each leaf is connected to the stem stele by one or more traces; these run throughout the rachis, giving rise to branches that traverse the pinnae and pinnules.

In *Adiantum* the venation is dichotomous, while in *T. dentata* it is pinnate. Reticulate venation is thought to have been derived from the dichotomous pattern by development of branches between the dichotomies. Internally, the leaf blade consists of an upper and lower epidermis, the latter with abundant stomata, enclosing a relatively undifferentiated mesophyll.

Van Cotthem has made a comprehensive survey (510 species of 240 genera!) of the stomata of ferns and recognizes nine different types. The mesophyll of *Adiantum* is limited in extent; the abundant chloroplasts in the epidermal cells in this genus undoubtedly play a major role in the photosynthesis.

The veins are collateral in arrangement of xylem and phloem. The leaves arise close to the growing point of the stem and develop at first through the activity of an apical cell with three cutting faces. A new group of leaves is produced each season. The simple leaves of the walking fern, *Asplenium rhizophyllum*, function in propagation.

Reproduction: the sporophyte

After a series of entirely vegetative leaves has been produced from the stem of a young plant, all the leaves that develop subsequently in *Thelypteris* and *Adiantum*, and in most other genera, are usually both vegetative and fertile.

In both genera, groups of sporangia known as *sori* (Gr. *soros*, heap) develop on the undersurface of ordinary leaves. Some segregation of vegetative and reproductive functions is apparent in the distribution of sporogenous tissue in several other genera of polypodiaceous ferns.

In the Christmas fern, *Polystichum acrostichoides*, for example, only the distal pinnae of each frond are fertile. *Onoclea sensibilis*, the sensitive fern, and *Pteretis pensylvanicum*, the ostrich fern, superficially suggest *Osmunda cinnamonea*, the cinnamon fern, in that they produce sporangia on markedly modified fronds, the remaining leaves being purely vegetative.

In *Adiantum* and *Pteris*, the sori are almost marginal and are covered during development by a marginal flap of tissue known as a *false indusium.* (*L. indusium*, a woman's undergarment). The sporangia are actually borne on this false indusium in *Adiantum.*

In *Thelypteris dentata* the sori lie over the veins of the pinnules, and each is covered by a shieldlike flap of tissue, the *true indusium*, a single layer of cells in thickness and of epidermal origin. The sporangia in both genera arise from the lower leaf surface, and the region of their origin is known as the *receptacle.*

The order of development in both cases is said to be *mixed*, since sporangial development follows no definite sequence with relation to position on the receptacle, both immature and mature sporangia being present in contrast to the simultaneous maturation of the sporangia, which is called *simple*, some ferns, e.g., in *Osmunda.*

The process of development of a leptosporangiate sporangium is illustrated in Figures elsewhere in this chapter. Each sporangium arises from a superficial cell of the receptacle that projects above the surface and undergoes an oblique division.

The inner product of the division either may not divide again or it divides to form two cells, of which the innermost takes no further part in sporangial ontogeny; the outer of these two and the most distal cell undergo intercalary divisions, forming the sporangium, which consists of

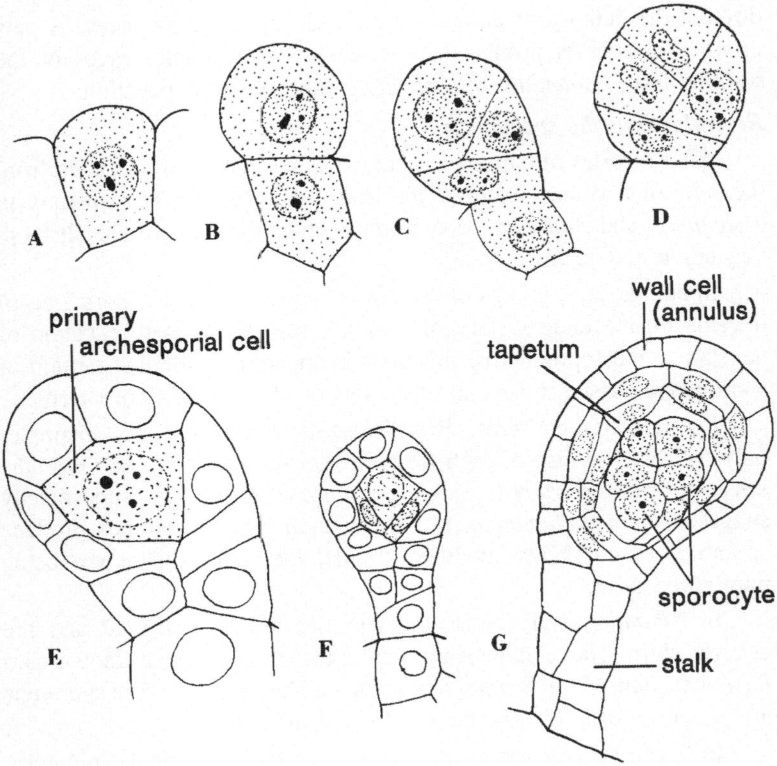

Figure 6.2: Thelypteris dentata. A-G. Successive stages in leptosporangiate sporangium development.

a stalk and an enlarged distal portion. A central tetrahedral cell gives rise by periclinal divisions to four cells, which subsequently undergo another periclinal division, forming two layers.

The outer usually serves as an inner layer of the sporangial wall, while the inner layer functions as a *tapetum*. The central cell (*primary archesporial cell*), enclosed by the tapetum, now divides repeatedly and forms the sporocytes, which vary in number from 12 to 16, the latter the most typical number.

Each of these separates and undergoes meiosis, forming a tetrad of spores that ultimately separate and thicken their walls. The chromosome number of the Venus maidenhair, *A. capillus-veneris*, has been determined to be $n = 30$, a rather low number among the leptosporangiate ferns.

The tapetal cells elongate radially during sporogenesis and finally become disorganized, presumably functioning in the nutrition of the developing spores. During sporogenesis, the cells of the sporangial

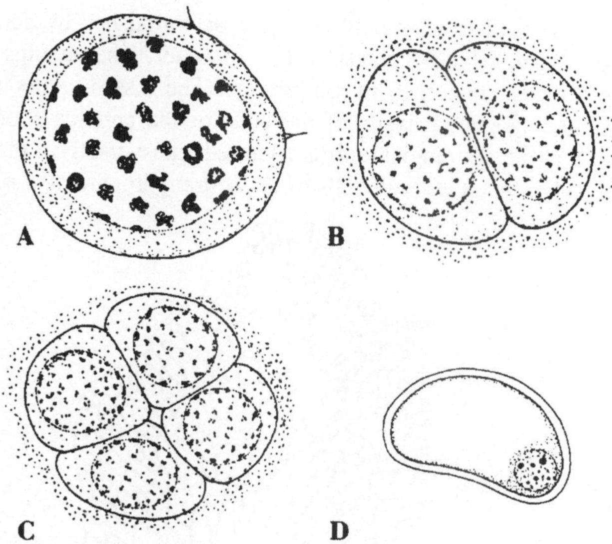

Figure 6.3: Thelypteris dentata. Sporogenesis. A. Sporocyte in prophase of meiosis. B. End of meiosis I. C. Spore tetrad. D. Immature spore.

jacket divide by anticlinal division and the products increase in size, as do the cells of the stalk. At maturity, the sporangium is a slightly flattened spheroid or ellipsoid.

The wall cells on the flattened faces are large and have undulate walls. A vertical row of specially differentiated cells, the *annulus*, forms an incomplete ring about the sporangium. The radial and inner tangential walls of these cells are markedly thickened.

Between the last cell of the annulus and the sporangial stalk there are a number (often four) of thin-walled cells, the *lip cells* or *stomium*. As the spores mature, they become invested wtih a yellow, rarely black, wall, and the color of the entire sorus changes from a delicate whitish-green to dark brown, rarely black.

The walls of the spores of ferns (and most other land plants) are differentiated into two layers, an inner (the endospore, or *intine*) and an outer (the exospore, or *exine*). The outer layer is variously ornamented, as revealed by electron microscopy.

In a few ferns a third layer, the *perispore*, surrounds the exospore. When the spores on a majority of the sporangia are mature, the indusium in *Thelypteris* contracts, exposing them to the air. In *Adiantum* and *Pteris* the revolute leaf edge unfolds slightly when the spores are mature.

Spore dissemination in both genera is accomplished by dehiscence of the sporangia, which depends on loss of water. The annulus and lip cells are directly concerned in the process. The loss of water through the thin outer tangential walls of the cells of the annulus shortens its length so that the sporangial wall is ruptured transversely in the region of the lip cells; the outer wall cells of the sporangium are also ruptured.

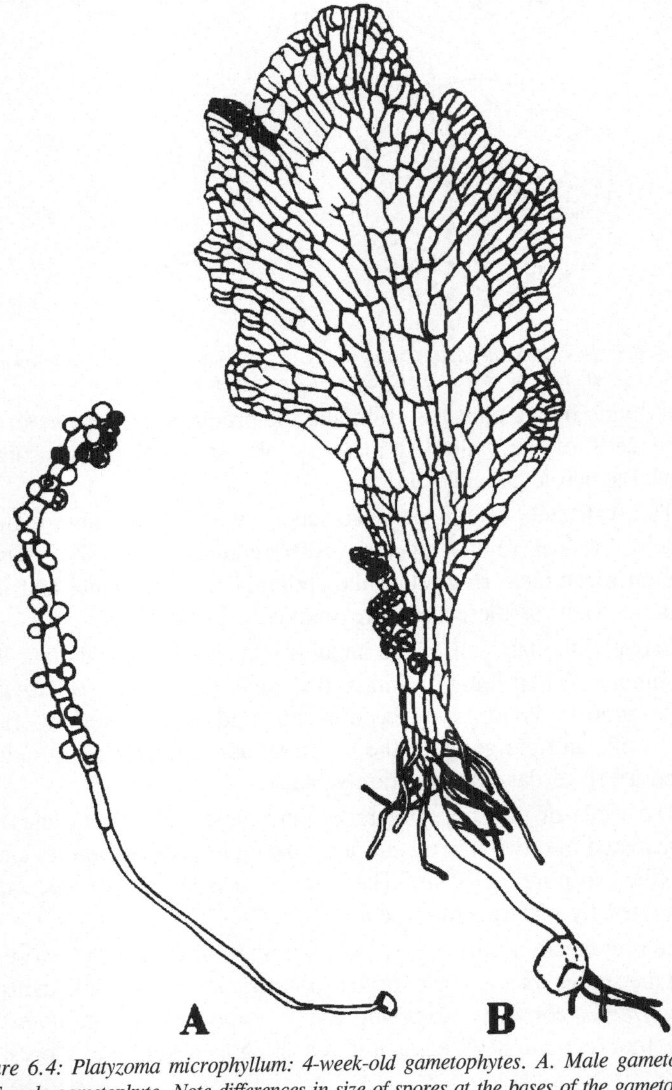

Figure 6.4: Platyzoma microphyllum: 4-week-old gametophytes. A. Male gametophyte. B. Female gametophyte. Note differences in size of spores at the bases of the gametophytes.

As the annulus continues to shorten, its outer tangential cell walls become increasingly concave, because they are adherent to the water within the annulus cells, the amount of which is lessening through evaporation.

Ultimately, a point is reached at which the tensile resistance of the water within the annulus cells is no longer sufficient to prevent the separation of the outer tangential walls from its surface; at this point the water vaporizes, reducing the tension on the outer tangential cell walls of the annulus, which snaps back or catapults to its original position, thus ejecting the spores.

Although the number of spores produced by a single sporangium in most leptosporangiate ferns is small, frequently 48-64, as compared with those of eusporangiate genera (1500-2000 in *Botrychium*, for example), the large number of sporangia in a sorus, along with the enormous number of sori on the pinnules of a single mature plant, results in the production of a surprisingly large number of spores by a single individual.

It has been estimated that one mature plant of *Thelypteris* produces 50 million spores each season. Farrar (1976) found that the ferns in a certain area in central Iowa matured and released most of their spores in a two-week period.

This was especially true of *Botrychium* and *Osmunda*, which mature all their spores simultaneously. Other species (e.g., of *Adiantum* and *Polypodium*), with nonsimultaneous (mixed) maturation of sporangia, shed their spores during the late summer and autumn.

Unique among the Filicales is an Australian fern, *Platyzoma microphyllum*, which produces spores of two size classes with a volume ratio of 1:7.5; in addition, spores of intermediate size are formed. Thirty-two spores are borne in some smaller sporangia and 16 in other larger sporangia.

These spores grow into unisexual gametophytes, the smaller into filamentous male gametophytes lacking rhizoids, and the larger into spatulate ones bearing archegonia and, later, antheridia. This distribution of sex organs is reminiscent of that in *Equisetum*.

Of additional interest is the report that the smaller spores may germinate within the sporangia.

Reproduction: the gametophyte

In spite of the enormous number of spores, relatively few complete their development into mature gametophytes in nature, because so many are borne by air currents to places unfavorable for germination. Gametophytes are sometimes present on moist soil or in rock crevices in the vicinity of fern colonies. As a matter of fact, fern gametophytes seem not to be abundant or conspicuous in the wild, at least in the temperate zone.

Germination of fern spores and their development into gametophytes were described first in 1827 by the German Kaulfuss. Davidonis and Ruddat (1973, 1974) reported that gametophytes of *Thelypteris normalis* do not grow under the sporophytic plants because of substances, Thelypterin A and B, diffusing from the roots.

Thelypterin A is an indole derivative that inhibits cell division, and hence cell numbers, in the gametophytes of T. *normalis* and also in the ferns, *Pteris*, and *Phlebodium*. It does not inhibit young sporophytes of *T. normalis*.

In this connection Petersen and Fairbrothers (1977) reported allelopathy between gametophytes of *Osmunda* species and *Dryopteris* species. The presence of the former decreases the growth and cell size of the latter by about 50%. Star and Weber (1978) found that the powdery, flavonoid exudate on the leaves of the fern *Pityrogramma calemolanos* inhibits spore germination and normal development of the gametophytes of the same species.

Most fern spores require light for their germination, especially red light (500 to 700 nm). The processes of spore germination and gametophyte development may be followed readily in laboratory cultures of spores of *Thelypteris*, *Adiantum*, and other leptosporangiate ferns planted on agar on moist soil, or on the surface of moist flowerpots or other crockery.

Some stages in their development are illustrated in Figure elsewhere in this chapter. In crowded cultures the developing gametophytes may remain irregularly filamentous, but when they are well spaced they typically become cordate.

Spore germination frequently results in the formation of a small, protonemalike chain of bulbous cells rich in chloroplasts. One or two rhizoids usually develop early from the basal cell, and the more rhizoids develop later from the ventral cells of the gametophyte.

Dyer and Cran (1976) have demonstrated that the walls of the rhizoids differ from those of other gametophytic cells. The walls of the latter have an oriented, fibrillar organization, while those of the former have a random network of fibrils within which are electron-dense deposits.

The form of the gametophyte and abundance of rhizoids are affected by quality and intensity of light. The spores of most ferns will not germinate in darkness. *Pteridium aquilinum* is exceptional in this respect. Higher intensities of white and blue light evoke the development of the flat, thallose form. They also increase the number of rhizoids.

In darkness or in low light intensities, especially of red light, the gametophyte remains filamentous and a few rhizoids form. Under favorable conditions, oblique divisions in the terminal cell of the young filamentous gametophyte result in the production of an apical cell that cuts off segments in two directions.

The derivatives continue to divide, forming a spatulate plant body one layer of cells in thickness, except in the central region near the apical notch. Mohr (1963) has reported that blue light (below 500 nm) is required for the initially filamentous stage to develop the spatulate phase of the gametophyte.

This type of development is just one of a number of patterns that have been recorded for ferns. The variations have been summarized by Nayar and Kaur (1971) and Atkinson (1973). It has been demonstrated that fern gametophytes (*Onoclea*) will grow in red light, provided sucrose is present in the culture medium, although they will not grow in its absence.

Accordingly, these gametophytes are facultatively heterotrophic in red light (but not in darkness). The *prothallia* or prothalli, as the gametophytes are often called, are usually monoecious but usually somewhat protandrous. This is especially noticeable in crowded cultures, in which minute filamentous gametophytes tend to develop antheridia precociously.

In uncrowded cultures, the sex organs appear in laboratory cultures on agar in about 35 to 40 days in *T. dentata*. Both types are normally borne on the ventral surface, although deviations may appear in the moist atmosphere of petri dish cultures.

In general, the antheridia of many gametophytes are produced before the archegonia (protandry) and develop nearer the posterior portion of the gametophyte than the archegonia, which develop on the thickened, central cushion nearer the apex.

Like the sporangia, the antheridia are protuberant, whereas only the necks of the archegonia project from the thallus surface. Both antheridia and archegonia originate from single superficial cells of the gametophyte.

The antheridial initial protrudes to form a hemispherical cell that undergoes transverse division. The outer product of division develops into the antheridium, as shown in Figure elsewhere in this chapter.

The antheridial wall is composed of three cells, two of them ringlike and the uppermost a *cover cell*, or cap cell. Liquid water is necessary for antheridial dehiscence, which is effected by the swelling of the component cells (both wall and sperm) and rupture of the cap cell.

The extruded multiflagellate sperms rapidly become motile and subsequently slough off their spheres of attached cytoplasm. Duckett (1975) has described the development and organization of the sperms of ferns at the ultrastructural level. Investigations by Dopp (1962); Naf (1962, 1968, 1969); Naf, Sullivan, and Cummins (1969); Voeller and Weinberg (1969); and Voeller (1971) have uncovered interesting data regarding the control of formation of fern antheridia.

Naf, Nakanishi, and Endo (1975) have summarized our knowledge of this. When spores of the bracken fern, *Pteridium aquilinum,*, germinate, some quickly give rise to two-dimensional and cordate gametophytes. These produce a substance, *antheridiogen*, which diffuses through the agar medium (a distance of 25 cm has been recorded) and stimulates other younger gametophytes to develop antheridia.

The gametophytes become insensitive to the antheridiogen as they become cordate, and, thus, those that secrete antheridiogen are themselves not induced to form antheridia, but they do form archegonia. Thus, a mechanism for early cross-fertilization is present.

Later, those gametophytes that have been induced by the antheridiogen to form antheridia develop archegonia, so that self-fertilization also may occur. Species of 20 genera in four different families of ferns produce antheridia in response to the antheridiogen from *P. aquilinum.*

An additional effect of this antheridiogen is that it evokes the germination of the spores of these same genera in darkness and obviates the usual requirement for light; *Pteridium* spores can germinate in darkness. Antheridiogens, chemically different from those of *Pteridium*, have been isolated from two other ferns, *Anemia phyllitidis* and *Lygodium japonicum*.

Both these antheridiogens are inactive in *Onoclea sensibilis*, the species used to assay for the antheridiogen of *Pteridium aquilinum. Anemia phyllitidis*, and *Lygodium japonicum* are distinct entities on the basis both of the criteria of cross-testing and chromatographic separation.

These antheridiogens are similar in their effect on gametophytic development to gibberellins GA_4 and GA_7. In addition to stimulating the development of antheridia in some fern species, these substances also can break the dormancy of their spores in darkness.

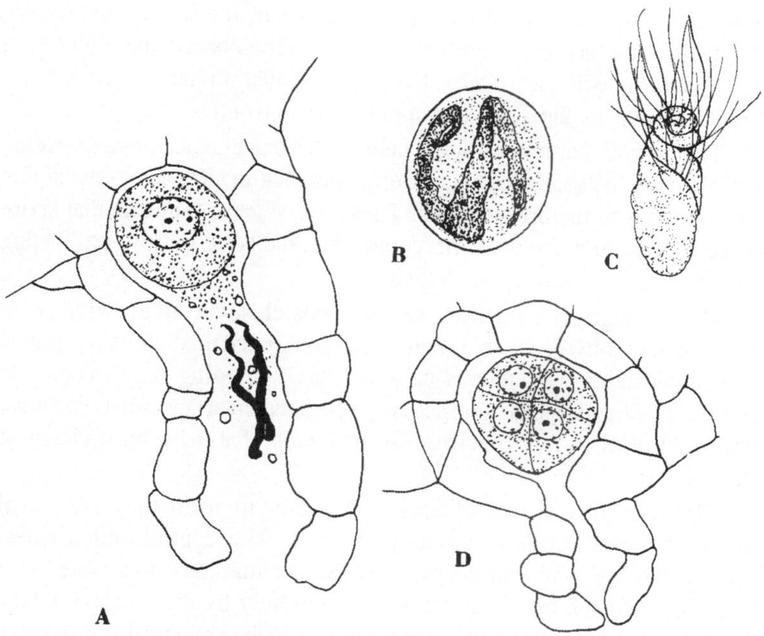

Figure 6.5: Thelypteris dentate. A. Median longitudinal section of mature archegonium, showing sperms in neck. B. Sperm in spermatogenous cell (aceto-carmine preparation). C. Free-swimming sperm. D. Median longitudinal section of archegonium with eight-celled embryo.

The antheridiogens differ not only chemically but also with respect to the species whose gametophytes and spores and antheridiogen from *Anemia* has been determined by Nakanishi, Endo, Naf, and Johnson (1971), the first chemical characterization of a fern antheridiogen and the fifth sexually related substance to be so characterized in the plant kingdom.

The chemical structure of *Anemia* antheridiogen is shown in Figure elsewhere in this chapter, and this substance is related to gibberellin, which also has antheridium inducing properties. The antheridiogen has been recovered in pure form.

It is active in inducing antheridial formation at a concentration as low as 10 μg/liter and in stimulating germination of spores in darkness at a concentration of 0.3 μg/liter. Tryon and Vitale (1977), on the basis of their studies of populations of gametophytes of two ferns, *Asplenium pimpernellifolium* and *Lygodium heterodoxum*, reported that an antheridiogen system is seemingly operative in nature.

Small (0.3 to 2.2 mm) gametophytes in colonies produced many antheridia, while widely spaced gametophytes of the same size (at least 15 cm from the nearest neighbor) had few. Schedlbauer and Klekowski (1972) and Schedlbauer (1976) have investigated antheridiogen activity and its results in the fern *Ceratopteris thalictroides*.

They found that in multispore cultures bisexual gametophytes develop first; they are the source of the antheridiogen that induces later-developing gametophytes to mature as males. These investigators suggest that spore size is an important factor in this connection, the large spores germinating first into hermaphroditic gametophytes.

The archegonia arise from surface cells close to the growing point of the gametophyte. Each initial undergoes periclinal division into a superficial and a hypogenous cell, the latter dividing only once. The outermost cell undergoes two successive perpendicular anticlinal divisions, forming initials of the four rows of neck cells that arise by division of these initials.

The hypogenous cell divides periclinally to form the neck canal nuclei, but cytokinesis is often suppressed. The central cell divides, forming the egg and ventral canal cells. On immersion in water, the distal tiers of neck cells are ruptured, apparently by the swelling of the disintegrated neck and ventral canal cells, which are extruded and leave a canallike passageway to the egg.

It was demonstrated long ago that the movement of sperms toward archegonia is not fortuitous but the result of a chemotactic response. The chemical stimulant secreted from the archegonium can be replaced by malic acid in laboratory experiments.

Duckett and Bell (1972a,b) investigated fertilization in the fern *Pteridium aquilinum* with the electron microscope. According to them, the sperms lose their plastid during their passage through the archegonial neck and only one sperm enters the egg cytoplasm.

The moist habitat of the gametophytes, along with the ventral position of the sex organs, enhances the opportunities for fertilization. Further growth of the gametophyte ceases after its archegonia have been fertilized. Nayar and Kaur (1971) have summarized the organization of the gametophytes in homosporous ferns.

Fern gametophytes are seemingly not obvious in nature, but Farrar and Gooth (1975), on the basis of their investigation of reproduction of ferns in an Iowa canyon, found that numbers of gametophytes in the wild differed in different species.

Thus, in plots within 5 meters of sporophytes of *Cystopteris bulbifera*, *Adiantum pedatum*, and *Woodsia obtusa*, between 500 and 3000

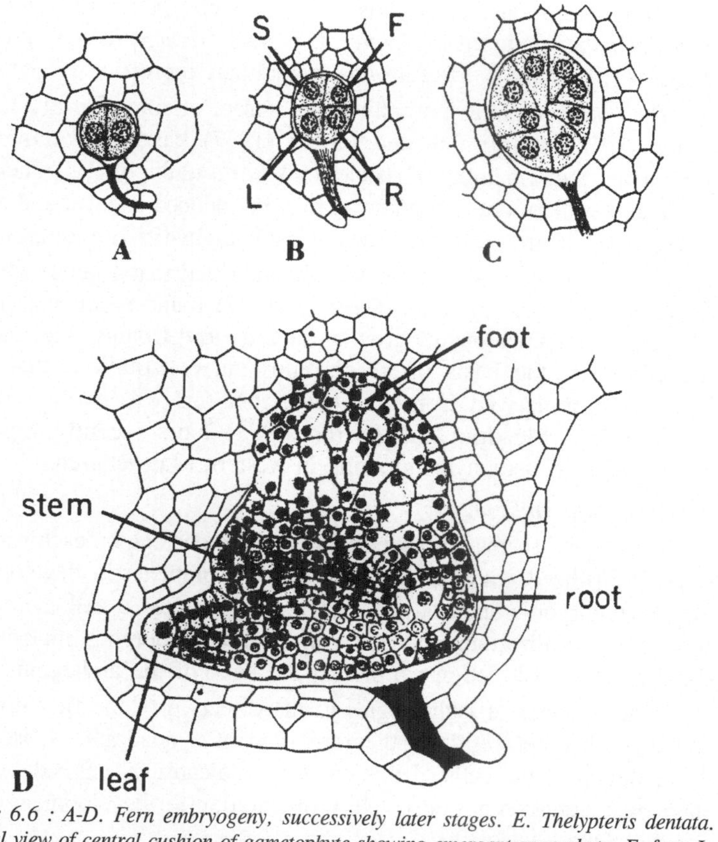

Figure 6.6 : A-D. Fern embryogeny, successively later stages. E. Thelypteris dentata. Ventral view of central cushion of gametophyte showing emergent sporophyte. F, foot; L, primary leaf; R, root; S, stem.

gametophytes were present in September, but the numbers diminished because of erosion, and gametophytes were present in only protected pockets by November.

Seventy-five gametophytes of *Cystopteris bulbifera* were examined carefully, of which 67 were sexually mature. Of these, 46 bore antheridia and archegonia and 21 only antheridia, so that both self- and crossfertilization could occur.

Evans and Bazzone (1977) have reported that gametophytes may develop and survive at acid pH's between 5.8 and 2.2 but fertilization, as evidenced by numbers of sporophytes, is reduced below pH 4.2. Thus, acidic precipitation, such as may occur in New England, would limit fertilizations in nature.

Although fern gametophytes are usually transitory, there are interesting exceptions. Thus, those of four species (*Gramnitis nimbata*, *Hymenophyllum tunbridgense*, *Vittaria* sp., and *Trichomanes* sp.) grow in nature at Highlands, North Carolina, where they reproduce by gemmae.

The corresponding sporophytes are absent or rare (Farrar, 1967). Farrar (1974) and Emigh and Farrar (1977) have shown that the gametophytes of a number of species of *Vittaria* multiply by filamentous gemmae. Furthermore, the gemmae may be induced to form antheridia precociously if grown in proximity to gametophytes with antheridia.

Tests with other species of *Vittaria* indicated that a genus specific antheridiogen is in operation. Gastony (1977) found specimens of the "Appalachian gametophyte" growing in Crawford County, Indiana. He suggested, on the basis of its chromosome constitution, that it is conspecific or derived from *V. lineata*, but this will require further confirmation. McAlpin and Farrar (1978) have recently reported *Trichomanes* gametophytes growing in western Massachusetts.

Reproduction: embryogeny

Although it seems probable that more than one egg on each gametophyte is fertilized, only one zygote normally completes its development into an embryonic sporophyte. The zygote secretes a cell membrane soon after fertilization, and after an interval undergoes mitosis and cytokinesis in a direction parallel to the neck of the archegonium.

Cell divisions at right angles to the direction of the first division and to each other result in the formation of a quadrant. Subsequent development of the cells of this quadrant indicates that already at this stage differentiation has occurred in preparation for development of the organs of the older embryo.

In some species there is doubt that the organs of the juvenile sporophyte are blocked out as early as the quadrant stage. The origin and development of these organs are depicted in Figure elsewhere in this chapter and explained in its labeling.

The archegonial venter and sterile gametophytic tissue keep pace for a short time with the developing embryo, but soon the root and primary leaf burst forth, the former penetrating the substratum and the latter emerging, usually through the apical notch.

The gametophyte persists in some cases until several leaves have been formed, but it ultimately turns brown, and the embryonic sporophyte initiates an independent existence. The early embryonic leaves are simpler in form than the mature leaves of the parent species, but leaves are gradually produced that are characteristic of the mature plant.

Other than the primary root, fern roots are adventitious. Once established, the young sporophyte embarks on a perennial existence in most leptosporangiate ferns. The time required for spores (planted in inorganic salt agar) of ten species of ferns to grow into mature gametophytes and to produce young sporophytes varies from 53 to 113 days.

After this, an additional 136 to 498 days, depending on the species, are required for the sporophyte to reach maturity (as evidenced by spore production). *Ceratopteris thalictroides*, a floating aquatic fern, completed a cycle from spore to spore in 3.5 months, the most rapid completion of a complete fern life cycle on record; in this fern the gametophytes became sexually mature 15 days after the spores had been sown.

De Maggio (1968) was able to induce sporogenesis and meiosis in juvenile, axenic plants of Todea barbara growing in an agarized culture medium for 24 months without transfer; control plants which had been transplanted periodically failed to form spores.

Analyses of the sporebearing plantlets revealed that they were senescent and contained less chlorophyll and cellular nitrogen. From this, De Maggio concluded that sporogenesis was evoked by depletion of nutriments.

However, it is difficult to apply this conclusion to plants growing in nature or in pots in the green house, especially the latter, where it has been observed repeatedly that new leaves produced on *Thelypteris dentata* develop abundant spores soon after the plants have been transplanted into fresh, newly fertilized soil.

Summary

A number of significant and incisive investigations of the reproductive process and genetics of ferns have been reported by Klekowski and Klekowski and Lloyd. This has been summarized to some degree by Lloyd. Klekowski has shown that a number of species have gametophytes that undergo self-fertilization, and their zygotes grow into vigorous, completely homozygous sporophytes.

One adaptation favoring selffertilization is the curvature of the archegonial necks toward the antheridia of the monoecious gametophytes. Self-fertilized gametophytes always give rise to homozygous (genetically homogeneous) sporophytes.

In most homosporous ferns the gametophytes are initially antheridial (protandrous) and later bisexual, but a few (e.g., some species of *Woodwardia*) are protogynous. In *Pteridium aquilinum*, the bisexual gametophytes are self-incompatible, so that the intergametophytic ("*cross*") fertilization is obligatory.

Of 18 ferns investigated, 83.3% exhibited intergametophytic mating. It has also been demonstrated by Klekowski that self-fertilizations in gametophytes may not produce as many sporophytes in the population as cross-fertilizations.

This is probably a result of the bringing together in self-fertilization of lethal genes which result in sporophyte abnormality or abortion during development. Finally, it has been demonstrated that populations of some ferns (*Osmunda regalis*) are adapted to intergametophytic, rather than to intragametophytic, sexual reproduction.

The genera *Thelypteris* and *Adiantum* described above have been chosen to serve as representative of the more advanced leptosporangiate ferns, the Polypodiaceae. Their distinctive characteristics are their method of sporangium development from a single cell; the mixed sori; the size, the annulus position, and the transverse dehiscence of the sporangium; and the small number of spores produced in each.

The gametophytes of these genera, as compared with the photosynthetic gametophytes of the eusporangiate Marattiales, differ in their more delicate structure, less massive form, absence of a midrib, and protuberant and smaller antheridia.

Furthermore, they are more rapid in their development and more ephemeral in their existence. Their doriventrality is marked. The precocity with which the organs of the embryo are organized in the early divisions of the zygote is also unlike the embryogeny of the eusporangiate ferns and *Osmunda*, in which differentiation appears later.

The independence of chromosome constitution (*n* or *2n*) of morphological expression of the sporophytic versus the gametophytic phase has previously been emphasized. Thus, De Maggio et al. (*1971*) had in culture *In*, *2n*, and *4n* gametophytes of the fern *Todea barbara*, a member of the Osmundaceae.

Recent analysis of these indicates that cell and nuclear volume increase with increase in chromosome number but such biochemical processes as respiration and photosynthesis are not altered markedly.

Other Filicales

The family Polypodiaceae, as represented *by Adiantum* and *Thelypteris* described above, is the largest family of the Filicales in number of genera and species. Most of the attributes described for *Adiantum* and *Thelypteris* are in marked contrast to those of the eusporangiate ferns.

Some of the other families of Filicales to be described briefly below are in some respects intermediate in several of their attributes between the *eusporangiate* and *leptosporangiate ferns*.

Family 2. Osmundaceae Osmunda

Vegetative morphology. In most classifications of the Filicales, the Osmundaceae, including *Osmunda* (*Osmunder*, Saxon equivalent to the god Thor) and *Todea* (after Henry Tode, German botanist), are placed at the beginning of the series in recognition of certain attributes that are interpreted as being intermediate between the eusporangiate and leptosporangiate Pteridophyta.

The genus *Osmunda is* cosmopolitan. Three species are distributed widely in the United States: *O. regalis*, the royal or flowering fern; *O. cinnamomea*, the cinnamon fern; and *O. claytoniana*, the interrupted fern.

These perennial ferns are found usually in rather hydric habitats, in which the magnificent ascending fronds attain a large size, often reaching 2 m in length. In the northeastern United States, the several species of *Osmunda* are planted as ornamentals in semishaded locations.

The striking leaves of *Osmunda* are either once or twice pinnately compound, depending on the species. Each growing season, the underground stem produces a group of circinately coiled fronds, which unfold, photosynthesize, and produce spores during the fifth year after they have been initiated as leaf primordia in the stem.

The leaves are annual and die at the end of the season; but the longpersistent leaf bases surround the stem and, together with the wiry roots, form prominent mounds. Mature pinnae are rather leathery in texture. Their venation is opendichotomous, as in *Botrychium.*

The dense covering of the wiry roots and persistent leaf bases, noted above, effectively protect the vertical underground stem of *Osmunda.* The roots, leaf bases, and stem are so intimately associated that sections of all are usually available for study in a single preparation.

The vascular tissue of the mature *Osmunda* stem, as viewed in transverse section, is composed of a circle of strands separated by narrow parenchymatous leaf gaps. Leaf traces that have occasioned the gaps may be observed in section at various points in the cortex, through which they pass into the leaf bases.

Three-dimensional and longitudinal views of the stele indicate that it is a siphonostele dissected by leaf gaps, as in *Ophioglossum.* The xylem strands are mesarch, with the protoxylem surrounded by metaxylem, the latter composed largely of scalariform-pitted tracheids.

A prominent endodermis delimits the stele from the cortical region of the stem. Within it there are several layers of parenchyma cells, the pericycle, the phloem cells, and the mesarch xylem. The inner cortex

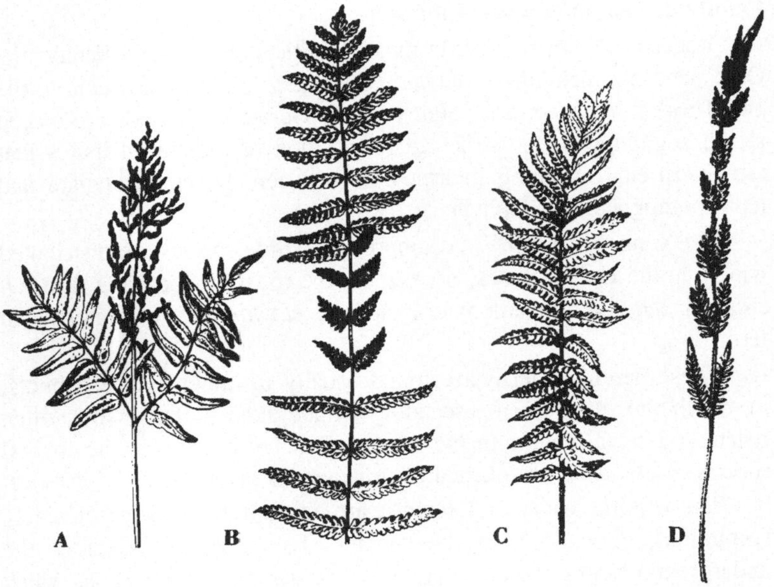

Figure 6.7 : A. Osmunda regalis. The royal or flowering fern. B. Osmunda claytoniana. The interrupted fern. C, D. Osmunda cinnamomea. The cinnamon fern; sterile frond at C; fertile frond at D. A. × 0.3.

is composed of parenchyma and darkly stained sclerenchyma tissue. The spirally arranged leaves are connected to the stele by C-shaped traces. Near each leaf base, two roots, with their vascular supply derived from the leaf trace, originate endogenously and grow between the leaf bases into the soil.

The roots contain exarch protosteles that are diarch or triarch. The development of both root and stem is localized in single apical cells. In certain individual roots, however, as many as four apical cells may be present, an attribute suggestive of ferns of the *Marattia* group.

Reproduction: the sporophyte

Further striking modifications of leaf structure are associated with sporangium production in *Osmunda*. The location of the sporangia varies in the several species. In all cases the sporangia do not occur in sori but are in marginal zones without indusia. In *O. regalis*, only the most distal pinnae and pinnules are fertile.

In *O. claytoniana*, on the other hand, certain intermediate pairs or pinnae bear sporangia, whereas the proximal and distal ones are sterile. Finally, in *O. cinnamomea*, the sporangia are borne only on special, fertile, spore-bearing leaves, the vegetative tissues and functions of

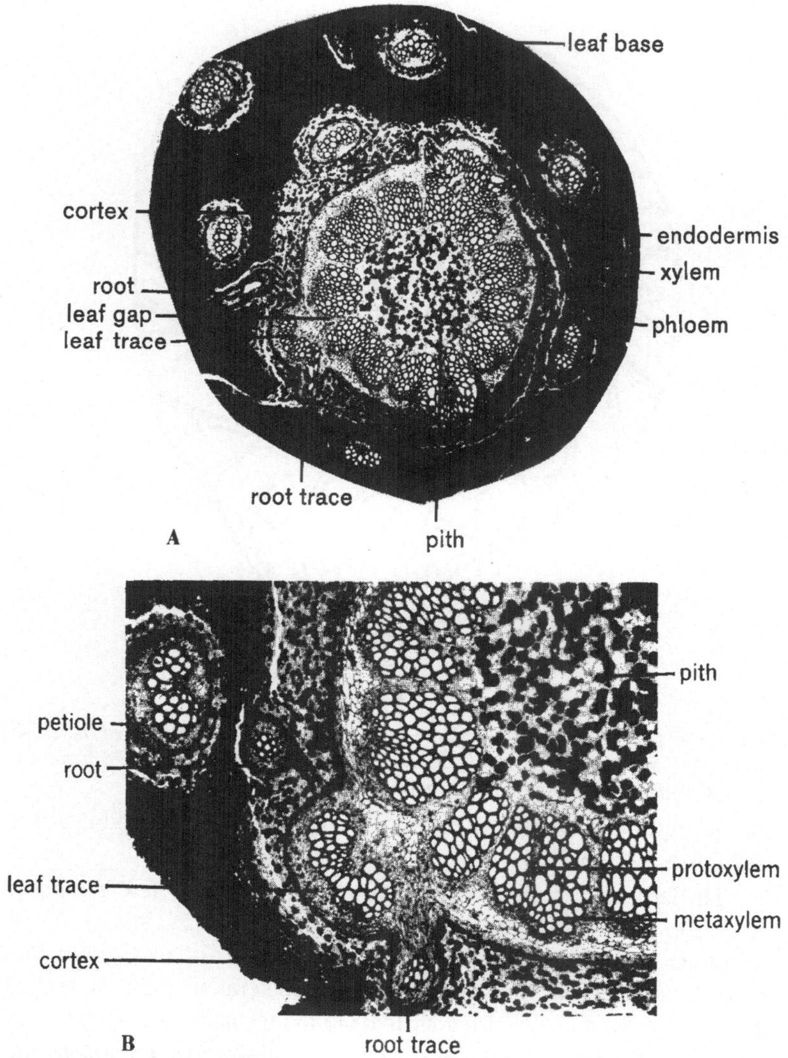

Figure 6.8: Osmunda sp. A. Transection of rhizome; note associated toots and leaf bases. B. Portion of stele enlarged; note mesarch xylem and stages in departure of leaf and root traces.

which are greatly restricted. Intermediate stages in these dimorphic phenomena are readily observable on examination of several individuals.

The sporangia themselves originate superficially on the pinnae surface. Although prominent single initial cells may be present sporogenous cells are produced. The outermost layer of these functions somewhat

Figure 6.9: Osmunda regalis. A. Section of sporangium at sporocyte stage; note two-layered wall and bulging, unilateral annulus (left), tapetum, sporocytes, and sporangial stalk. B. Wall of mature sporangium showing unilateral annulus.

as a tapetal plasmodium during sporogenesis, and, in addition, a true tapetum is present.

The large and prominent chromosomes are relatively few in number (n = 22). Each sporangium produces between 256 and 512 spores. These are green at maturity and are shed by dehiscence of the sporangium along a vertical line running between a unilateral in each sporangial precursor, adjacent cells also contribute to the formation of the *sporangium*, which becomes protuberant and rather massive in comparison with that in other leptosporangiate ferns.

Furthermore, the sporangial stalk is also thicker than in other leptosporangiate ferns, and the wall is two-layered. A central sporogenous cell in each sporangium undergoes repeated divisions until approximately 128 group of thick-walled annulus cells and the stalk of the sporangium.

Reproduction: the gametophyte

As is the case with the chlorophyllous spores of *Equisetum*, those

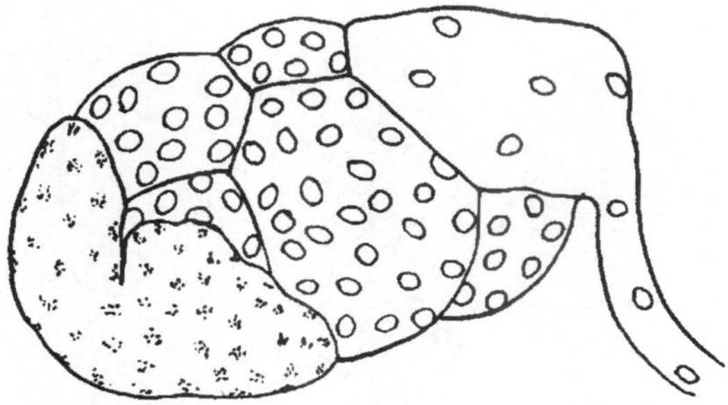

Figure 6.10: Osmunda regalis. Spore germination, 2 weeks after spores were planted on agar.

of *Osmunda* do not remain viable very long. They germinate very readily, however, if transferred to agar, soil, or other environments with adequate moisture.

The young gametophyte at first consists of a short chain of cells with a basal rhizoid, but an apical cell is organized soon by successive oblique division of the terminal cell. This gives rise to a spatulate gametophyte up to several centimeters long, at the tip of which several apical cells may function.

Their derivatives build up a relatively massive green gametophyte suggestive of those *Marattia* and *Angiopteris*. Prominent ventrally projecting midribs are present in the gametophytes of *Osmunda*, which are liverwortlike and long-lived and may be perennial.

Vegetative propagation of the gametophytes by separation of marginal lobes has been observed. There is some evidence that the gametophytes are protandrous; well-separated individuals are always monoecious. The antheridia are borne on the underside of the gametophyte near the margins, and the archegonia are on or near the midrib.

The protuberant antheridia have a single layer of jacket cells, one of which, near the apex, is thrown off as the antheridium dehisces. Approximately 100 spermatogenous cells fill the antheridium; each gives rise to a single, coiled, multiflagellate sperm.

The archegonial venters are sunken in the superficial tissue on the ventral surface of the gametophytes. The single binucleate neck canal cell is surrounded by four rows of neck cells about six to eight tiers high.

Reproduction: embryogeny

The zygote undergoes two successive vertical divisions parallel in direction to the axis of the archegonium but perpendicular to each other.

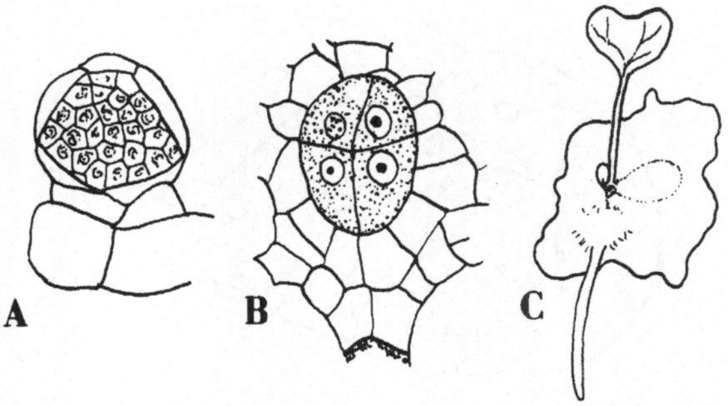

Figure 6.11: A. Osmunda cinnamomea. Mature antheridium. B. Osmunda claytoniana. Section of eight-celled embryo in archegonium. C. Osmunda claytoniana. Gametophyte with young sporophyte emerging.

The next divisions are transverse, so that an octant stage develops. The outermost four cells (nearest the neck) gradually develop the stem, leaf, and primary root of the embryo, and the four basal cells form a foot.

Growth of the embryo is relatively slow in *Osmunda* as compared with other leptosporangiate ferns. The archegonium functions as a calyptra during early embryogeny, but it is ultimately ruptured by the developing embryo, which protrudes from the gametophyte and becomes established as an independent plant.

The primary embryonic leaf and those that follow it during the juvenile phases of development are much simpler than those of the adult plant. The stem of the young sporophyte is protostelic at first, and the dissected siphonstelic condition does not arise until considerable development has occurred.

Summary

Osmunda and the Osmundaceae differ from Polypodiaceous ferns such *Adiantum* and *Thelypteris* in a number of respects. The sporangia are not in sori, and all mature their spores simultaneously as in eusporangiate ferns.

Furthermore, the sporangia, which have two wall layers, are not typically leptosporangiate in development because several cells, in addition to the initial cell, function in its development. In addition, as many as 512 spores may mature in each sporangium.

The spores are thin-walled and green, like those of *Equisetum*. The sporangium opens by a vertical cleft, and the annulus consists of a terminal and pseudolateral group of thickwalled cells.

The gametophytes are longer-lived and more massive than those of leptosporangiate ferns. The antheridia produce more sperms and the rhizoids contain chloroplasts. The archegonial necks are straight instead of curved, as in the Polypodiaceae.

The embryo of *Osmunda* differentiates later in development than the quadrant or octant stage. Finally, the primary leaf does not grow up through the apical notch, as in the Polypodiaceae, but laterally around the margin of the gametophyte.

Family 3. Schizaeaceae

Of the genera of this family, *Lygodium* (Gr. *lygodes*, like a willow) and *Anemia* (Gr. *aneimon*, unclad, referring to the naked sporangia), are perhaps the best known and most readily available for study. Although a single species of *Lygodium*, the climbing fern, *L. palmatum*, is native to the United States, *L. japonicum* is widely cultivated in conservatories and in many gardens in the southern United States and in some places (Georgia and Texas) has escaped from cultivation to become a wild fern.

The petioles and rachises of the compound leaves of *Lygodium* are of almost indeterminate growth, in some species forming leaves almost 30 m long. The subterranean stems are short. *Anemia mexicana* is native to the extreme southern United States (southern Florida and Texas); its sporangia occur on much-reduced leaf segments. In these ferns the sporangia are borne on the leaf margins and either lack an indusium or have a false one.

The sporangia produce up to 216 spores; an apical group of thickwalled cells serves as an annulus. Sporangial dehiscence is vertical. All the sporangia mature simultaneously (simple type), as in the eusporangiate ferns and Osmundaceae. One species of *Schizaea* (Gr. *schizein*, to split) is native to the United States, occurring in the Pine Barrens of New Jersey.

FIGURE 17-34

Schizaea. A. S. pusilla. B. Leaf of S. *elegans*. x0.3. (*After Smith.*)

The gametophytes of *Schizaea-like* ferns are of great interest and

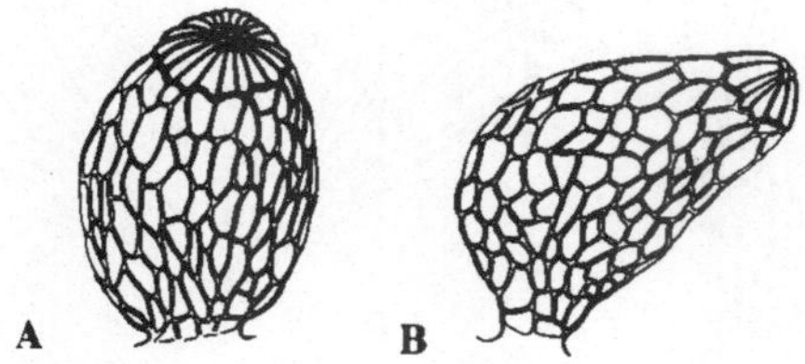

Figure 6.12: A. Anemia mexicana, sporangium. B. Lygodium palmatum, sporangium.

of two types. Some, like those of *S. pusilla*, are chlorophyllous and filamentous, much like moss protonemata. Species with such photosynthetic gametophytes have been retained in the genus *Schizaea.*

However, a number of ferns, formerly included in *Schizaea*, have been reassigned to the genus *Actinostachys*, because their gametophytes are subterranean and fleshy, cylindrical structures much like those of *Psilotum*. Furthermore, subterranean gametophytes of *A. melanesica* contain endophytic fungi.

The occurrence of such radially symmetrical gametophytes in the Pteridophyta is interpreted as a primitive attribute which may indicate common ancestry with other vascular cryptogams with similar gametophytes.

Family 4. Stromatopteridaceae

The family Stromatopteridaceae has only a single member, *Stromatopteris moniliformis*, native to New Caledonia; it has been studied intensively by Bierhorst. This plant is characterized by lack of clear distinction between leaf petioles and various irregularly branched underground axes and roots.

Like the gametophytes of *Psilotum*, *Tmesipteris*, *Ophioglossum*, and *Actinostachys*, those of *Stromatopteris* are subterranean and cylindrical and lack chlorophyll. Fungi are present in both the subterranean sporophytic axes and gametophytes.

As noted earlier, Bierhorst has emphasized a number of similarities between *Psilotum*, *Tmesipteris*, and *Stromatopteris* and considers all these to be primitive Pteridophyta.

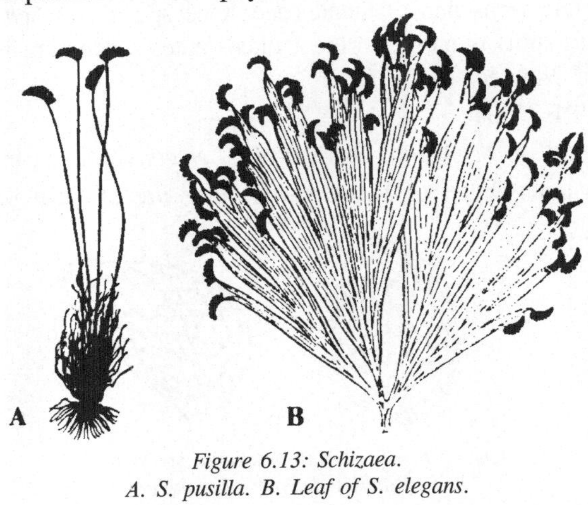

Figure 6.13: Schizaea.
A. S. pusilla. B. Leaf of S. elegans.

Family 5. Hymenophyllaceae

The Hymenophyllaceae, the filmy ferns, are largely tropical and include (among others) two genera of delicate-leaved ferns, *Hymenophyllum* (Gr. *hymen*, membrane, + Gr. *phylon*, leaf) and *Trichomanes* (Gr. for waterwort), both of which are represented in the flora of the United States. *Trichomanes* occurs in extremely moist habitats such as on rocks bathed in spray from waterfalls.

As the familial name implies, the leaves are delicate, often only a single layer of cells thick except at the midveins. The sporangia are borne at the margin of the leaves on elongate receptacles covered during development by cuplike or two-lipped indusia. Development of the sporangia on the receptacle is orderly, the oldest being at the apex and the younger sporangia arising on the flanks of the receptacle, with the youngest at the base.

This represents gradate organization of the sorus, in contrast to the simple (all spores maturing simultaneously) sori of the Ophioglossales. Up to *512* spores may be produced in each sporangium. The annulus is obliquely vertical, and the sporangium opens transversely.

The spores may undergo the early stages of germination before they are shed from the sporangia. The green gametophytes are branching and straplike (*Hymenophyllum*) or branching filaments (*Trichomanes*) with erect, fleshy, gemmiferous branches.

In *Trichomanes holopterium* the gametophyte is more abundant than the sporophyte and selfreproducing.

Family 6. Gleicheniaceae

The Gleicheniaceae are ferns of the tropical and south temperate parts of the earth and comprise more than 100 species, by some classified as four genera, but by others included in the single genus *Gleichenia.* This fern has prostrate, dichotomously branching rhizomes with long internodes.

The rhizomes contain haplostelic protosteles with mesarch xylem. The leaves, which are twice or more times pinnately compound, grow for long periods and are vinelike; they may attain a length of 50 m. Their leaflets have open-dichotomous venation.

The sori, which are borne in two ranks near the midrib of the pinnule, have few (4 to 8) sporangia and are not covered with an indusium. An annulus of elongate, thickwalled cells develops transversely and slightly obliquely the rather globose sporangium.

This is correlated with vertical dehiscence of the latter. Bierhorst

(1971b) has investigated soral and pinnule ontogeny in *G. linearis.*

Spore germination, which requires several weeks, results in a cordate gametophyte with a thickened midregion. The antheridia produce large numbers of sperm (up to 500).

The prolonged growth of the leaves, the protostelic rhizome, and the large number of spores (up to 1024) in the sporangia, among other features, suggest that *Gleichenia is* primitive.

Family 7. Cyatheaceae

To this family belong the tree ferns (as well as some species with massive prostrate stems). Tree ferns grow natively in tropical rain forests, where large specimens may exceed *20* m in height. They are widely cultivated in conservatories and outof-doors in mild, moist climates like that of the Pacific coast.' *Cyathea* (Gr. *kyathos*, *cup*), *Alsophila* (Gr. *alsos*, grove, + Gr. *philein*, to live), and *Cibotium* (Gr. *kibotion*, little box) are often present in conservatory collections.

The trunks (stems) are rarely branched and are covered by a dense mat of adventitious roots, which arise in association with the leaf bases. Roots at the distal portion of the trunk never reach the soil. Creeping stems arise on the trunks some distance above the soil, run downward and then outward, and initiate new erect stems.

The lower portion of the stem, which is smaller in diameter than the upper, is supported by a dense, buttresslike covering of persistent roots. In spite of their massive size, tree ferns lack a cambium and secondary growth.

Anatomically, the young stems are simple and protostelic, but as the stem continues to grow, the stele increases in diameter, becoming dictyostelic and, finally, polystelic and quite complex.

The apex of the trunk supports a crown of leaves, which are circinately vernate when young. The leaves may approach 4 m in length and are pinnately compound.

The sporangia are borne in gradate sori. In the Dicksoniaceae these are marginal and subtended by cuplike indusia, while in the Cyatheaceae they are abaxial and may or may not have indusia. The annulus is obliquely vertical, and the transverse sporangial dehiscence is initiated in the region of special thin-walled lip cells or stomium, as in the Polypodiaceae.

The gametophytes are heart shaped and organized much like those of the Polypodiaceae. The archegonia have long, slightly curved necks like those of *Osmunda.*

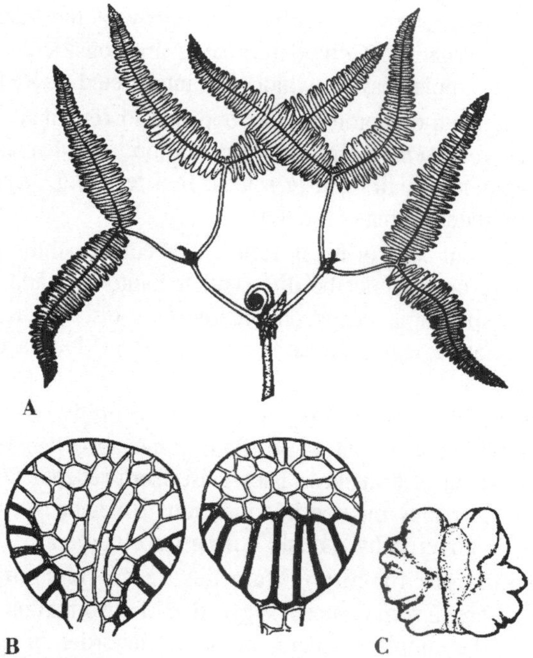

Figure 6.14: Gleichenia. A, B. G. pectinata. A. Segment of leaf. B. Sporangium, ventral (left) and dorsal views. C. G. dichotoma. Dorsal view of gametophyte.

Summary of Filicales

The Filicales include all the homosporous leptosporangiate ferns. They are widely distributed in both the tropics and temperate zones and are almost exclusively perennial plants. In colder climates, with few exceptions (*Cyrtomium* and *Polystichum*, for example), the leaves die at the end of the growing season and are replaced by a new set of leaves the following spring.

The stems of Filicales may be prominent and trunklike (Cyatheaceae) or rhizomes, or underground, vertical stems. They may be dichotomously or irregularly branched. Their ontogeny may be traced in every case to an apical cell.

This may be tetrahedral, with derivatives arising on three sides, or with derivatives arising only on two sides. The stele in juvenile sporophytes is usually a protostele. As the stem increases in size, a siphonostele, dictyostele, or complex polystele may develop. Secondary growth is absent.

The roots of Filicales are adventitious. All develop from the activity of prominent (tetrahedral) apical cells and have exarch protosteles.

Filicalean leaves are formed early in ontogeny at the stem apex and have circinate vernation. Compound leaves are considered to be more primitive than simple leaves, which are interpreted as reductions.

Similarly, open-dichotomous, as opposed to reticulate, venation is considered to represent the primitive condition. The leaves and stems often have epidermal hairs and/or scales. In a few (e.g., *Lygodium*) the leaves are of indeterminate growth.

The epidermal cells of many fern leaves contain chloroplasts; their mesophyll may or may not be differentiated into palisade and spongy regions. The sporangia occur on the margins or abaxial surfaces of ordinary vegetative leaves or somewhat modified leaves or segments thereof.

Marginal sori are considered to be more primitive than superficial ones because they correspond in position, in megaphyllous leaves, to the terminal sporangia of branches. They arise from receptacles in discrete groups or sori, or they may be in continuous zones or rows. They may or may not be covered by indusia during development.

The sporangia in certain families (e.g., Osmundaceae and Schizaeaceae) are in some aspects suggestive of eusporangiate sporangia. The sori may be simple, gradate, or mixed in order of development. Dehiscence is either vertical or oblique.

This is correlated with the position of thick-walled annulus. The gametophytes of Filicales show considerable range of organization. There are differences in spore germination and early development (bipolar, tripolar, and unipolar germination and time of initiation of spatulate stage).

The gametophytes may be filamentous (*Schizaea*), ribbonlike (*Hymenophyllum*), cylindrical, subterranean, and achlorophyllose (*Actinostachys*, *Stromatopteris*), or cordate, the latter with entire or incised margins, and they may bear unicellular and/or multicellular branched or unbranched hairs.

The gametophytes may be massive and long-lived (Osmundaceae) or rather delicate and ephemeral (Schizaeceae, Hymenophyllaceae, and Polypodiaceae). The rhizoids may be brown-walled or colorless. The gametophytes of almost all Filicales are monoecious.

The antheridia may have many wall cells (Osmundaceae) or only three (Polypodiaceae) or four. The archegonia may have long, straight necks (Osmundaceae) or shorter, curved ones (Polypodiaceae). The taxonomy of Filicales is based largely on sporophytic attributes, but gametophytic characteristics are being increasingly studied.

Many aspects of the reproductive cycle in ferns have been summarized succinctly by Miller (1968). Finally, in the embryogeny of the Filicales, differentiation into the organs of the young sporophyte may occur as early as the quadrant or octant stage, or it may be delayed.

THE FERN LIFE CYCLE

The life cycle of *Adiantum* and *Thelypteris* and of most other Filicales is fundamentally similar to that of other vascular cryptogams in that it involves a regular alternation of a diploid, spore-producing generation and a haploid, gamete-producing one.

This type of life cycle has been so greatly emphasized in biological teaching that we often gain the impression that it is obligate and inexorable. Furthermore, we are so prone to contrast the two alternates in the life cycle that they sometimes seem like different organisms rather than merely successive morphological expressions of the same one.

This tendency to contrast has, of course, been enhanced by the antithetic theory of alternation of generations discussed at previous points in this text. The purpose of the following paragraphs is to present a somewhat different interpretation of life cycle phenomena, with the ferns as a point of departure.

Bell (1959) and Voeller (1971) have reviewed a number of aspects of the life cycle in ferns. Deviations from the life cycle described for *Adiantum* and *Thelypteris* occur in nature, or they may be induced. These deviations have been grouped together under the phenomena apogamy and apospory, alluded to earlier.

Apogamy denotes a deviation from the life cycle in which the transition from the gametophytic phase to the sporophyte is accomplished without sexual union of gametes and their nuclei. By *apospory*, on the other hand, is meant the transition- from sporophyte to gametophyte in a manner other than through the medium of spores and occurrence of meiosis.

Apospory is known to occur among both Hepatophyta and Bryophyta, as well as in the vascular cryptogams and seed plants. Injured sporophytes of *Anthoceros* develop gametophytic thalli, and injured moss setae and capsules may develop protonemata.

In certain fern varieties, prothallia may develop at the leaf margins or from transformed sporangia, or they may be induced to develop by injuring juvenile leaves. Examples of apogamy are best known from certain varieties of ferns.

In most of these, the gametophytes do not produce archegonia, although antheridia may be developed abundantly. The thickened central portion of the gametophyte develops directly into a sporophyte without the occurrence of sexual union.

The phenomena of apogamy and apospory have an important bearing on such fundamental questions as the nature and relation of the alternating generations and the chromosome cycle. Are apogamously produced sporophytes haploid or diploid?

If the former is the case, what is the nature of the chromosome behavior during sporogenesis? In the latter case, are the prothallia diploid or haploid, and if diploid, what is the origin of the diploid condition?

In spite of the investigations of numerous cytologists, the chromosome cycle in apogamous and aposporous ferns has not been clarified until relatively recently. It has been shown for the holly fern, *Cyrtomium falcatum*, for example, that the chromosome number of both sporophytes and gametophytes is the same, both being diploid.

The gametophytes give rise to sporophytes apogamously. However, only the spores from certain types of sporangia in a sorus develop into gametophytes. Spores from other types of sporangia usually abort. In the sporangia that produce fertile spores, the first three divisions of the primary archesporial cell are normal; hence, eight cells are produced.

When these undergo nuclear division in preparation for the formation of 16 sporocytes, nuclear division is arrested at prophase or metaphase, with the result that in all eight sporogenous cells the nuclei are precociously reorganized. These contain double the chromosome complement of the original cells.

These eight cells (second eight-celled stage) now function directly as sporocytes, undergoing meiosis with regular chromosome pairing and production of 32 spores, each of which, however, contains a nucleus with the chromosome number characteristic of the sporophyte.

This temporary doubling, in the abortive fourth nuclear division, makes normal meiosis possible and also explains the similarity of chromosome number in gametophyte and sporophyte. A number of other ferns have been shown to have a similar chromosome cycle.

Another type of apogamous fern life cycle has recently been described in which the basic (presumably diploid) chromosome number is preserved by mitosis throughout both generations; 'meiosis is absent. In *Polypodium dispersum*, both sporophyte and gametophyte are diploid, the sporophytes arising from gametophytes lacking sex organs.

No change of chromosomes occurs at spore production or at the time the sporophyte is initiated by the gametophyte. Thus, at least three types of life cycle occur among leptosporangiate ferns:

(1) the widespread cycle that involves regular alternation of diploid sporophytes and haploid gametophytes, as in *Thelypteris* and *Adiantum;*

(2) the *Cyrtomium falcatum* type, in which both sporophyte and gametophyte are diploid and meiosis occurs; and

(3) the *Polypodium dispersum* type, in which both sporophyte and gametophyte are diploid but meiosis is absent. The last two life cycles involve obligate apogamy.

Apogamy may be induced at will in other, normally sexual species. This has been accomplished by withholding water from the surface of gametophyte cultures, thus preventing swimming and functioning of the sperms.

It has been demonstrated by Whittier and Steeves and by Whittier (*1964*) that when gametophytes of 14 species of ferns (including *Pteridium aquilinum*, *Osmunda cinnamomea*, *Dryopteris [Thelypteris] marginalia*, and *Adiantum pedatum*) are grown in an inorganic medium supplemented with about 2.5% sugar (glucose, fructose, sucrose, or maltose), they produce sporophytes apogamously.

The role of the sugar is not one of effecting a change in osmotic pressure but probably acting as a respiratory substrate. Control cultures grown in an inorganic medium without sugar did not show apogamy.

Elmore and Whittier (1975a,b and earlier) found that certain fern gametophytes produce ethylene in culture. Investigating nine gametophytic strains of *Pteridium aquilinum*, the bracken fern, they found that all nine produced ethylene in culture and that, when the cultures were sealed, eight of the nine produced apogamous buds.

The same strains responded similarly to exogenous ethylene. Apogamy in this case, according to Elmore and Whittier, depends on capacity of the plants to respond to ethylene. A further factor effecting apogamy has been shown to be high light intensity and quality.

It has been suggested that this operates by increasing the rate of photosynthesis. Adding sugars to an inorganic medium may thus replace the factor of intense illumination. Apospory, which occurs less frequently in nature than apogamy, also may be induced in many ferns.

This is most readily accomplished by removing the leaves from young sporophytes and placing them on agar medium. After an interval, leaf cells in contact with the agar give rise to filaments, which ultimately grow into typical cordate gametophytes.

Hirsch (1976) investigated regeneration of juvenile leaves (from callus) of the fern *Microgramma vaciniifolia*. She found three types of structures developed from regenerative divisions of the epidermal cells of the leaf: apogamous gametophytes, sporophytic plantlets, and intermediates.

Chlorophyllous gametophytes have been induced to develop on the excised, colorless roots in root cultures of the bracken fern (*Pteridium aquilinum*) (Munroe and Sussex, 1969). These gametophytes were diploid and produced sex organs.

The apogamous production of sporophytes and the aposporous development of gametophytes, such that gametophytes and sporophytes have the same chromosomal constitution, are strong evidence in support of the homologous, or transformation, theory of alternation of generations.

The facts that sporophytes can directly transform some of their tissue into gametophytes (apospory) and that the same chromosome complement may be present in both phases without modifying their fundamental morphology seem to indicate that the two alternating generations are fundamentally similar.

In evidence of this may be cited the work of Bristow (1962), who reported that the presence of less than 0.1 g/liter of sucrose, glucose, or fructose caused diploid callus (derived from leaves of *Pteris cretica*) to develop gametophytes, which in a greater concentration of these sugars formed sporophytes.

Furthermore, Morel (1963) found that juvenile leaves of *Adiantum pedatum* regenerate gametophytes, while adult leaves regenerate sporophytes in the same culture medium. This indicates an internal change in the leaf tissues as they mature. These phenomena, then, serve to focus our attention once again on the nature of alternation of generations and on the causal relationships involved.

It was suggested early in this century, on the basis of the isomorphic alternation known for certain algae, that the explanation for the profound morphological differences between the sporophyte and gametophyte in land plants was environmental.

In the algae, it was argued, both generations develop as free-living plants from reproductive cells set free in the same environment; thus, the morphology of these algal sporophytes and gametophytes was similar. (Heteromorphic alternation in algae such as the kelps, certain red algae, and some species of *Bryopsis* was unknown at the time.)

In contrast, it was suggested that while the spore of land plants germinated freely into the gametophyte in nature, the zygote always underwent the early phases of its development into a sporophyte within the confines of a pressure-exerting archegonium or calyptra.

This difference of environment during development of sporophyte and gametophyte of land plants was suggested as the cause of their divergence in morphology.

A number of investigators have studied the morphogenetic factors involved in fern life cycle, including, among others, Ward and Wetmore, 1954; Ward, 1963; De Maggio, 1963; De Maggio, Wetmore, and Morel, 1963; and White, 1971a,b.

In efforts to test this hypothesis, spores have been injected into the thickened midregion of fern gametophytes; although gametophytes ultimately arose from the injection site, it has not been possible to trace their origin with certainty.

On the other hand, surgical removal of the archegonial neck, with less pressure and constraint on the zygote, resulted in the latter's producing a mass of tissue in which differentiation into organs of the sporophyte was somewhat delayed but finally did occur. However, zygotes removed completely from archegonia before they had initiated cell division developed into two-dimensional prothalloid masses, which did not become organized as sporophytes.

There is evidence then, that the retention of the zygote within the calyptra and gametophyte has an important morphogenetic role. It was long ago suggested that the chromosomal differences that normally obtain (the gametophyte being haploid and the sporophyte diploid) determine the difference in morphological expression, and this often is strongly emphasized.

Several lines of evidence are available, however, in opposition to this suggestion. The occurrence in nature of gametophytes and sporophytes with the same chromosome complement, as in the case of *Cyrtomium falcatum* and *Polypodium dispersum* already discussed, is one negating factor. A second is the induction in apospory of regeneration of diploid fern leaves into diploid gametophytes.

Finally, a polyploid series of haploid, diploid, and tetraploid gametophytes and diploid, tetraploid, and octoploid sporophytes of the same species has been obtained by experimental induction of apospory (followed by fertilizations) in the laboratory, a striking demonstration of the similar potentialities of gametophytes and sporophytes.

In these investigations, gametophytes were still gametophytes whether haploid, diploid, or tetraploid, and diploid, tetraploid, and octoploid sporophytes themselves were little modified in morphology. These last results suggest that chromosomal or differences in quantity of DNA of themselves do not explain the differences between sporophyte and gametophyte.

It has been suggested (Bell, 1959) that the cytoplasm of the egg cell itself may be the site of morphogenetic determination. In the later discussion of data from electron microscopy, Bell (1970, 1975) has summarized the profound reorganizations that occur during the ontogeny of both the egg (oogenesis) and the spore (sporogenesis) in the fern life cycle.

He ascribes to this reorganization the physical basis for differences between gametophyte and sporophyte and discounts other hypotheses that seek to explain them. The most significant causal agent so far discovered may be the enclosure of the zygote and the young embryo by the archegonial jacket or. calyptra.

A similar force seems to be involved in the regeneration of juvenile plants from undifferentiated callus of angiosperms. It has been suggested (De Maggio, 1963) that the differences in sporophyte and gametophyte may be occasioned by the "lessened availability of some cell substrate" in the haploid gametophyte that does not permit the development of the more complex sporophyte.

Two phenomena argue against this hypothesis: the greater complexity of the gametophyte, as compared with the sporophyte, in certain liverworts and mosses, and the typical morphology of polyploid gametophytes. Finally, the increase in apogamous production of sporophytes by addition of sugar to the culture medium has suggested that an adequate nutritional level is a factor in the development of the sporophyte, at least in vascular plants.

In addition to the evidences of similarity of the alternates provided by apogamy and apospory, one additional point is relevant. It has been demonstrated that fern gametophytes may be stimulated to form vascular tissue (tracheids) by treatments with sucrose and an auxin (naphthalene acetic acid).

Furthermore, by planting them in an erect position in inorganic agar medium with a 1.0% supplement of sucrose, the gametophytes become cylindrical and develop tracheids. They thus approach in organization the axes of sporophytes and, at the same time, suggest the cylindrical organization of the gametophytes of *Psilotum* and *Ophioglossum.*

Accordingly, although the phenomenon of alternation of generations has been described and investigated for more than a century, we still lack precise data regarding the causal factors involved.

It seems increasingly clear, however, on the basis of the evidence at hand, that sporophytes and gametophytes in a given life cycle are not so fundamentally different from each other as sometimes has been suggested or implied.

While the phylogenetic aspects of alternation were emphasized before 1960, an increasing number of experimental morphogenetic investigations have helped since then to shed light on this important phenomenon. White (1971a,b) has reviewed a number of experimental studies of the fern sporophyte.

7

Vascular Cryptogams IV: Division Pteridophyta III

It should be reiterated at this point that the division Pteridophyta contains three classes-Ophioglossopsida, Marattiopsida, and Filicopsida-of which the third was discussed, in part, in the preceding chapter. (The homosporous Filicopsida, the Filicales, were treated in the preceding chapter.)

The present chapter includes a discussion of the heterosporous orders, Marsileales and Salviniales, sometimes called the water ferns.

ORDER 2. MARSILEALES

The order Marsileales contains the single family Marsileaceae.

Marsilea, Regnellidum, and Pilularia

Introduction and vegetative morphology. The genera *Marsilea* (after Count F. L. Marsigli, an Italian naturalist), *Regnellidium* (after A. F. Regnell), and *Pilularia* (*L. pilula*, little ball') constitute the single family Marsileaceae.

All are amphibious, growing in shallow ponds and ditches, and are also able to survive when the water level falls, as long as the soil is moist; one species of *Marsilea*, however, is xerophytic. *Marsilea*, with about 70 species, widely distributed throughout the world, occurs in the southern and Pacific regions of the United States; it is emphasized in the following account.

Regnellidium, with a single species, is native to the Amazon region of Brazil; *Pilularia* (with six species), the pillwort, occurs in Europe, Africa, and Australia; in the United States it grows natively in Texas, Oregon, California, Kansas, Arkansas, and Georgia. Bonnet (1955) summarized the organization and reproduction of *P. globulifera* and *P. minuta.*

Marsilea at first glance is decidedly unfernlike in appearance; its compound leaves frequently suggest four-leaf clovers to the unitiated. It grows readily under greenhouse conditions and is fairly hardy in colder climates, where it perennates by means of its stems, which are embedded in soil or mud.

The plant body consists of an elongate, branching, stolonlike stem, which grows either on the surface of the mud or slightly below it. The leaves are in two rows, alternately inserted on opposite sides of the stem, from which they arise in circinate fashion.

The internodes are very long in aquatic habits. In mature plants, three kinds of leaves may develop:

(1) floating leaves,

(2) submerged leaves, and

(3) aerial leaves

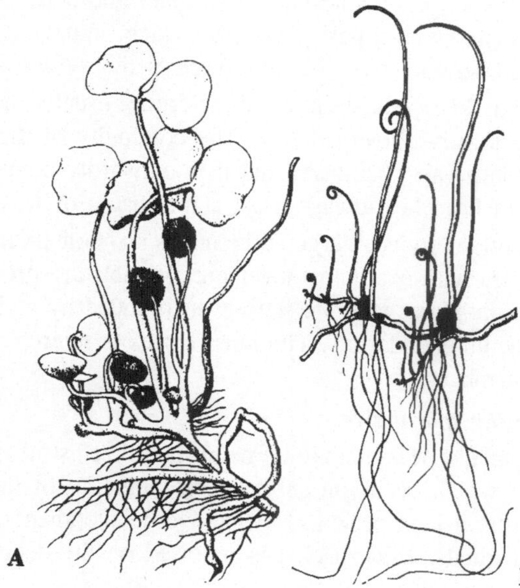

Figure 7.1: A. Regnellidium diphyllum. B. Pilularia sp. Both with sporocarps.

The first two, of course, occur in aquatic habitats and the last when the plant is terrestrial. In submerged plants the petioles are relatively flaccid and have air chambers, and the leaflets float on the surface of the water; stomata are restricted to the upper surface of the leaflets.

The petioles of aerial leaves, however, lack air chambers and are sufficiently rigid to support the leaflets in an erect position; here sunken stomata occur on both the dorsal and ventral leaf surfaces.

The four leaflets of each leaf do not actually arise at one locus from the petiole; two are slightly higher than the others and are inserted in alternate fashion, the leaflet veins dichotomously branched but laterally and marginally united to some extent to form a loose reticulum.

A transection of the leaf reveals the presence of an upper and lower epidermis, both with slightly sunken stomata. The mesophyll is differentiated into palisade and spongy areas.

Each petiole is traversed by a V-shaped vascular trace that leaves a gap above the place of its departure from the stem stele. The submerged leaves have smaller blades than either of the other two types and lack a cuticle and differentiation into palisade and spongy mesophyll.

Growth of leaves, stem, and root originates in apical cells and their derivatives. The vascular tissue of the mature stem is arranged in the form of an amphiphloic siphonostele. Both inner and outer phloem are covered by a single layer of pericycle cells, which, in turn, are covered by a single endodermal layer. In some species the xylem is exarch.

The pith may be parenchymatous or sclerotic, usually the latter, in stems growing in nonsubmerged soil. The continuity of the cortex is interrupted by large air chambers, and it is outwardly bounded by an epidermis. Stem branches always arise at the bases of leaves.

The adventitious roots emerge at the nodes and contain monarch or diarch protosteles with exarch arrangement. Vessels are present in the roots of *Marsilea*. Here, too, the stele is surrounded by a single layer of pericycle and an endodermis. The inner cortex is sclerotic; the outer contains air chambers.

Reproduction: the sporophyte

The sporangia of *Marsilea* are borne in specialized structures known as *sporocarps*, which occur on short lateral branches of the petioles. They appear after a long period of vegetative development, usually on terrestrial individuals. Bilderback has reported on the details of their development.

The sporocarps at first are relatively soft and green, but they become hard, brown, and nutlike at maturity. They may be borne singly or in clusters, depending on the species. Anatomical and ontogenetic evidence indicates that the sporocarp probably represents a fertile pinna that has become folded with the margins united, thus enclosing the fertile (abaxial) surface of the leaflet.

Each lateral half of the sporocarp bears a row of elongate sori with ridgelike receptacles. The sori of one half alternate with those of the other, but all are close together and there is overlapping. Each sorus is covered with a delicate indusium; the indusia of adjacent sori are partially fused together, so that each receptacle and its sporangia lie in a cavity.

Sporangial initials develop first at the apex of each ridgelike receptacle; subsequently, additional initials on the flanks initiate sporangium development in gradate order.

The sporangia develop according to the leptosporangiate method, and all produce between 32 and 64 spores. In the sporangia at the apex of the receptacle, however, all the spores except one degenerate, their contents mingling with those of the tapetal cells, which have formed a plasmodium late in sporogenesis.

The surviving spore, probably as a result of absorbing large quantities of nutriment, increases to many times its original size, becoming somewhat elipsoidal. A single megaspore, therefore, matures in each of the sporangia at the apex of the linear receptacle.

Three abortive megaspores are sometimes visible near the apex of the functional megaspores. The mature megaspore has a rounded

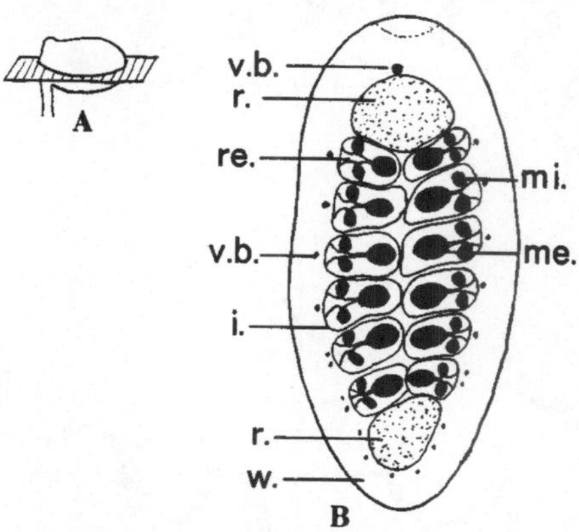

Figure 7.2: Marsilea sp. A. Diagram indicating sectional plane. B. Section of sporocarp. i., indusium; me., megasporangium; mi., microsporangium; r., gelatinous ring; re., receptacle; v. b., vascular bundle; w., wall of sporocarp.

protuberance or papilla at one end on which the triradiate ridges remain visible. The wall in this region is delicate, but over the remainder of the spore protoplast it is extremely thick.

The megaspores are sufficiently large to be readily visible to the unaided eye. The single nucleus of the megaspore lies in dense cytoplasm and in the region of the protuberance. The bulk of the spore cavity is filled with starch grains; only a small amount of cytoplasm is present.

All the spores in the sporangia on the flanks of the receptacle mature; they are many times smaller than the megaspores. Each of these microspores has a single central nucleus and rather dense cytoplasm containing starch grains.

Hence, *Marsilea* is heterosporous, as are *Selaginella* and *Isoetes* among extant microphyllous plants. As the spores mature, changes occur in the sterile tissues of the sporocarp. The outer layers become stony, and their cell walls thicken markedly.

The vacuoles and cytoplasm of a zone of cells within the sporocarp become filled with polysaccharide and make up the structure later to expand as the sorophore. Both microsporangia and megasporangia lack a highly differentiated annulus, an indication of the fact that the spores are not discharged vigorously and explosively from the sporangia.

In nature, the sporocarps persist in the water and soil after the vegetative portions of the plants that produced them have disappeared. It is probable that bacterial action plays a role in rotting the sporocarp wall and in thus effecting spore dissemination.

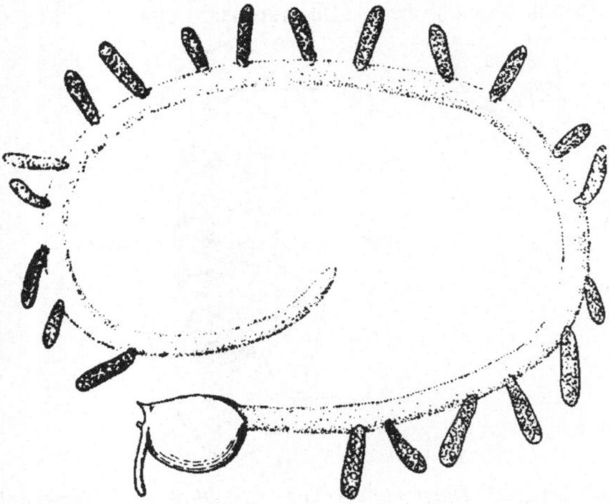

Figure 7.3: Masilea sp. Germinated sporocarp; note sorophore (ring) with sori.

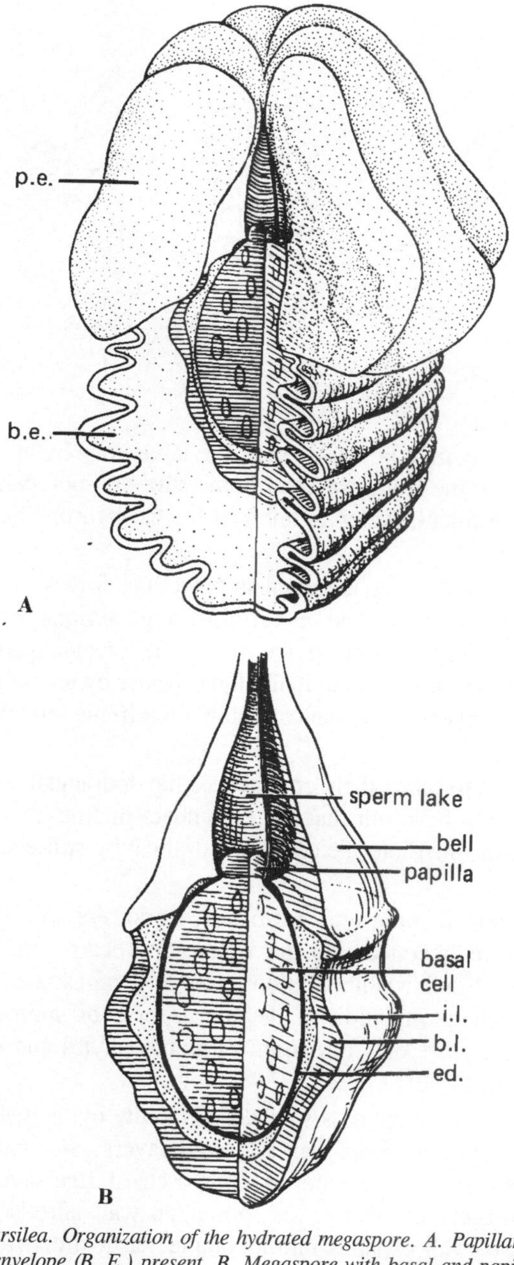

Figure 7.4: Marsilea. Organization of the hydrated megaspore. A. Papillar envelope (P. E.) and basal envelope (B. E.) present. B. Megaspore with basal and papillar envelopes removed.

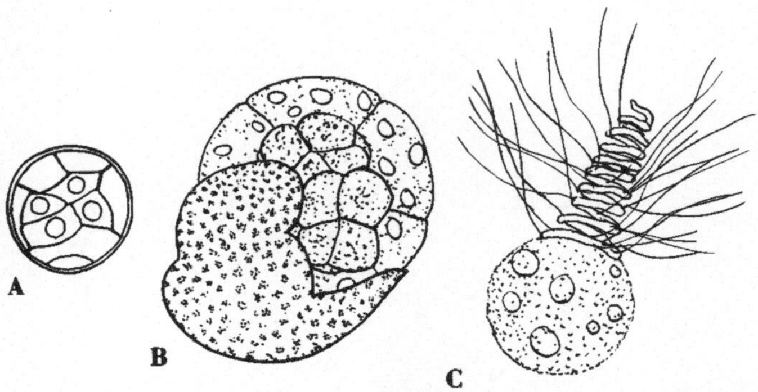

Figure 7.5: Marsilea vestita: Development of the gametophyte. A. Section of the microspore with d gametophyte; note prothallial cell and two rudimentary antheridia. B. Microspore with emergent d gametophyte. C. Living sperm.

This process may be hastened in the laboratory by cutting away a small portion of the stony wall and immersing the sporocarps in water. After such treatment, water is imbibed by the hydrophilic colloids in the sporocarp.

Within a short time, the attendant swelling forces the two halves of the sporocarp apart and a vermiform gelatinous structure, the sporophore, emerges, bearing the sori. The great expansion of the sorophore is occasioned by the inhibition of water by the polysaccharides within the sorophore cells, which results in extreme stretching of their walls.

Several hours after their emergence, the sporangial walls become gelatinous, with the result that large numbers of free microspores and megaspores are shed into the common soral cavity still enclosed by the indusium.

The latter disintegrates ultimately, and the microspores and megaspores are liberated into the water. Sporocarps are well known for retention of their viability. Bloom (1955) demonstrated opening the sporocarp with germination of the megaspores of sporocarps of M. *quadrifolia* 32 years old; formation of gametophytes and development of embryos followed.

The mature megaspore is surrounded closely by the megasporangial wall. The megaspore itself has two wall layers, an inner *endospore* and outer *exospore*. The latter is composed of five layers. When it comes in contact with water, the sporangial wall unrolls rapidly, and the megaspore wall expands into a complex structure, which has been described by Machlis and Rawitscher-Kunkel.

Soon after the megasporangial wall is cast off, two extensive gelatinous envelopes appear, the basal envelope (folded horizontally) and the papillar envelope (folded longitudinally).

Within the papilla envelope and over the papilla, a bell-shaped gelatinous structure develops; in its center is an elongate fluid region, the *sperm lake*. Although sperms may be observed throughout the gelatinous envelopes at the papillar region, they are concentrated in the sperm lake in which they swim actively.

Reproduction: The Gametophytes

Unlike those of *Selaginella* but like those of *Isoetes*, the spores of *Marsilea* do not germinate until they have been shed from the sporocarp. Development into gametophytes is then very rapid. Hepler (1976); Myles and Hepler (1977); and Myles, Southworth, and Hepler (1978) have recently investigated incisively the development of the male gametophyte and spermatogenesis in *Marsilea vestita.*

Formation of the male gametophyte by the microspore is initiated by a nuclear and cell division to form unequal cells within the microspore wall; the smaller cell is the prothallial cell. As in *Isoetes* and *Selaginella*, this cell fails to divide again and is often interpreted as the sole remnant of vegetative tissue in the male gametophyte.

The large cell divides in two, and each of the resulting cells, by further division, forms an antheridium that is covered with jacket cells, which surround the 16 spermatogenous cells. Late in the divisions of the spermatogenous cells, deeply staining organelles, the *blepharoplasts*, arise *de novo* near the nuclei and ultimately function (as in the cycad, *Zamia*) in forming the procentrioles and basal bodies of the 100 to 150 flagella of the mature sperms.

The microspore wall now ruptures, and the mature antheridia protrude. The prothallial cells and jacket cells disintegrate, and the large sperms, which have previously developed singly in each spermatogenous cell, become actively motile and swim away.

The sperms are tightly coiled and have their flagella at the apical nuclear portion. Myles (1975) reported that the motile sperms lose their ball of cytoplasm before they reach the eggs. The development of the male gametophyte and liberation of the sperms may take place in as short a time as from 11 to 15 hours, depending on the species.

In the development of the female gametophyte by the megaspore, a limited number of nuclear and cell divisions occur within the hemispherical protuberance, resulting in the formation of a small amount of vegetative tissue bearing a single apical archegonium. Enlargement of these cells ruptures the megaspore wall, which is delicate in the region of the protuberance.

The megaspore that bears the mature female gametophyte becomes surrounded by a gelatinous matrix, which is usually thickest in the region of the female gametophyte. The liberated sperms, apparently attracted chemotactically, swarm into the matrix in the vicinity of the archegonium. One of them makes its way to the egg cell through the sperm lake, and fertilization occurs.

Reproduction: embryogeny

Development of the embryo is initiated several hours after fertilization by nuclear and cell division of the zygote. Cytokinesis is usually in a direction parallel to the long axis of the archegonium and megaspore, which are typically horizontal.

A second division, also parallel to the archegonial axis but in a plane perpendicular to that of the first division, results in a formation of four cells. By further division these develop the foot, leaf (cotyledon), stem, and root of the embryonic sporophyte, as indicated in Figures elsewhere in this chapter.

The vegetative cells of the gametophyte are stimulated to divide as an embryonic sporophyte develops, and they form a sheathing calyptra around the latter. The surface cells of this gametophytic tissue develop rhizoids; both rhizoids and other gametophytic cells develop chloroplasts.

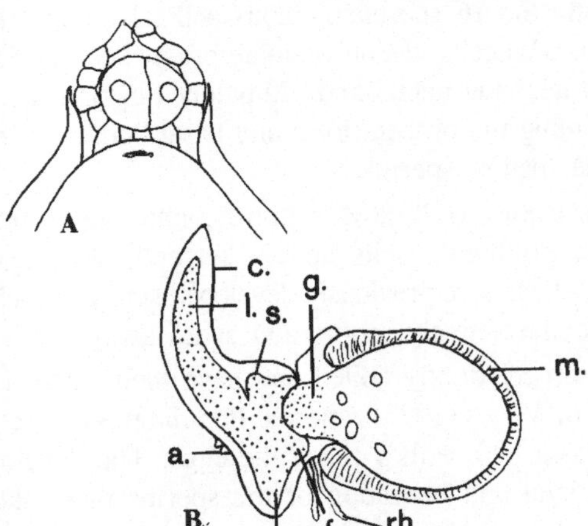

Figure 7.6: A. Marsilea vestita. Median longitudinal section of 9 gametophyte; archegonium with early embryo. B. Marsilea sp. Median longitudinal section of megaspore, 4 gametophyte, and embryo. a., archegonium; c., calyptralike sheath; g., 9 gametophyte; 1., primary leaf or cotyledon; m., megaspore wall; r., root; rh., rhizoid; s., stem.

The calyptra is relatively persistent, but disappears about the same time that the embryonic root penetrates the substratum.

Growth of the embryonic sporophyte is rapid. One series of germling sporophytes of *M. vestita* planted in April produced mature plants bearing sporocarps by the following October.

The genera of Marsileales form an interesting evolutionary series with respect to their leaves. *Marsilea* usually has two pairs of pinnae on its compound leaves, but occasionally it may have three pairs. In *Regnellidium* a deeply bilobed leaf occurs. Finally, in *Pilularia* no leaf blade develops, and the petiole and rachis are the photosynthetic organs.

The organization of the sporocarp, maturation of the gametophytes, and the embryogeny of *Regnellidium* and *Pilularia*, in general, resemble corresponding phases in *Marsilea.*

Summary of Marsileales

Although decidedly not fernlike in appearance, the vegetative structure and sporangial development of *Marsilea* are very similar to those of other leptosporangiate ferns. The cloverlike leaves represent sterile pinnae with a dichotomous venation that is closed at the margins and to some extent laterally.

Vernation of the leaves is circinate. The stems are amphipholoic siphonosteles, interrupted by leaf gaps, which usually do not overlap because of the great length of the internodes. The leaves arise alternately in two rows from the stolonlike stems.

Both roots and stems afford anatomical evidence of aquatic habitat in the form of air chambers; the vascular tissue, however, is unusually abundant for a hydrophytic plant. The roots contain vessels. *Marsilea is* representative of the leptosporangiate ferns in which heterospory has been developed.

The sporangia are borne in sclerotic, modified, fused pinnae which constitute the sporocarp. With it have appeared such concomitant attributes as dioecious gametophytes, reduction in vegetative functions and tissue, and duration of the gametophytes. Gametogenesis and embryogeny are extremely rapid in *Marsilea.*

Order 3. Salviniales

The order Salviniales contains two genera, *Salvinia* (after Antonio M. Salvini) and *Azolla* (Gr. *azo*, parched, killed by drought), both small, floating aquatics. Most species of *Salvinia* are native to Africa, but one species occurs in the United States. *Salvinia* is widely distributed in

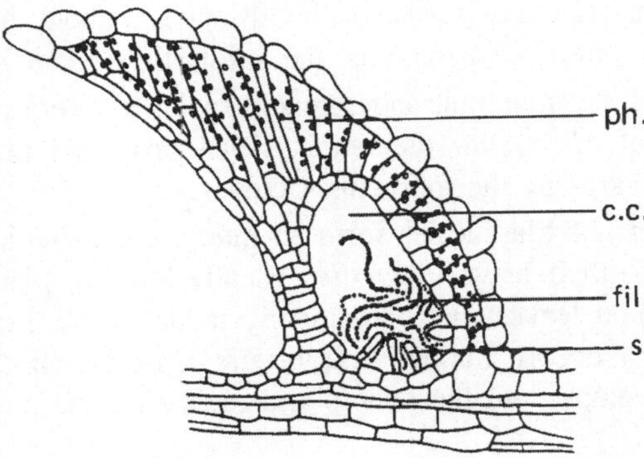

Figure 7.7: Longisection of dorsal leaf lobe showing cavity containing Anabaena. *ph., photosynthetic tissue. c.c., central cavity. fil.,* Anabaena *filaments. s., secretory hair.*

greenhouses and aquaria. Two species of *Azolla* occur in the United States, *A. caroliniana* in the eastern states and *A. filiculoides* in the western states. Ponds and swamps are often colored red by "blooms" of *Azolla* in intense light.

Salvinia is rootless, the apparent roots being morphologically filiform leaf segments. The leaves are in whorls of three, two of which are floating and the third submerged. It is the latter that is divided into rootlike lobes. The floating leaves are concave and covered with hairs and waxy papillae. The slender floating stems of *Salvinia* have a small pith (which is encircled by tracheids) and are, accordingly, siphonostelic. Gaudet (1973) succeeded in growing *S. minima* in axenic culture.

Azolla consists of branching stems densely clothed with alternate bilobed leaves that suggest those of certain Jungermanniaceae. Each leaf is composed of a chlorophyllous dorsal lobe and a submerged achlorophyllous ventral lobe.

The dorsal lobes contain cavities in which occur filaments of the blue-green alga *Anabaena*; there is good evidence that the alga fixes nitrogen. *Azolla* growing in strong sunlight often becomes orange-red. Holst (1977) has identified the pigment of *A. mexicana* as an anthocyanin, luteolinidin-5-glycoside.

This pigment is apparently always present in the plants but increases with the increase of incident light. Pieterse, Delange, and Van Vliet (1977) reported that anthocyanin production is influenced by temperature and water composition, not by photoperiod.

True roots, which arise endogenously. at intervals along the stem, occur in *Azolla*. The roots bear root hairs as long as they exist. Both stem and root have exarch protosteles.

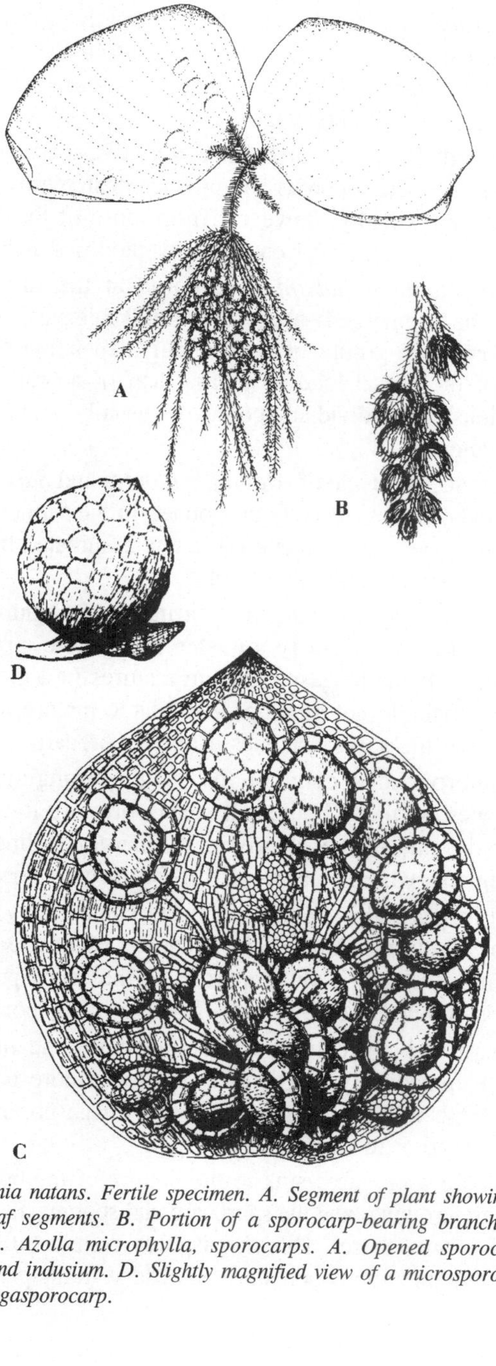

Figure 7.8: Salvinia natans. Fertile specimen. A. Segment of plant showing submerged sporocarps on leaf segments. B. Portion of a sporocarp-bearing branch more highly magnified. C, D. Azolla microphylla, sporocarps. A. Opened sporocarp showing microsporangia and indusium. D. Slightly magnified view of a microsporocarp (larger, spherical) and megasporocarp.

Both *Salvinia* and *Azolla* reproduce vegetatively because of their continuing apical growth, branching, and death of the older regions of the plants. Detachment of branches and their subsequent independent growth also increase the population.

Salvinia with 13 species and *Azolla* with 5 species, like the genera of Marsileales, are heterosporous and produce their spores in sporocarps. The latter differ markedly, however, from those of the Marsileales in that they represent single sori enclosed by modified indusium.

The sporocarps of *Salvinia* are borne at the tips of the short branches of the submerged, branching rootlike leaves, while those of *Azolla* are formed in groups of two or four (depending on the species) in the axil of the dorsal lobe of a basal leaf of a branch. The plants are monoecious, but individual sporocarps usually contain only micro- or megasporangia.

The reproductive cycle of *Azolla filiculoides* and *Salvinia auriculata* has been elucidated most recently by Bonnet. In the former, development of the essentially leptosporangiate sporangia is initiated by a single cell at the apex of a moundlike receptacle.

This first sporangia is potentially a megasporangium, while other sporangia initiated laterally on the receptacle are potentially microsporangia. If the megasporangium matures in a given sporocarp, the microsporangia do not develop; if it fails to mature, the microsporangia do so and the sorus becomes a microsporocarp.

Eight sporogenous cells in the megasporangium function as megasporocytes, so that 32 potential megaspores are formed. Only one of the potential megaspores survives. It enlarges, filling much of the megasporangium, which enlarges to fill the megasporocarp.

In both mega- and microsporangia the tapetal cells disintegrate to form a tapetal plasmodium. This becomes vacuolate at first, later hardened and alveolar, is quadripartite in the megasporangium, and sometimes is composed of more lobes in the microsporangium.

This hardened alveolar material constitutes the *massulae*. That portion of it immediately surrounding the megaspore is known as the *perispore*. Neither the microsporangial nor megasporangial walls are modified in relation to dehiscence.

The mature sporocarps sink to the bottom of the body of water in which they are growing, and the sporocarp and sporangial walls ultimately release the spores there. The megaspores remain attached to their massulae, while the microspores are embedded in the periphery of their massulae.

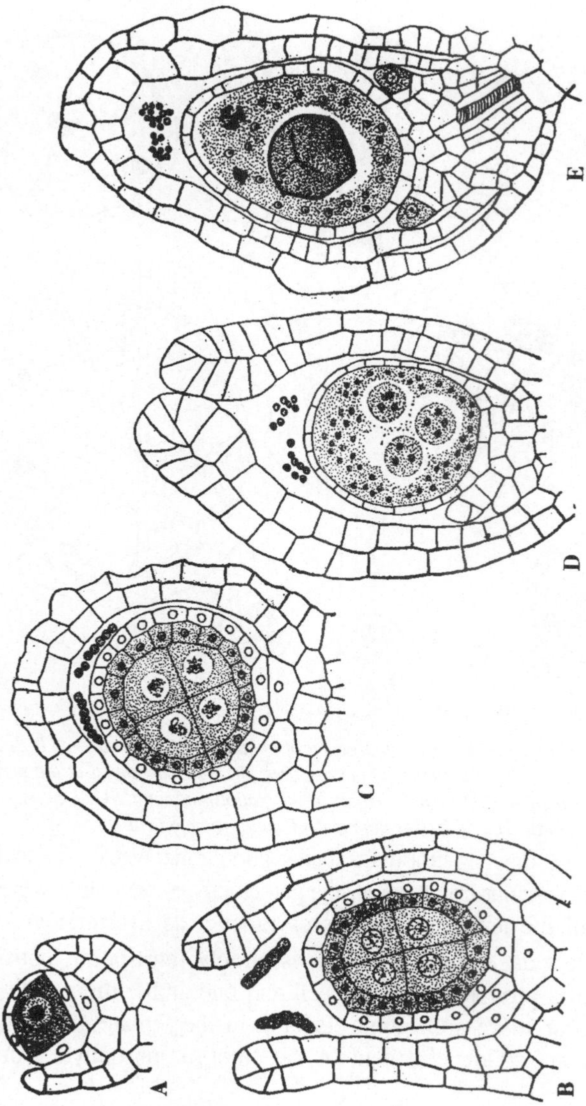

Figure 7.9: Azolla filiculoides. Stages in development of the megasporangium and indusium; note included Anabaena cells.

The latter in some species have protuberances known as *glochidia*, which apparently can become attached to a megasporic massulae or perispore.

Unlike those of many species of *Selaginella*, but like those of *Isoetes* and the Marsileales, the heterospores of *Azolla* and *Salvinia* do not germinate until they are liberated from their sporangia, and

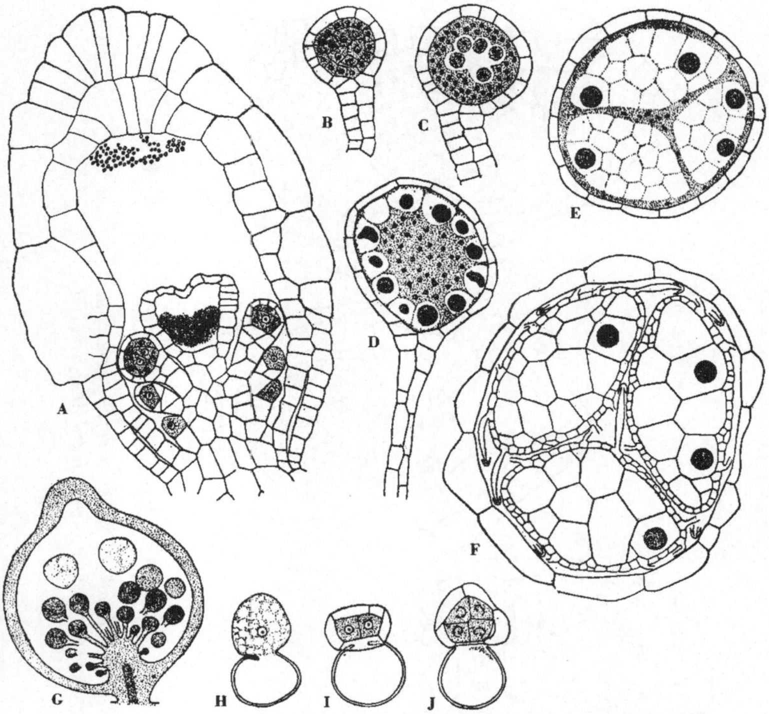

Figure 7.10: Azolla filiculoides. A. Longisection of immature microsporocarp. B-F. Stages in development of microsporangium and microspores, the latter arranged at the periphery of the microsporangium in D-F; note tripartite (in section) massulae. G. Longisection of maturing microsporocarp. H-J. Development of male gametophyte.

development of the gametophytes takes about one week. As in other heterosporous vascular cryptogams, the gametophytes have little vegetative tissue, that of the female being photosynthetic, as in *Marsilea*.

The male gametophyte of *Azolla* is largely intrasporal, consisting at maturity of a prothallial (sterile) cell and one antheridium with eight sperms. One or more archegonia develop in the female gametophyte, which is the site of development of the embryo sporophyte from the zygote.

Reproductive material of *Salvinia* and *Azolla* is not frequently encountered. It could probably be evoked in laboratory culture where temperature, photoperiod, and nutrients could be controlled.

It should be clear from the above brief account that although it is fundamentally similar to that in other heterosporous vascular cryptogams, especially the Marsileales, the reproductive process in the Salviniales

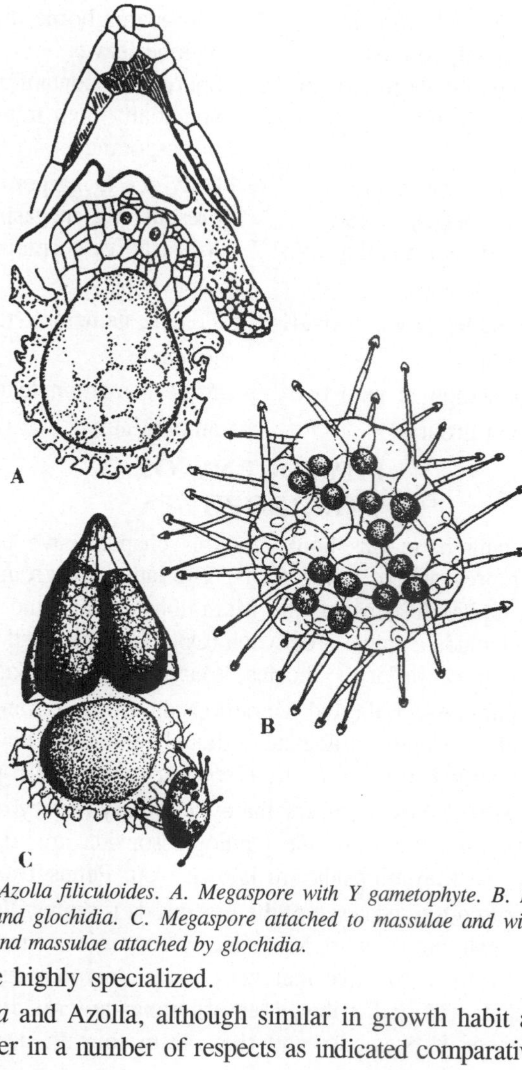

Figure 7.11: Azolla filiculoides. A. Megaspore with Y gametophyte. B. Massulae with microspores and glochidia. C. Megaspore attached to massulae and with a group of microspores and massulae attached by glochidia.

has become highly specialized.

Salvinia and Azolla, although similar in growth habit and aquatic habitat, differ in a number of respects as indicated comparatively below:

Salvinia	*Azolla*
1. Simple, whorled leaves	1. Leaves overlap ping, each with floating and sub mersed lobe
2. Roots lacking, one leaf at each node rootlike	2. Roots with root hairs and root caps present
3. Siphonostelic stem	3. Protostelic stem

4. Sporocarps at branch tips of submersed, rootlike	4. Sporocarps borne on the apex of lobe leaves
5. Sporocarps *either* micro- or mega-sporangiate	5. Sporocarps containing potentially both micro- and megasporangia
6. Several megasporangia present in megasporocarp	6. Only one megasporangium present in a megaspor ocarp
7. Megaspores germinating at the water surface	7. Megaspores germinating when submersed
8. Female gametophyte strongly photosynthetic	8. Female gametophyte barely green
9. Male gametophyte with two antheridial groups	9. Male gametophyte with one antheridium

PHYLOGENY OF PTERIDOPHYTA

Other chapters in this book and this chapter have presented an account of representative living ferns. The latter are grouped in three classes, the Ophioglossopsida, the Marattiopsida, and the Filicopsida; the first two include a single order each (Ophioglossales and Marattiales) and the last, three orders (Filicales, Marsileales, and Salviniales).

The Ophioglossopsida and Marattiopsida are eusporangiate, while the Filicopsida are leptosporangiate, although sporangial development is somewhat modified in some (e.g., *Osmunda*) of the Filicopsida.

The most sound evidence for the evolutionary history of a group is the fossil record. Fossils of the Ophioglossopsida are unknown, but members of the Marattiopsida are known from Pennsylvanian times.

One family (Osmundaceae) of the Filicopsida is represented beginning with the Permian, but most are Mesozoic or Cenozoic in first appearance. It is important to realize that members of the Polypodiaceae-today the most dominant, widely distributed leptosporangiate ferns-did not appear until the Upper Cretaceous, and they seem thus to be as recently evolved as are the angiosperms.

For this reason, they are often spoken of as "modern ferns." The fossil record of ferns and their supposed precursors gives some indication of characteristics that may be considered to be primitive. These include elaborate, compound (branched) leaves, presumably modified from branch systems; erect, epiterranean stems; massive sporangia, lacking annuli, with several-layered walls and indefinitely large numbers of tetrahedral spores; the sporangia borne marginally on the leaves and at the ends of veins. Because these features characterized many ancient ferns, deviations from them have come to be considered to be further evolved or "advanced."

Such characteristics are simple leaves, prostrate, often dorsiventral, rhizomatous stems, small sporangia with annuli, one- to two-layered walls and fewer spores, the sporangia borne on the abaxial surface of leaves instead of marginally. A number of additional characteristics have been inferred to be, either primitive or advanced.

Among the latter are thin-walled, green, rapidly germinating spores; direct formation of a platelike gametophyte (rather than a filameint); small, thin delicate, ephemeral gametophytes lacking a midrib; small antheridia with 24-156 sperms (in contrast to several hundred), with 4 or fewer wall cells; and archegonia with relatively long necks.

Many other characteristics have been cited as illustrative of relative primitiveness or advancement. Thus, Wagner (1974) presented, at a symposium on phylogeny of ferns and their classification, a table of over 70 evolutionary "trends" or characteristics, sporo phytic and gametophytic, vegetative and reproductive, which he considered valid.

He (1974) and others have found the form and ornamentation of fern spores to be important taxonomically and indicative of phylogeny. Since "nature mocks at human categories," once again we find, as anticipated, that the putative "primitive" and/or "advanced" characteristics are not neatly correlated in one or another genus, family, or order.

Although the primitive nature of some characteristics may be reasonably inferred from the fossil record of ferns, the validity of their criteria of advancement and primitiveness has been questioned. Even at the symposium cited above, Holttum, a leading investigator of the taxonomy of ferns, stated: "As regards the great majority of ferns, their probable phylogeny can be inferred only from their classification; there is little other evidence available."

At a later point in the same Symposium another specialist (Wagner) in pteridology said: "There is simply no 'royal road' to classification, and the way it is done is every man's special prerogative." In an earlier symposium (1964) the same investigator had remarked: "Such patterns as we can construct of the origin and evolution of the ferns are based almost exclusively on data from the living members of the class."

In conclusion, when one is considering phylogeny or the probable course of evolution among the higher categories (more-embracing taxa), Holttum's statement might well be a sobering consideration. More extensive discussion of the evolution and phologeny of ferns is available in the following references cited in the Bibliography: Delevoryas (1964), Jermy, Crabbe, and Thomas (1973), Bierhorst (1974), Lloyd (1974), Mickel (1974), Stidd (1974), Wagner (1974), and White (1974).

8

VASCULAR CRYPTOGAMS: RECAPITULATION AND FOSSIL RECORD

Other chapters in this book have presented a discussion of the structure and reproduction of living representatives of the divisions Psilotophyta, Microphyllophyta, Arthrophyta, and Pteridophyta. The present chapter presents a brief comparative summary of the more important features of these organisms, the vascular cryptogams, and discusses their phylogenetic implications.

THE LIFE CYCLE

In earlier schemes of classification (other than the one used in this book; see inside back cover), the seedless vascular plants were grouped together in a single division, Pteridophyta. Although the plants so classified have been regrouped as four separate phyletic lines (divisions) in the present volume, it should be emphasized that they do have in common the same balance between alternating generations or phases in their life cycles.

In almost all vascular cryptogams the sporophyte is the dominant and persistent (usually perennial) phase in the life cycle; the gametophyte is clearly simpler and more ephemeral. In all cases, however, the latter is separated ultimately from the parent sporophyte, unlike the female gametophyte in the seed plants, in which it is permanently retained.

In the Hepatophyta, Anthocerotophyta, and Bryophyta, on the other hand, the gametophyte is dominant. That the life cycle is not entirely inflexible and obligate is evidenced by numerous examples of apogamy and some of apospory. *Apogamy*, the development of a sporophyte from a gametophyte in which no fertilization takes place, occurs regularly in certain species of polypodiaceous ferns, and there is evidence of its presence in species of *Marsilea* and *Selaginella* as well.

Furthermore, apogamy has been induced in normally sexual genera. *Apospory*, the development of a gametophyte directly from sporophytic tissue, and not from a spore, is less widespread. It, too, occurs in nature and may be induced.

These phenomena have focused attention on the question of the origin and relation of the two alternating phases and have resulted in speculations regarding the type of life cycle in the first land plants or their immediate ancestors. There seems to be rather general agreement that primitive plants were at least potentially sexual, gametophytic, and haploid.

The initiation of the sexual process would obviously result in the existence of a diploid cell, the zygote. In organisms with zygotic meiosis, the diploid zygote is only a transitory phase, which is obliterated in the meiotic process.

It seems clear that the inception of sexuality and the first occurrence of meiosis must have been closely related in time, if not simultaneous, in view of their complementary functions and invariable co-existence. An extensive diploid sporophyte generation appears to have been a secondary adjunct to the life cycle with sexuality.

Its origin is postulated to have been occasioned by a delay in meiosis in the zygote and by the interpolation of a more or less extensive series of mitoses and cytokineses between fertilization and meiosis, with the result that diploid cells other than the zygote arose for the first time.

Meiosis then occurred in all these diploid cells, however numerous. This, of course, represents the type of life cycle present in all organisms with sporic meiosis. Finally, gradual extension of the duration and importance of the diploid sporophytic phase, concomitant with the suppression of the haploid phase, is thought to have resulted in the type of life cycle in which gametic meiosis occurs.

It should be emphasized that the preceding statements are mere conjectures, none of which is verifiable experimentally. The credence with which they frequently are received and repeated might well be tempered by this consideration and others, among them the following:

The great majority of animals are diploid organisms with gametic

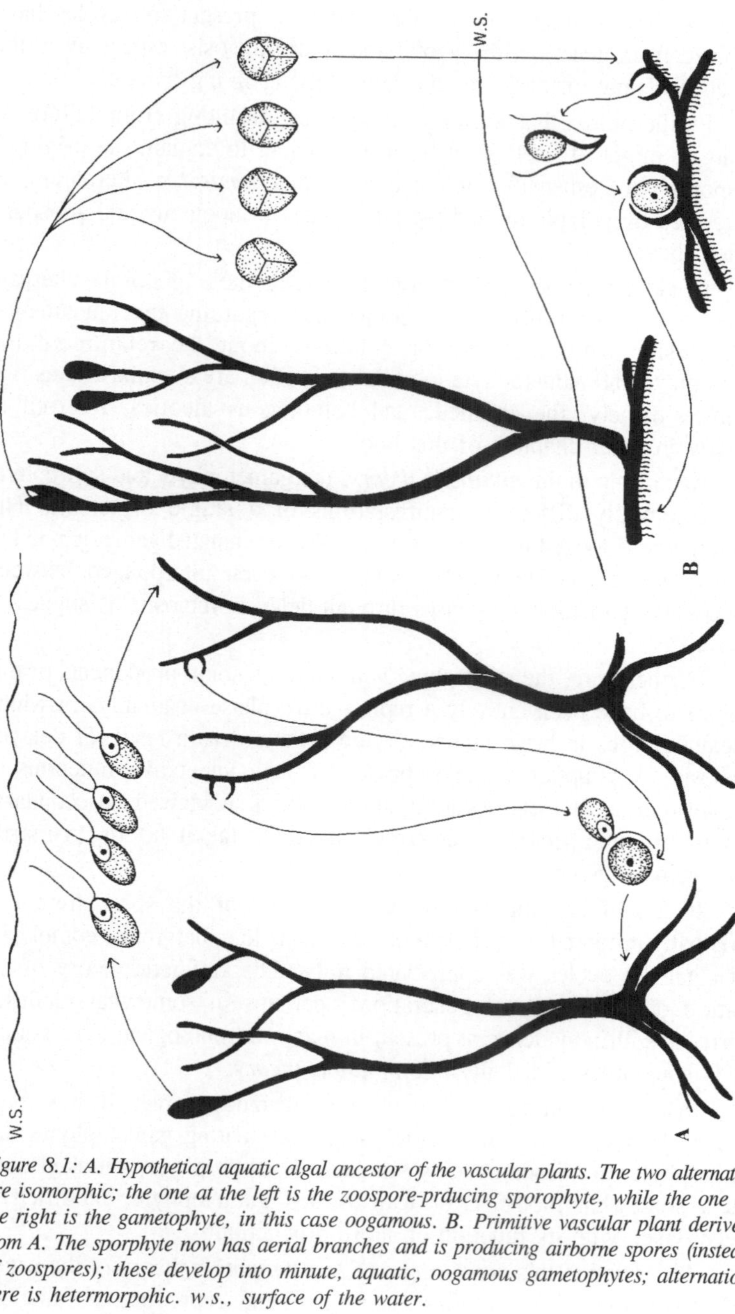

Figure 8.1: A. Hypothetical aquatic algal ancestor of the vascular plants. The two alternates are isomorphic; the one at the left is the zoospore-prducing sporophyte, while the one at the right is the gametophyte, in this case oogamous. B. Primitive vascular plant derived from A. The sporphyte now has aerial branches and is producing airborne spores (instead of zoospores); these develop into minute, aquatic, oogamous gametophytes; alternation here is hetermorpohic. w.s., surface of the water.

meiosis. It is scarcely conceivable that their present life cycles have evolved from genera with zygotic and sporic meiosis, especially in the absence of any examples of the latter among living animals.

Furthermore, that diploidy of zygotes, resulting from failure of meiosis, might of itself have been insufficient to explain the origin of a sporophyte, especially of the type in *heteromorphic* alternation, is suggested by polyploidy and the phenomena of apogamy and apospory noted above.

In addition to these speculations concerning the origin of the alternate phases, there have been many conjectures regarding the fundamental relationship between them. Speculations about the relation of the sporophyte and gametophyte to each other often are summarized as two theories-namely, the antithetic and homologous theories, referred to briefly in other chapters of this book.

According to the *antithetic theory*, the gametophyte and sporophyte are essentially different manifestations of a single organism. The sporophyte is looked upon not as a modified or changed gametophyte but rather as a phase *sui generis*, which has been interpolated between successive gametophytic phases through delay in meiosis, as suggested above.

Furthermore, the sporophyte is thought by some proponents of this theory to have been entirely a reproductive phase originally, in which asexual spores in large numbers were produced as a result of delayed meiosis. Assumption by sporophytes of such vegetative functions as photosynthesis and translocation, among others, is viewed as secondary. These are interpreted as acquired functions taken up by primarily sporogenous tissues.

It should be emphasized that this view of the sporophyte was originally proposed by a student of land plants long before the complexity of algal life cycles was appreciated fully. The antithetic theory of the nature of alternation of generations, perhaps in somewhat modified form, is still in evidence at present in many morphological discussions. It is sometimes called the inter*polation theory*.

In opposition to the views summarized above, it has been emphasized by some morphologists that alternating gametophytes and sporophytes are fundamentally similar. The sporophyte is looked upon as a somewhat modified or transformed gametophyte, modified in accordance with its function of spore production.

According to this *homologous* or *transformation* theory of the nature of alternation of generations, vegetative and reproductive functions coexist in primitive sporophytes, although the balance between them may be variable. Certainly algal sporophytes are photosynthetic.

Conceding that the alternates among the land plants are, indeed, heteromorphic, possibly because of the stimulus of a terrestrial environment, proponents of this theory also point to the algae, in which numerous cases of both isomorphic and heteromorphic alternation of generations are known in a uniform aquatic habitat.

It has been suggested that one important factor effecting heteromorphism is the permanent retention of the sporophyte within or on the gametophyte, as in the diploid carposporophyte of the *Rhodophycophyta* and the *sporophytes* of *Hepatophyta*, *Anthocerotophyta*, and *Bryophyta*, and its dretention during *embryogeny* in the *vascular cryptogams* and seed plants.

However, marked heteromorphism is present in the kelps (*Laminaria*), in which the two generations are entirely independent of each other. This discussion of alternation of generations has been presented not with the purpose of settling the problem, but rather to indicate the complexity of the considerations involved.

The apparent independence of alternation of generations from chromosome number has already been emphasized. It seems quite possible that different life cycle patterns may have arisen as a result of different circumstances and different stimuli in different organisms, and that a comprehensive explanation may be unattainable. Wahl (1965) has presented a comprehensive discussion of the phenomenon of alternation of generations.

MORPHOLOGY OF THE VEGETATIVE ORGANS OF THE SPOROPHYTE

Comparison of the several divisions in which the vascular cryptogams have been classified indicates that the stem is certainly the dominant organ of the sporophyte, except in the Pteridophyta, in which it may be equaled or surpassed in stature and anatomical complexity by the megaphyllous leaves.

In the living Psilotophyta, Microphyllophyta, and Arthrophyta, examples of erect and ascending, vinelike, rhizomatous, and stolonlike stems occur. With the exception of the tree ferns, the stems of the Pteridophyta are mostly subterranean, vertical or horizontal, or at the surface of the ground.

Dichotomous branching of the stems, by the equal division of single apical cells or groups of meristematic cells, is considered primitive as compared with monopodial and sympodial types. *Equisetum*, with its whorls of branches and leaves, the latter alternating in origin with the former (i.e., they are not actually axillary), is unique among living vascular plants.

A considerable range in disposition of the vascular tissues is apparent in the members of the several divisions. Many primitive genera and the juvenile stages of most others usually have stems that contain protosteles. Examples of increasingly complex types of steles-siphonosteles, both amphiphloic and ectophloic, dictyosteles, eusteles, polysteles, and atactosteles-have been described.

Foliar gaps are present only in the Pteridophyta (and in other plants with siphonostelic

stems). Thickening of the stem by addition of secondary tissues through the activity of a cambium is rare among living vascular cryptogams, and where it occurs (*Isoetes*, *Botrychium*), it does not result in any considerable increase in girth.

The unicellular tracheid is the conducting element of the xylem of all these forms. In the stems of *Selaginella*, *Equisetum*, and *Pteridium*, and in the roots of *Marsilea*, however, perforation of walls of tracheids has resulted in the formation of vessels.

It is clear that the structures designated by the term "leaf' are not necessarily morphologically equivalent in the vascular plants. It will be recalled that in contrast with the microphyllous leaves of such plants as *Lycopodium* and *Selaginella*, which are relatively small, determinate in growth, and traversed by unbranched veins that leave no leaf gaps in the stem steles, *megaphyllous* leaves are typically larger, their development is more extended, if not indeterminate (*Lygodium*, *Gleichenia*), their vascular system is richly branched, and their traces profoundly modify the stem stele from which they depart, leaving parenchymatous gaps.

Furthermore, the vascular tissue is usually organized in the axes (petioles, rachis) of megaphyllous leaves in a pattern different from that in the stems on which they are borne. Because both these structures are called "leaves," are we, therefore, to consider them homologous? Morphologists have given different answers to this question. They have long speculated about the origin and evolution of the plant body of vascular plants.

According to the telome theory, five fundamental processes occurred in the evolution of the plant body. These are illustrated in the Figure

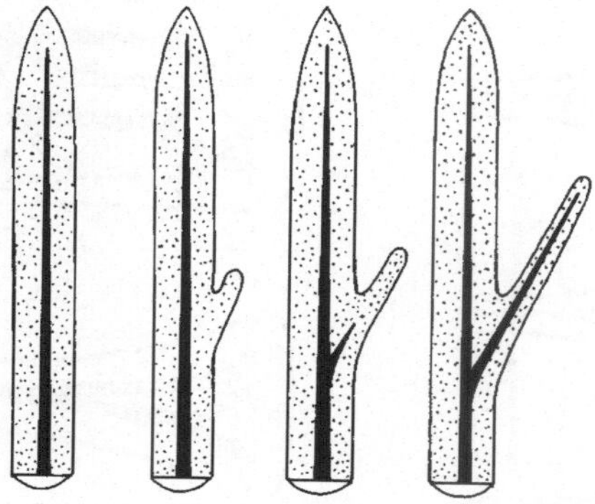

Figure 8.2: A-D. Evolutionary origin of a microphyllous leaf, according to the enation theory; the emergence at C corresponds to that occurring sometimes in Psilotum; that at D corresponds to leaves of Lycopodium and Selaginella.

elsewhere in this chapter and summarized in its caption. Fusion or union of parts of axes is postulated to have occurred both in leaflike and stemlike portions of axes.

The order of the illustrations does not necessarily indicate the order in which these phenomena occurred. Some of them, such as fusion, recurvation, and reduction, also are postulated to have affected the reproductive systems of plants.

Organization of leaves has been considered by morphologists as affected by these five phenomena. It is argued by some that microphylls are to be interpreted as localized, superficial enations of stems, which ultimately become vascularized.

Possible examples of this occur in *Psilotum*. Megaphylls, by contrast, are to be interpreted as branches of stems that have undergone planation by limitation of branching to one plane and webbing by extension of parenchymatous tissues between the branching axes.

The evidence for this interpretation of the megaphyllous leaf is based on its extensive, much-branched, vascular supply; on the fact that its trace, like the branch trace of microphyllous plants, effects a break in the stele where it originates; and finally, on its relatively large size and indeterminate development, all supported by the study of the fossil record and of such primitive living ferns as *Stromatopteris*, in which the distinction between axes and leaves is not well defined.

Accordingly, at least the main branching veins even of an undivided fern leaf represent the direction of the branching of a primitive axis which has become webbed between the vein branches. These views regarding leaves are in accord with the telome theory, which emphasizes

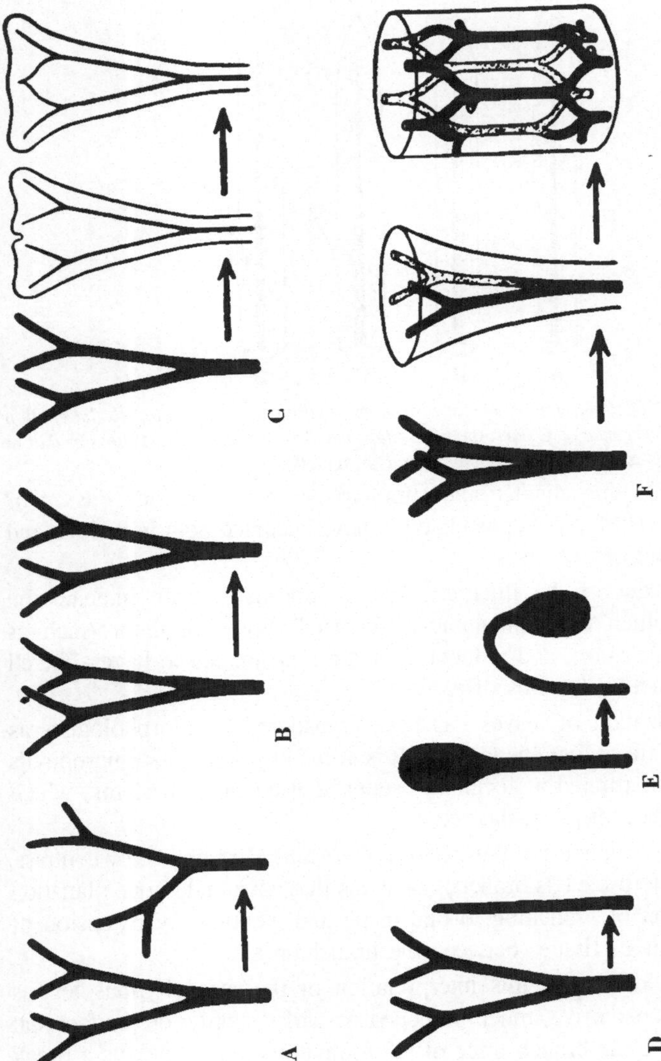

Figure 8.3: Five elementary evolutionary processes in the development of the body of vascular plants. A. Overtopping. B. Planation. C. Coalescence and webbing in the leaf. D. Reduction. E. Recurvation. F. Coalescence in the axis.

the shoot or axis as the fundamental unit in the organization of plants. Roots are present in all the divisions of vascular cryptogams except the Psilotophyta, in which the underground rhizomes, provided with rhizoidal appendages, carry on the function of absorption with sufficient efficiency to support the aerial portions of the plant.

That the root is probably an organ of the vascular cryptogams that developed later than their leaves and stems is suggested by the minor and relatively transitory role of the primary root or radicle in many genera; furthermore, the root sometimes arises in embryogeny later than the stem, never vice versa.

The root system of the vascular cryptogams is almost exclusively adventitious in origin. Internally, the roots are exarch and protostelic without exception, and they develop entirely from primary meristems. It has been suggested that the root arose as a modified rhizome branch that became covered with a root cap.

Reproduction: the sporophyte

Review of other chapters elsewhere in this chapter reveals considerable variation in the location and nature of the sporogenous tissues in the extant vascular cryptogams. Examples of little or no segregation of vegetative and sporogenous tissues are available in such instances as *Lycopodium lucidulum* and many Polypodiaceous and Marattiaceous ferns.

Even in *Psilotum* and *Tmesipteris*, however, sporogenous tissue is restricted to special, determinate lateral branches. The dimorphism observable in such plants as *L. complanatum*, species of *Osmunda*, the fertile spike of the *Ophioglossum-Botrychium* type, and the strobili of the Microphyllophyta and *Equisetum is* a manifestation of segregation of vegetative and reproductive functions at the organ level.

Furthermore, examples of both cauline (*Psilotum*) and foliar (Microphyllophyta, Polypodiaceous ferns) sporangia are present. With reference to their sporangia and method of ontogeny, two types, albeit with intermediates, may be distinguished among the vascular cryptogams.

These have usually been designated eusporangiate and leptosporangiate, but Bierhorst argues that the terms ought to be abandoned, because the distinguishing characteristics are not reliable in all cases. This apparent distinction still serves a useful purpose, however.

There is good evidence that heterospory developed independently in the Microphyllophyta, the Arthrophyta (fossil forms), and the Pteridophyta. Spore ontogeny in the heterosporous genera indicates that the *immediate* cause of heterospory lies in differences in spore number and nutrition and that these are expressed ultimately by spore size, but certainly more subtle genetic mechanisms are operating.

Reproduction: gametophyte and embryo

Considerable morphological and physiological variation is apparent among the gametophytes of the vascular cryptogams. Cylindrical form, radial symmetry, and saprophytism characterize the gametophytes of

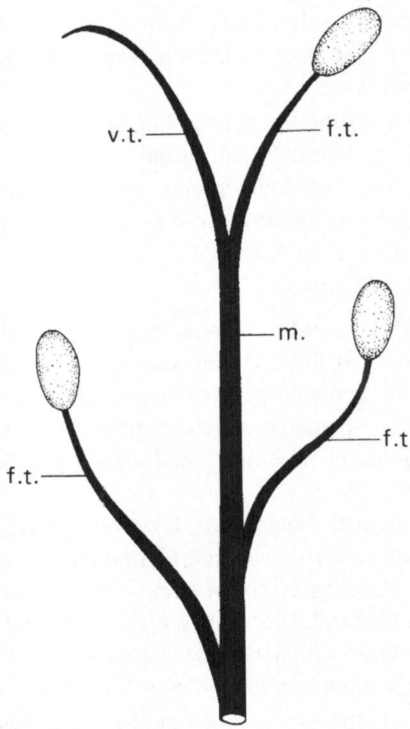

Figure 8.4: Telomes and Mesomes. f t., fertile telome; m., mesome; v.t., vegetative or sterile telome.

Psilotum, of certain species of *Lycopodium*, *Ophioglossum*, *Stromatopteris*, and *Schizaea*. Dorsiventral and photosynthetic gametophytes are present in *Equisetum* and in Marattiaceous and homosporous leptosporangiate ferns.

The presence of heterospory is associated with marked reduction in the morphological complexity and duration of the gametophyte, as is evident in *Selaginella*, *Isoetes*, and *Marsilea*. Furthermore, unisexual gametophytes inevitably accompany heterospory.

The nutrition in these gametophytes is based largely on metabolites stored by the parent sporophyte in the spores. Although the gametophytes of *Psilotum* and species of *Lycopodium*, *Ophioglossum*, and *Botrychium* are relatively long-lived as compared with those of other genera, the gametophyte generation, in general, is of lesser duration and complexity than are the persistent, perennial sporophytes of the vascular cryptogams.

The archegonia of the female gametophytes produced in heterosporous ferns are in general smaller and less complex than those in homosporous

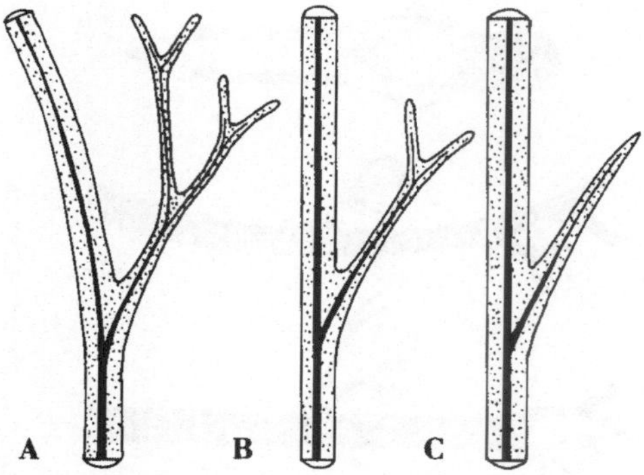

Figure 8.5: A-C. Hypothetical origin of a microphyllous leaf by reduction.

types. Both biflagellate (*Lycopodium*, *Selaginella*) and multiflagellate sperms (*Isoetes*, *Equisetum*, *Pteridophyta*) occur among vascular cryptogams.

The embryogeny of the vascular cryptogams exemplifies both slow (*Lycopodium*, *Psilotum*, *Ophioglossum*) and relatively rapidly growing (*Selaginella*, *Equisetum*, Polypodiaceous ferns) types. Nutrition of the embryo in heterosporous forms is based on metabolites of the parent sporophyte stored in the megaspores.

PHYLOGENETIC CONSIDERATIONS

The preceding paragraphs and Chapters any where else in this book have reviewed the ontogeny of the vegetative organs of the vascular plant—its stem, root, and leaf-and the reproductive features of representatives of the several groups of vascular cryptogams.

At this point it is appropriate to turn to a consideration of the phylogenetic origin of vascular plants and that of their component organs. The fossil record indicates clearly that life was aquatic in origin, and that it was largely restricted to an aquatic habitat for about 2.5 billion years.

At the end of this period, colonization of the land began. The emigrants were with great probability algae or modified algal descendants. There have been many suggestions regarding the course of evolution of the land flora from its algal progenitors.

These have largely been incor porated in a synthesis known as the telome theory by the eminent morphologist Walter Zimmerman (1952, 1965) and discussed by Stewart (1964). The telome theory attempts to

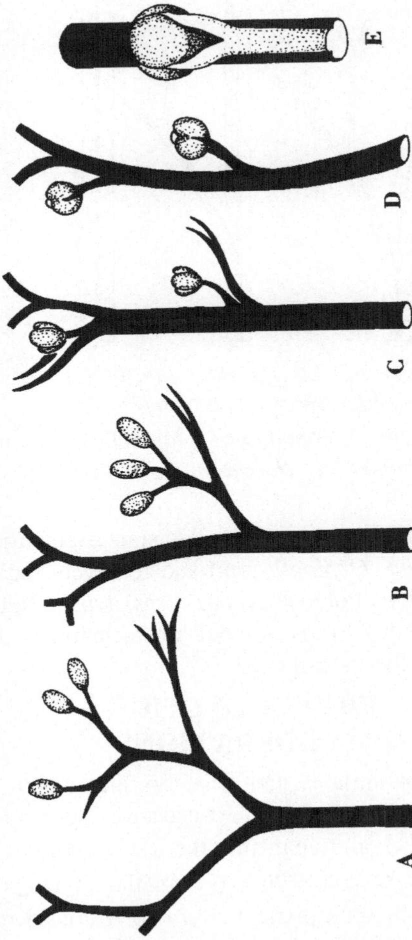

Figure 8.6: A-E. Proposed evolutionary steps leading to the development of the Psilotum type of synangium.

interpret extant plants in terms of their origin from extinct precursors. The major components of this concept will now be summarized.

According to the telome concept, the vascular plants evolved from algal precursors. The ultimate branchlets of the dichotomies are called *telomes*, and the connecting axes between dichotomies are called *mesomes*. Telomes may be sterile or fertile.

The Rhyniophyta are, perhaps, closest to the hypothetical ancestor. In these extinct plants, as exemplified by *Rhynia*, there are no leaves or roots, the plant body consisting of a three-dimensional system of mesomes and telomes.

The vascular tissue is in the form of a simple protostele. With the

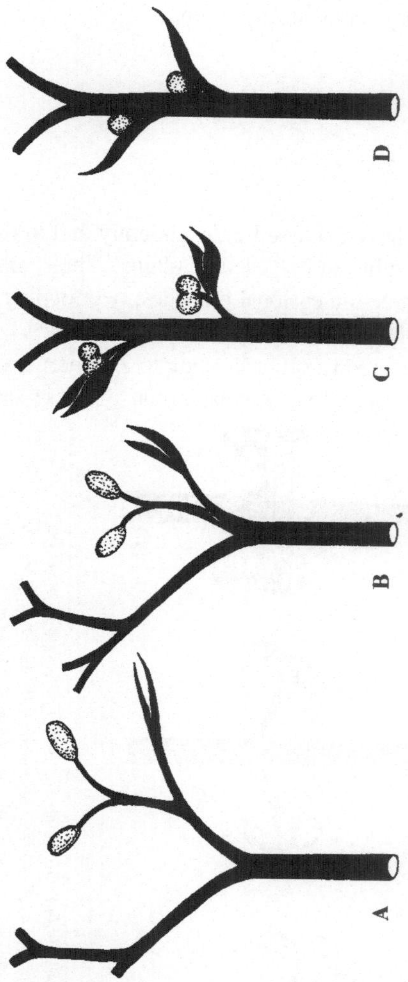

Figure 8.7: A-D. Proposed evolutionary steps in modification of a primitive axis (composed of fertile and sterile telomes) into the Tmesipteris (C) and Lycopodium (D) type of sporangial position. (After Stewart, from Zimmerman.)

land habit, there developed cuticle and stomata on the aerial meson7es, and telomes and rhizoids in the subterranean ones. The gametophytes of primitive land plants generally were not preserved in the fossil record, perhaps because of their delicate nature, or in their algal precursor.

Evolution of the primitive type of sporophyte just described, which was present also in the Devonian Zosterophyllophyta and Trimerophytophyta, into such diverse plant bodies as those of Microphyllophyta, Arthrophyta and Pteridophyta, the Microphyllophytan, Arthrophytan, and Pteridophytan types of plant body' is postulated by the telome concept to have involved the fundamental processes illustrated in Figure elsewhere in this chapter, among them the following:

(1) overtopping,
(2) planation,
(3) webbing,
(4) recurvation, and
(5) reduction.

These processes have occurred independently and in differing order and number in the evolution of vascular plants. Thus, in the evolution of megaphylls from three-dimensional branches, overtopping and planation have probably occurred, and in that order.

On the other hand, reduction, according to Zimmerman, may account for the origin of microphyllous leaves. Some of these same processes

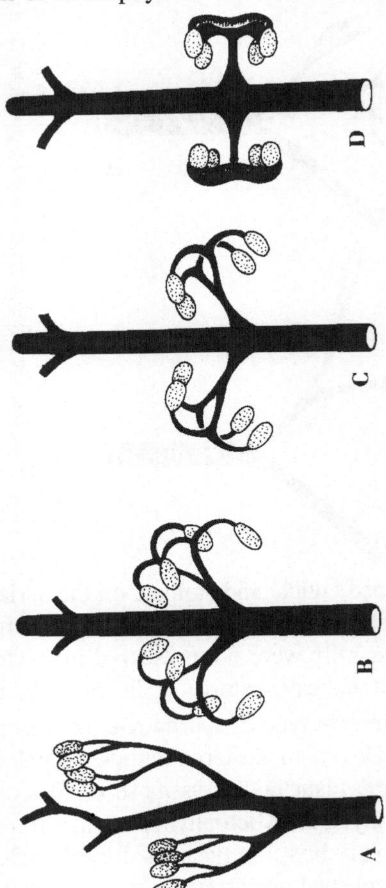

Figure 8.8: A-D. Proposed evolutionary steps in development of a primitive axis (A), composed of fertile and sterile telomes, into several types of arthrophytan sporangiophores. (After Stewart, from Zimmerman.) gial arrangement seen in Cladoxylon scoparium.

have operated in the evolution of the reproductive organs of vascular plants according to the telome concept.

The cauline sporangium of the Psilotophyta and the axillary or foliar sporangium of the Microphyllophyta, according to this concept, arose as a result of reduction. The arthrophytan sporangiophore, it is proposed, also arose through these modifying forces.

In the Pteridophyta, planation and webbing may well have developed the type of sporangial arrangement seen in Cladoxylon scoparium. Zimmerman has also interpreted the vascular system in light of the telome theory.' For example, he looked upon polystelic stems as having resulted from syngenesis or fusions of haplosteles.

However, his conclusions with respect to the origin of stelar types have not been received with enthusiasm. The telome concept is a unifying synthesis that seeks to interpret the diversities of organization of extant plants as modifications from a primitive stock of Devonian plants.

With respect to its postulates regarding the origin of microphylls by reduction, it is in marked contradiction to the enation theory and the evidence on which the latter is based. Perhaps, if microphylls and megaphylls are fundamentally similar in organization, differing only in number of component telomes, then we ought not to contrast them as strongly as we do.

The same argument has been applied to sporangial position, which, in the last analysis, is really always at the tip of a telome. Similarly, the telome theory disagrees with the interpretation of the evolution of stelar types accepted by most morphologists.

In spite of these difficulties, the telome concept certainly is and has been a stimulating and thought-provoking synthesis that has played and continues to play an important role in morphology.

In concluding this brief summary of the extant vascular cryptogams, it seems clear that comparison of representatives of the divisions Psilotophyta, Microphyllophyta, Arthrophyta, and Pteridophyta offers little evidence for close relationship of these plants.

The fossil record indicates that these four phyletic series had been established by the Devonian (inside front cover). Psilotophyta-like organisms may perhaps have been the precursors from which these four lines developed, but, as noted earlier, 400 million years separates these Devonian plants from the extant Psilotophyta.

Their diversities seem clearly to overshadow in significance the combination of attributes they share: vascular tissue, lack of seeds, and similarity in balance of the alternating generations.

THE FOSSIL RECORD

Although comparative morphology of living plants is an indispensable tool in attempts to determine morphological relationships and possible evolutionary pathways, the only real evidence concerning the course of change in plant form through time is preserved in the fossil record.

This record is, at best, extremely fragmentary; nevertheless we have learned a great deal about the history of the plant kingdom through a study of plant remains preserved in rocks.

A person who studies living plants primarily may be disappointed with the nature of the fossil record because so much is missing.

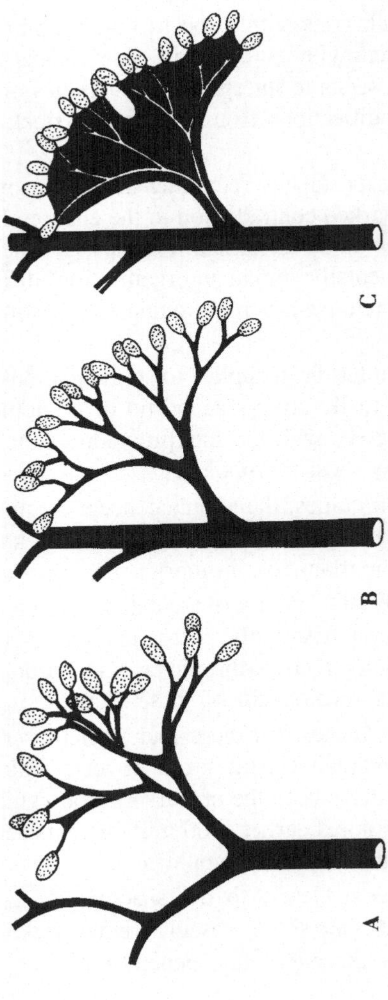

Figure 8.9: A-C. Proposed course of evolutionary development of a pterophytan pinnule with marginal sporangia from a primitive axis composed of fertile and sterile telomes.

Furthermore, it is seldom that an entire plant is preserved. The conditions under which plants are fossilized frequently involve factors that tend to break the plant into pieces, which are then preserved.

Thus, leaves may be separated from stems that are nowhere near reproductive parts that may have been borne on the plants. Also, only those plants that are near appropriate conditions that are conducive to preservation are represented in the fossil record.

Undoubtedly countless plants that grew some distance from ideal preservational situations have not entered into the fossil picture. Plants are preserved in a variety of ways in the rocks.

Probably the most frequently occurring type of fossil preservation is one that results from plant parts that are carried into basins (e.g., lagoons, abandoned stream channels in a delta) into which suspended sedimentary particles are also being transported.

Accumulation of considerable sediment (e.g., during storms and floods) eventually produced sufficient pressure to squeeze the plant parts until they were nothing but thin films of carbon and other chemicals that are degradation products of the original plant material.

This type of fossil is called a *compression* and is valuable in showing external features. At times, however, the cuticle that covers aerial parts of most land plants may resist distortion or decay and may survive the fossilization process intact.

This cuticle faithfully reproduces the surface features of a plant organ-such as a leaf, for exampleand when removed and mounted for microscopic examination, the cuticle may show quite dramatically the epidermal features of the fossilized plant part.

At times, plant parts that were compressed and preserved as fossils undergo further modification in that the organic material left behind does not hold together and is lost. There is left, then, a negative imprint on the surface of the rock matrix next to where the plant part was.

Even when organic material is present, splitting open the rock often leaves one surface devoid of organic remains with an imprint of the flattened plant part. Such a fossil is called an *impression*. Like a compression, an impression shows only surface features.

In some instances, the rock matrix is composed of such fine grains (clay, for example) that epidermal features are preserved faithfully as imprints in the rock, and these features may be transferred to a sheet of latex or similar material and then examined with a scanning electron microscope. Even though there is nothing left of the actual plant part, many details of the epidermis may be observed.

When the plant part carried into the basin of accumulating sediment happens to be relatively three-dimensional, in many instances the surrounding sediment is compressed and hardened before the plant fragment was compressed.

Subsequently there may have been a decay of the plant part, with a hollow negative resulting. This negative three-dimensional structure in the rock is called a *mold*. Subsequently the mold may have been filled with other sediment that conformed to the contours of the mold and produced a three-dimensional, positive replica of the original plant part.

This kind of fossil is referred to as a *cast*. Again, only surface details are evident, and there generally is nothing of the original plant part preserved. (Occasionally a thin film of carbon may surround the cast.) A very interesting type of process of fossilization permits the observation of internal structure in plant parts.

Such a fossil is formed when a plant part settles in a basin of water with a high concentration of dissolved mineral material or, when covered with sediment, is still surrounded by dissolved minerals. After a certain period of exposure to these conditions, the plant part became infiltrated with the liquid with the high charge of mineral material.

Subsequently the mineral salts precipitated (no one yet fully understands why) and the plant part became entombed in a solid mass of solidified mineral matter. Most often cellular contents are not preserved, with the mineral having infiltrated into cell lumens and intercellular spaces, leaving the cell wall structure more or less intact.

In a few instances, however, nuclei and cytoplasm survive the preservational process. This permineralized fossil is called a *petrifaction*. Minerals involved in petrifaction include silicon dioxide, calcium, magnesium, or iron carbonate, ferric sulfide, and occasionally others. The most common method of investigation of plant fragments preserved in this manner involves making a thin section of the rock matrix and its contained plant material.

This involves cutting a piece of the petrified material with a special saw that incorporates diamond particles in the blade. The piece is then polished on one surface, which is then cemented to a glass slide with a transparent adhesive.

With the slide then firmly clamped in the saw, the specimen is cut once again as thin as is reasonably possible. Then while the petrified material is still cemented to the slide, it is ground thinner and thinner with appropriate abrasives until it eventually becomes transparent enough to permit transmission of light. Addition of mounting medium and a cover glass then makes it possible to examine the thin section with a light microscope. This technique is essentially that of geologists who study thin sections of various kinds of rock.

When the embedding matrix is a carbonate (usually calcium carbonate), a simple but ingenious technique may be employed to prepare sections. The cut surface of the petrified material is polished and then etched in dilute hydrochloric acid.

This process removes some of the surface carbonate but leaves the cell wall material unaffected. After a short period of etching, the cell walls project above the surface of the rock. The acid is then washed off with water and the surface allowed to dry.

The surface is then flooded with acetone and a thin sheet of clear cellulose acetate is laid on the surface, with care taken to avoid air bubbles. Acetone partially dissolves the lower surface of the acetate sheet, and it now envelops the cell walls projecting from the surface.

Because acetone is quite volatile, it evaporates in a short time, once again rendering the lower surface of the cellulose acetate into solid form. The cell walls now are partially embedded in the sheet of cellulose acetate. After it is completely dry, the sheet may be pulled away gently, and it then carries with it a very thin section of the petrified material embedded in it.

This type of preparation is called a *"peel,"* and it permits examination of the sectioned plant material with a microscope. If the petrifying mineral is something other than calcium carbonate, other kinds of acids may be employed for the etching process.

Occasionally, in the past, plant parts may have been carried into basins of accumulating sediment and buried with extremely finegrained material. Air was excluded and conditions were unsatisfactory for growth of decaying organisms.

As a result, plant parts may have survived for millions of years in a relatively unaltered state. It is possible to section wood or other plant fragments preserved in such a manner with equipment used for sectioning tissues of present-day plants.

Plant parts preserved in peat bogs are also relatively unaltered. Pieces may be fragmentary or slightly compressed, but internal tissues are intact and may be sectioned for microscopic examination. The above are simply the most frequent types of preservation of fossil plants.

Less common kinds are sometimes encountered, as well as

combinations of the types cited above. Despite the vagaries of preservation of plants in the past and the incompleteness of the fossil record, a considerable body of knowledge concerning the earliest vascular plants and their subsequent evolution has been gathered by paleobotanists.

The first indisputable vascular plants were on land at the end of the Silurian period (some 405-410 million years ago; see inside front cover). There are some reports (e.g., Gray and Boucot, 1971; Mortimer and Chaloner, 1972; Gray, Laufeld, and Boucot, 1974) of the possible earlier existence of vascular plants in the form of resistant spores or peculiar tubelike structures that resemble xylem cells.

However, it is necessary to demonstrate more than cutinized spores to prove that they belonged to a vascular plant. Such a resistant spore simply signifies that it was probably exposed to the air during some time in the life cycle of the plant. Furthermore, the tubelike structures that have been compared to tracheids are quite different and are not unquestionably tissues of vascular plants.

Admittedly, the first vascular plants may have settled on land before the end of the Silurian, but convincing evidence for that occurrence is still absent. After the first appearance of vascular plants, there was a rapid diversification, and during the following period, the Devonian (about 345-405 million years ago; see inside front cover), all the major groups of vascular cryptogams were present in the earth's flora.

This section will present a brief summary' of representative vascular cryptogams. Our knowledge of these ancient plants has been greatly augmented during the last three decades. Many of the early vascular cryptogams belonged to divisions of the plant kingdom that are now extinct.

Members of the divisions Rhyniophyta, Zosterophyllophyta, Trimerophytophyta, Microphyllophyta, Arthrophyta, Pteridophyta, and Progymnospermophyta will be discussed in the following presentation. Members of all these divisions were present during the Devonian period, while one genus (*Cooks onia*) of the Rhyniophyta, discussed below, occurred in the Silurian.

DIVISION RHYNIOPHYTA

Members of the Rhyniophyta are among the simplest known vascular plants. Their plant bodies consisted of simple, slender, leafless, dichotomizing, photosynthetic axes.

Roots were absent, with the anchoring and absorbing functions assumed by the basal portion of the stem system. Sporangia were borne at the tips of some of the ultimate branches. All known members of the

Rhyniophyta were homosporous. Rhyniophytes were typically protostelic, with the smallest xylem elements in the center of the stele (centrarch); secondary vascular tissue was absent.

The best preserved members of the Rhyniophyta originate from a chert deposit near the town of Rhynie, in Aberdeenshire, Scotland. This chert, considered to be Lower Devonian in age, represents fossilized remains of a bog ' that seems to have been preserved with the plants in their growing positions.

One genus, *Rhynia* (named for the town of Rhynie), is extremely well known and serves as a typical example of the general habit of plants of the division Rhyniophyta. Two species of *Rhynia* are known from the Rhynie chert beds: *R. gwynne-vaughanii* and *R. major. Rhynia gwynne-vaughanii is* smaller and more slender, reaching a height of 17 cm, while the larger, more robust *R. major* was about three times as tall. Each plant had a horizontal branching stem from which originated erect, leafless, dichotomously branched aerial axes.

These rootless plants had tufts of slender, unicellular rhizoids, each of which was actually an extension of a single epidermal cell. It is assumed that the photosynthetic process took place in the aerial stem system and that these stems were green.

There is no evidence of this from the fossil, of course, but the fact that wellpreserved stomata occurred in the epidermis provides evidence along those lines. Internal structure is preserved with amazing fidelity. The vascular system of a *Rhynia* axis is exceedingly simple, consisting principally, in *R. gwynne-vaughanii*, of a slender central strand of just a few tracheids in thickness.

These tracheids are characterized by annular secondary thickenings. In the larger *R. major*, the centrarch central strand of the xylem is evident. Satterthwait and Schopf (1972) described what they considered to be a phloem zone surrounding the xylem core, but their conclusions have not found acceptance among all paleobotanists.

At the ends of some of the axes were borne sporangia that were actually swollen tips of the stem system. The cortex of the vegetative axis continued into the thick wall of the sporangium. That these plants were sporophytes is attested to by the occurrence of spores within the sporangia that, in some instances, were fossilized in the tetrad stage.

Hence they were obviously products of meiosis. Spores were produced in tetrahedral tetrads, and each shows a prominent trilete mark on the proximal face, with the flat faces in the angles of the trilete structure representing planes of contact with adjacent spores in

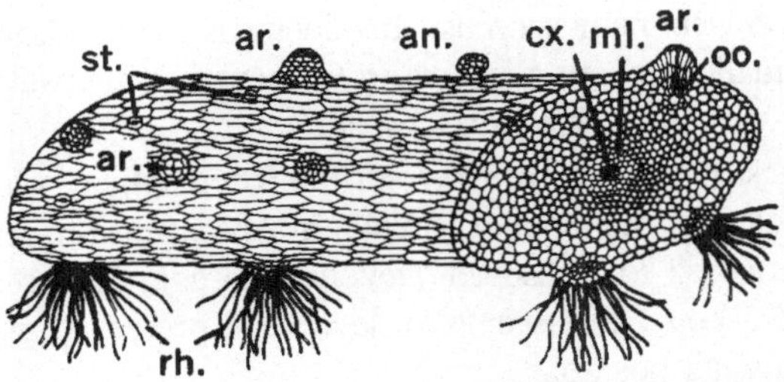

Figure 8.10: Rhynia gwynne-vaughanii. Schematic representation of the "gametophyte." an., antheridium; ar., archegonium; ex., stele; me., endodermis; rh., rhizoids; st., stomata.

the tetrad. While sporangium-bearing axes of *Rhynia* are undoubtedly sporophytes, there is no general agreement about the nature of the gametophyte phase.

It would be of considerable interest to know the structure of the gametophyte of these early vascular plants in order to understand the nature of the plants that were ancestral to the first land plants. Pant (1962) and Lemoigne (1970) feel that certain of the vascularized axes of *Rhynia* that had been interpreted to be rhizomes of the sporophyte may actually be vascularized gametophytes.

Swellings on the surface of the axes with what appears to be a canal leading to the interior of the axis have been called archegonia. If they were, indeed, archegonia, the necks would have been much more massive than any others known among vascular plants.

There is not universal agreement that these structures were archegonia, and Bierhorst *sug*gests that these "archegonia" may have been hydathodes or some other kind of secretory structures.

Similarly, spherical bumps on the surface of certain axes were described as antheridia by Lemoigne, but not all paleobotanists are prepared to accept that interpretation. If these axes are actually gametophytes, they would have much in common with those of *Psilotum* and *Tmesipteris as* well as those of *Actinostachys*.

A second genus, *Horneophyton* (named for *a* Dr. Horne), resembles *Rhynia* to some extent, but there are some signficant differences. In *Horneophyton*, the basal part of the plant consisted of a number of swollen, bulblike structures from which the upright, dichotomizing, aerial shoots arose.

Hairlike rhizoids attached to the bottoms of the swollen portions served as absorbing structures. Terminating some of the aerial shoots were elongated, sometimes branched sporangia that were truncated at the tips. A slender columella extended through the middle of each

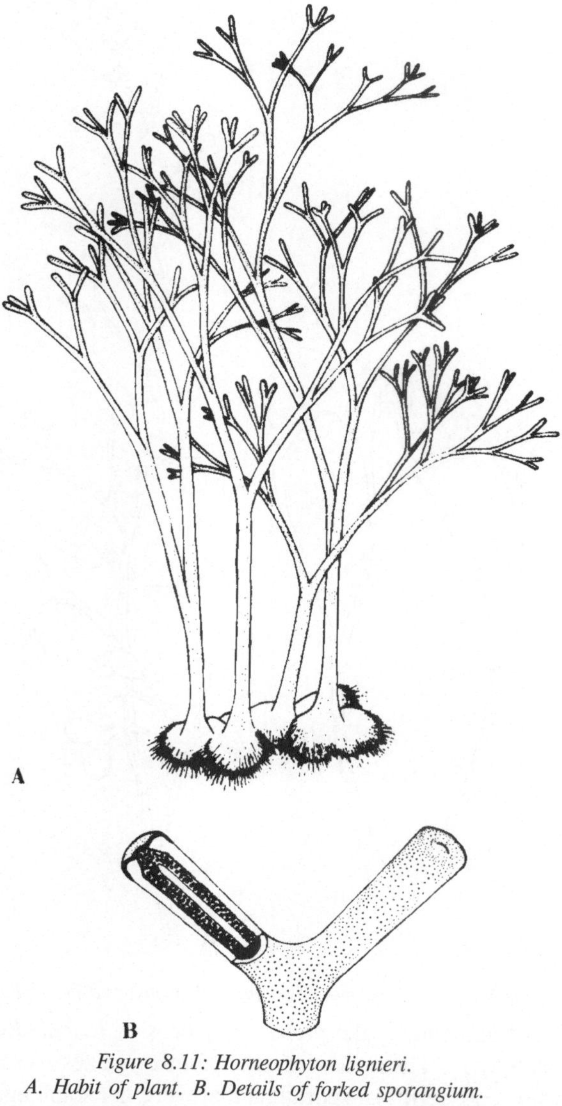

A

B

Figure 8.11: Horneophyton lignieri.
A. Habit of plant. B. Details of forked sporangium.

sporangium. The trilete spores were of one type. *Cooksonia* (named for Isabel C. Cookson, an Australian paleobotanist) is known from less well-preserved material than that in which the Rhynie chert plants occur, but enough is known to place it in the Rhyniophyta.

It is the oldest genus of *bona fide* vascular plants, with two known species from Upper Silurian and Lower Devonian strata. Although the

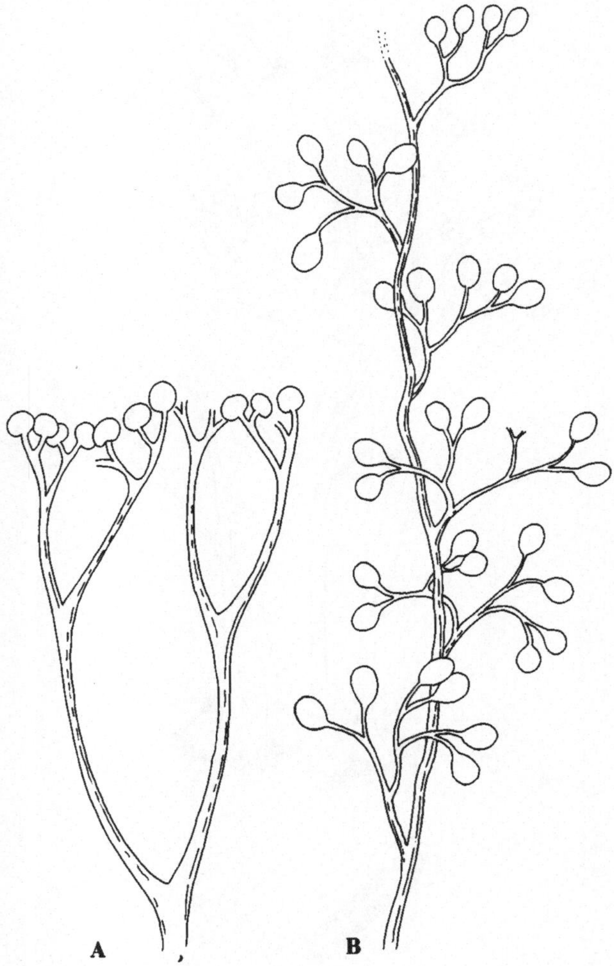

Figure 8.12: A. Cooksonia caledonica. B. Cooksonia hemisphaerica.

material is fragmentary, the preserved pieces of *C. caledonica* may be as long as 6.5 cm. These slender, dichotomizing axes were naked, and, like *Rhynia*, bore terminal sporangia that were not so elongated as those in the latter genus. *Cooksonia hemisphaerica* is illustrated by Ananiev and Stepanov (1969) as having a principal axis with lesser lateral, dichotomously branched fertile branches.

An example that plants do not always "fit" into categories erected by human beings is the Lower Devonian *Renalia*. It resembles *Cooksonia* in having a dichotomously branched plant body and swollen terminal

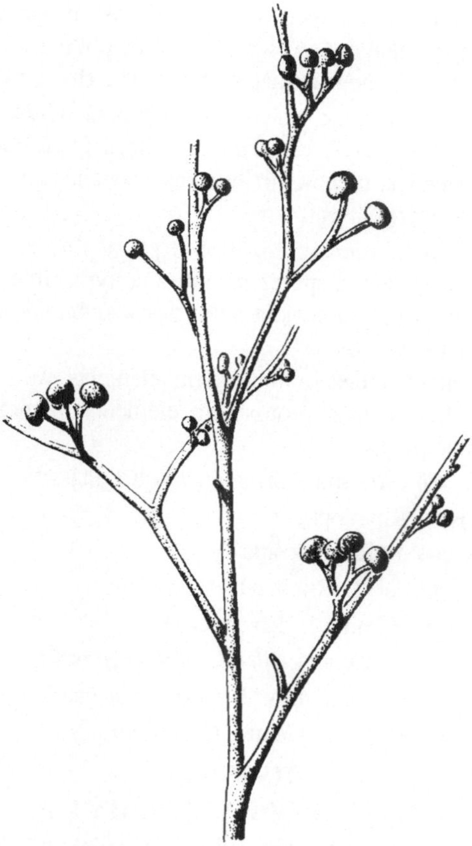

Figure 8.13: Renalia hueberi.
Habit of portion of plant.

sporangia. The mode of dehiscence of the sporangium, however, more closely resembles that in the division Zosterophyllophyta (see below) in that splitting occurs along the distal margin, with the line of dehiscence bordered by a row of thickwalled cells. *Renalia* was homosporous.

For more than half a century such genera as *Cooksonia*, *Rhynia*, and *Horneophyton* were considered to be similar, morphologically, to the living genus *Psilotum.* All these genera appear to have axes without vascularized leaves and roots, have rhizoid-bearing rhizomes (actually not demonstrated in *Cooksonia*), and have sporangia terminating branches.

These similarities have caused many botanists to consider *Psilotum* as a persistently primitive type of plant that is, in essence, a living rhyniophyte. More likely, however, is the adoption by *Psilotum* of a habit that superficially approximates that of the rhyniophytes.

In summary, it may be stated that members of the Rhyniophyta exhibit an extremely simple construction with a plant body consisting only of naked, slender, dichotomizing axes. Appendages in the form of leaves and roots were absent.

Sporangia were merely swollen tips of branch axes, were thickwalled, and contained spores *of* only one type. Internal structure, too, is simple, with only a slender solid vascular bundle traversing the axis throughout its length.

Secondary thickenings of the xylem elements were annular, the type found on first-formed protoxylem elements in more specialized kinds of vascular plants.

Cooksonia, *Rhynia*, and *Horneophyton* are classified as follows:

Division Rhyniophyta
Class 1. Rhyniopsida
Order 1. Rhyniales
Family 1. Rhyniaceae
Genera: *Rhynia*, *Horneophyton*
Family 2. Cooksoniaceae
Genus: *Cooksonia*

DIVISION ZOSTEROPHYLLOPHYTA

Before the work of Banks (1968), in which he reclassified the earliest vascular plants, members of the Zosterophyllophyta were included in the same group of plants as that containing the Rhyniophyta. Contemporaneous in the Lower and Middle Devonian with the Rhyniophyta, the Zosterophyllophyta differed from the former in that their sporangia were borne along the sides of the dichotomously branching stem system rather than terminally.

These sporangia, often reniform, opened transversely. Another difference between the two divisions is that in the zosterophyllophytes the xylem of the protostele is exarch. Otherwise there is much similarity, with the body habit of both divisions involving a leafless and rootless stem system that was photosynthetic and had dichotomous or near-dichotomous branching.

Some of the members had spinelike projections on the surface of the aerial stem systems, but they were not vascularized, nor were

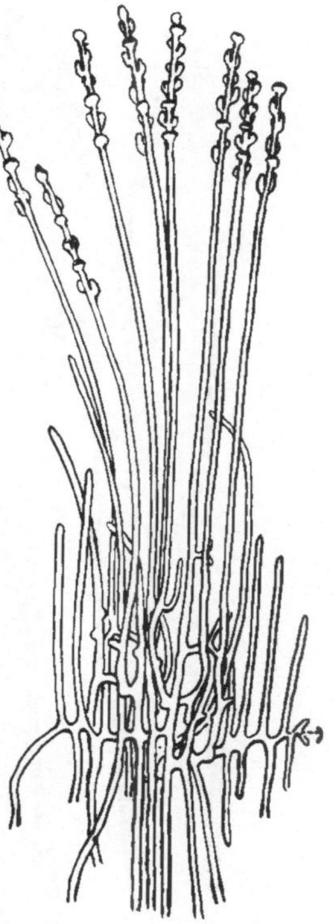

Figure 8.14: Zosterophyllum myretonianum.

sporangia associated with them in any consistent pattern. *Zosterophyllum* (from *Zostera*, eelgrass, a marine angiosperm, + Gr. *phyllon*, leaf) from which the name of the division is derived, was a Lower Devonian genus that had what appeared to have been a prostrate stem system from which arose aerial axes.

The basal part demonstrates an unusual kind of branching pattern in that from one axis a lateral branches off and from that lateral there are frequently two branch axes, one growing upward and one downward so that there is the appearance of "H-branches".

It is conceivable that this so-called "H branching" may be a preservational phenomenon, however. Reniform sporangia were aggregated at the tips of some of the aerial shoots and were borne along the surfaces of these.axes. These plants were homosporous, and one species is known to have had a cuticle and stomata, thus indicating a terrestrial habit.

Sawdonia ornata is an example of a Devonian zosterophyllophyte that had spiny projections on the stem surface. The dichotomously

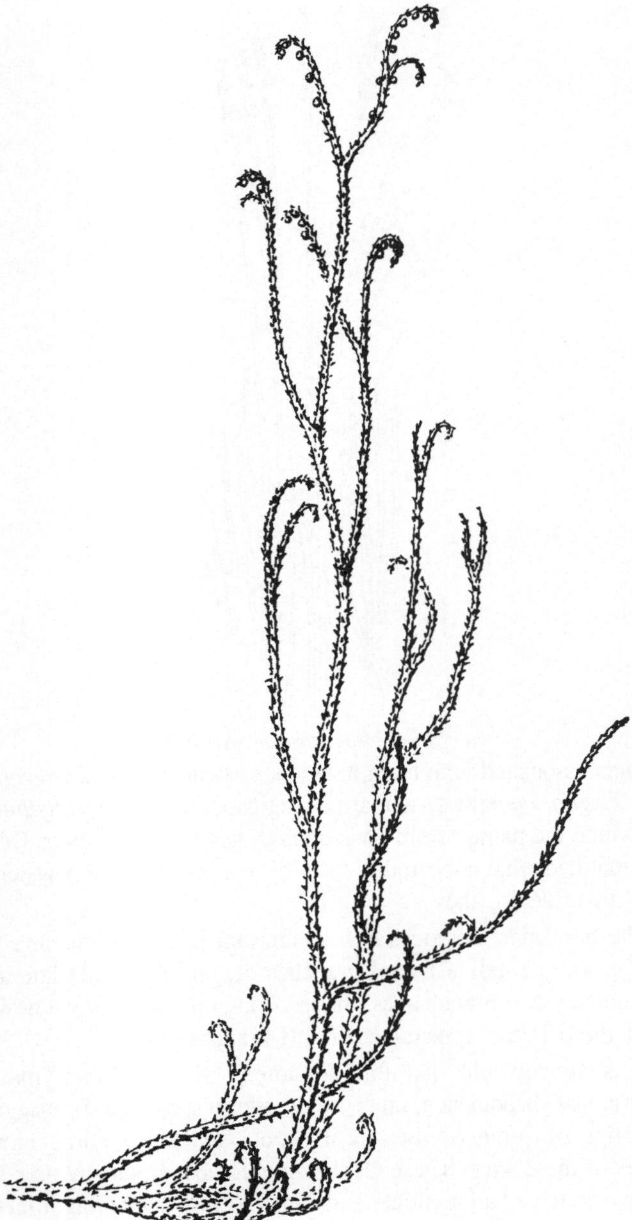

Figure 8.15: Sawdonia ornata.

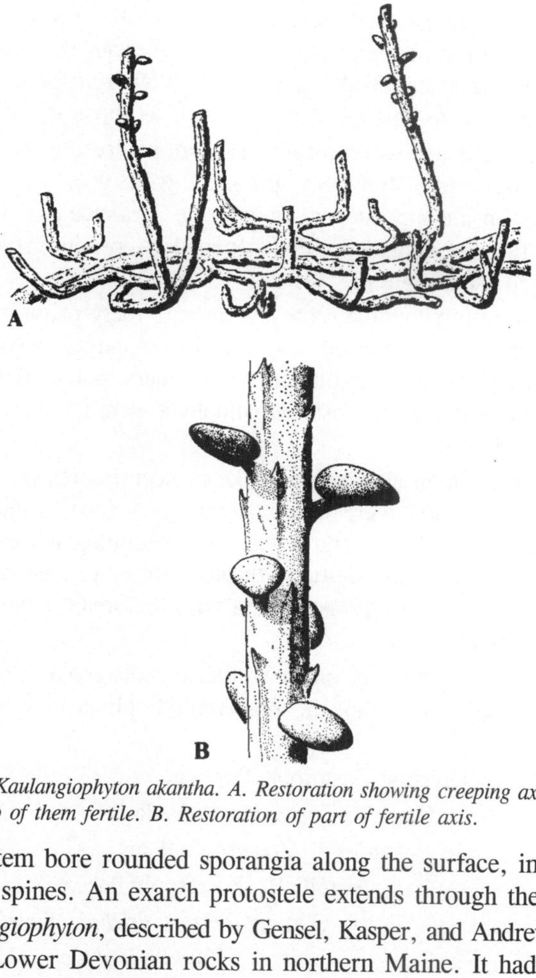

A

B

Figure 8.16: Kaulangiophyton akantha. A. Restoration showing creeping axes with erect branches, two of them fertile. B. Restoration of part of fertile axis.

branched stem bore rounded sporangia along the surface, interspersed among the spines. An exarch protostele extends through the stem.

Kaulangiophyton, described by Gensel, Kasper, and Andrews (1969), occurs in Lower Devonian rocks in northern Maine. It had a robust, prostrate stem system that was supposed to have exhibited "H-branching," from which originated erect axes, 5-9 mm wide.

These erect branches bore stout spines with no discernible phyllotaxy and large, ovoid sporangia that seem to have been concentrated in fertile zones. Except for the fact that sporangia had no relationship to leaves, the plant must have resembled quite closely certain creeping species of *Lycopodium*.

One more zosterophyllophyte genus, *Crenaticaulis*, may be mentioned here because of certain peculiarities in its structure. These pseudomonopodially and dichotomously branching plants bore toothlike projections, but only on opposite sides of the axes. Swollen tubercles occurred at the region of branching of the axes, and these tubercles show evidence of having borne branches. Banks and Davis (1969) remarked about their close resemblance to rhizophore bases such as those in *Selaginella.*

Within the axes were terete, exarch protosteles with chiefly scalariform tracheids. Reniform sporangia were grouped on some of the branches in an opposite or subopposite arrangement. Each had a transverse line of dehiscence that opened to produce two unequal portions of the sporangium.

The Zosterophyllophyta represent an extremely primitive group of vascular plants that coexisted with the Rhyniophyta, also primitive, but each group probably exhibited evolutionary potential in different directions. Most likely the Zosterophyllophyta were the ancestral source of the Microphyllophyta.

The former often showed spinelike projections resembling minute leaves, and sporangia were borne laterally. A modification of these spines would result in structures closely resembling leaves of certain *Lycopodium* species. In addition, through time, the sporangia could have come to be intimately associated with the small leaves, as in the microphyllophytes.

Anatomically, there is much similarity between the two groups. The genera discussed within the Zosterophyllophyta may be classified as follows:

Division Zosterophyllophyta
Class 1. Zosterophyllopsida
Order 1. Zosterophyllales
Family 1. Zosterophyllaceae
Genera: *Zosterophyllum*, *Sawdonia*, *Kaulangiophyton*, *Crenaticaulis*

DIVISION TRIMEROPHYTOPHYTA

While in many aspects the Trimerophytophyta have much in common with the Rhyniophyta, there seems to be good reason for separating them. As in the Rhyniophyta, members of the trimerophytophytes are typically leafless and rootless, bear terminal sporangia, and have centrarch protosteles.

The distinction, however, lies in the branching pattern. Trimerophytophytes tend to show a principal axis from which laterals arose. These laterals may have retained the dichotomous pattern of branching, however.

A

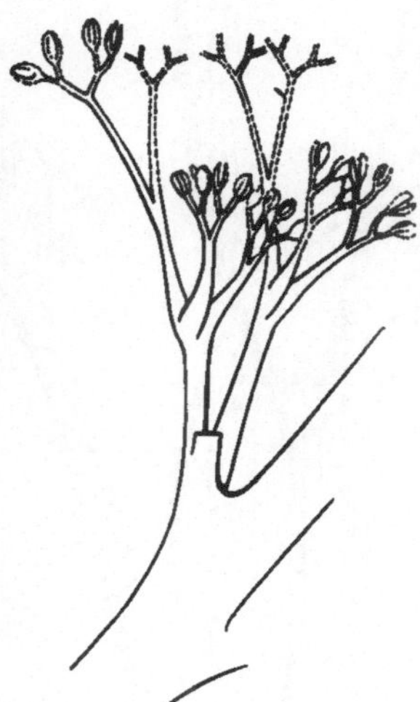

B

Figure 8.17: Trimerophyton robustius.
A. Branching axes. B. Lateral branch with sporangia.

The origin of the Trimerophytophyta is most likely from forms such as those in the Rhyniophyta; indeed, some members of the latter tend to show a departure from a strict dichotomous pattern of branching (e.g., *Cooksonia hemisphaerica*).

Trimerophyton (Gr. *treis*, three, + *meros*, part, + *phyton*) is the genus on which the circumscription of the division is based. Although it is still imperfectly known, *Trimerophyton* had a fairly robust principal

Figure 8.18: Psilophyton princeps. Restoration by Hueber.

axis with laterals that tended to trichotomize. The tips of the branches terminated in a cluster of sporangia that dehisced longitudinally.

The best-known genus of the Trimerophytophyta, and the first well-known vascular plant, is *Psilophyton* (Gr. *psilos*, naked, + Gr. *phyton*, plant). *Psilophyton princeps* was first described by Sir J. W. Dawson, a Canadian geologist and university administrator, in 1859 from Lower Devonian rocks of the Gaspe peninsula in Quebec, Canada.

That first description depicted a slender, naked, dichotomously branched plant lacking leaves and roots and bearing terminal sporangia. He later modified his original diagnosis and described a new variety, *P. princeps* var. *ornatum*, that was said to have borne spines near the basal portions of the plant.

Painstaking and critical re-examination of Dawson's specimens and recent new collections of fossil plants from the area have resulted in the recognition of a number of changes in Dawson's original descriptions. For example, *P. princeps* var. *ornatum* has been transferred by Hueber to the genus *Sawdonia* in the Zosterophyllophyta, with *S. ornata* as the type species.

In addition, Hueber and Banks emended the description of *P. princeps* Dawson, and Hueber prepared the reconstruction reproduced herein as Figure elsewhere in this chapter. The new interpretation of *P. princeps* indicates that branching was not strictly dichotomous, but unequal branching resulted in a kind of pseudomonopodial pattern, with laterals less extensively developed than the principal axis.

Covering the leafless axes were robust, truncated, spinelike projections. The dichotomizing lateral appendages had pendulous, paired, terminal sporangia. Dehiscence of sporangia was longitudinal. The protostele was centrarch or mesarch.

Trimerophyton and *Psilophyton* are classified as follows:

Division Trimerophytophyta
- Class 1. Trimerophytopsida
  - Order 1. Trimerophytales
    - Family 1. Trimerophytaceae
      - Genera: *Trimerophyton*, *Psilophyton*

DIVISION MICROPHYLLOPHYTA

Although the *Rhyniophyta*, *Zosterophyllophyta*, and *Trimerophytophyta* represent the earliest and most primitive vascular plants, they apparently have no representatives in present-day vegetation.

The Microphyllophyta, which also originated in the Devonian period, include forms with features that link them to extant genera such as *Lycopodium* and *Selaginella*. The microphyllophytes, then, represent the oldest of the currently living divisions of vascular plants.

Members of the Microphyllophyta have certain characters reminiscent of those of the Zosterophyllophyta and most likely were derived from that group. Their closely spaced, generally simple leaves were probably derived from the spiny projections of the zosterophyllophytes. Sporangia are lateral along the axes, and in many they are localized in terminal zones to form strobili.

While in the Zosterophyllophyta the sporangia had no special association with the spines, in the Microphyllophyta, both fossil and extant, sporangia are intimately associated with leaves, either attached directly on the adaxial surface or situated in the axil.

Members of the Microphyllophyta most frequently have exarch protosteles. A relationship between Zosterophyllophyta and Microphyllophyta was suggested by Banks (1968) and Bierhorst (1971a).

Both herbaceous and arborescent fossil Microphyllophyta are known. In the following account, *Asteroxylon*, *Protolepidodendron*, *Baragwanathia*, *Leclercqia*, *Lepidodendron* (and other related genera in the Lepidodendrales), *Lycopodites*, *Selaginella*, *Pleuromeia*, and *Nathorstiana* are among the genera discussed briefly as examples of fossil Microphyllophyta.

Order 1. Asteroxylales

Asteroxylon

Asteroxylon is among the genera found in the famous Rhynie chert beds in Scotland. It was contemporaneous with *Rhynia* and *Horneophyton* and was originally included in one order with those two genera.

It is distinct enough, however, to warrant considering it among the Zosterophyllophyta or the Microphyllophyta. Its inclusion here within the latter is somewhat arbitrary because it has certain features more typical of those in the former.

From smooth, horizontal rhizomes arose erect branches. These upright stems were monopodial, although the laterals tended to dichotomize. Covering the aerial axes were closely spaced, small, *Lycopodium*-like, leaflike structures about 5 mm long.

Many botanists hesitate to call them leaves because they lacked vascular tissue. From the stele, traces extended upward and outward toward the leafy structures but stopped near the bases. This situation may be interpreted as one that shows the possible origin of microphylls from enations or spines.

Zosterophyllophyte spines, of course, were not vascularized. *Asteroxylon's* leaflike appendages lacked traces, but there were traces in the stem that were associated with them, and the usual situation in the Microphyllophyta is one in which the trace extends into the leaf.

The stele of *Asteroxylon* is more like that of herbaceous Microphyllophyta than it is like that in the Zosterophyllophyta. In cross section the xylem of the stele appears to be deeply lobed (more or less star-shapedhence the generic name), with protoxylem near the tips of the ridges.

Stalked sporangia were borne laterally along the aerial shoot, and there seems to be increasing evidence that there is some relationship between a sporangium and a leaflike scale.

The best known species of *Asteroxylon*, *A. mackiei*, probably reached a half meter in height. The organization is somewhat suggestive of the extant *Lycopodium lucidulum* and *L. selago*.

Order 2. Protolepidodendrales

The Protolepidodendrales include a single family, Protolepidodendraceae. Principally Devonian in age, members of the Protolepidodendrales were reminiscent of robust *Lycopodium* plants.

Once believed to be the oldest known vascular plant, *Baragwanathia* (named for the paleobotanist, W. Baragwanath) is now regarded to be Lower Devonian in age, and while still extremely old, it does not antidate the earliest rhyniophytes.

It was a robust plant, with stems 1-6.5 cm in diameter and with crowded, linear leaves up to 4 cm long and 1 mm wide. Reniform sporangia were borne in the axils of some of the leaves in zones.

The plant was probably homosporous. *Baragwanathia* was protostelic, with a xylem strand characterized by ridges and furrows and tracheids with annular thickenings. *Protolepidodendron* (Gr. *protos*, first, + *lepidos*, scale, + *dendron*, tree) specimens have been recovered from both Lower and Middle Devonian strata.

Plants were herbaceous, 20-30 cm tall, with a horizontal, creeping stem covered with closely spaced, helically arranged leaves, forked at the tips. Erect stems, dichotomously branched, were borne on the prostrate part of the plant and they, too, bore small, forked leaves, many of which bore ovoid sporangia on the median adaxial surface.

Stems had protosteles that were somewhat crenate in section, with protoxylem produced at the outer surfaces of the ridges. One interesting feature of *Protolepidodendron* is the manner in which leaves were attached to the stems. The leaf flared at the base, forming an axially elongated swollen portion.

At the time of abscission, the entire leaf did not fall off. Rather, the slender portion at the apex of the swollen base became detached, leaving the leaf base behind. Thus, on a twig from which leaves had

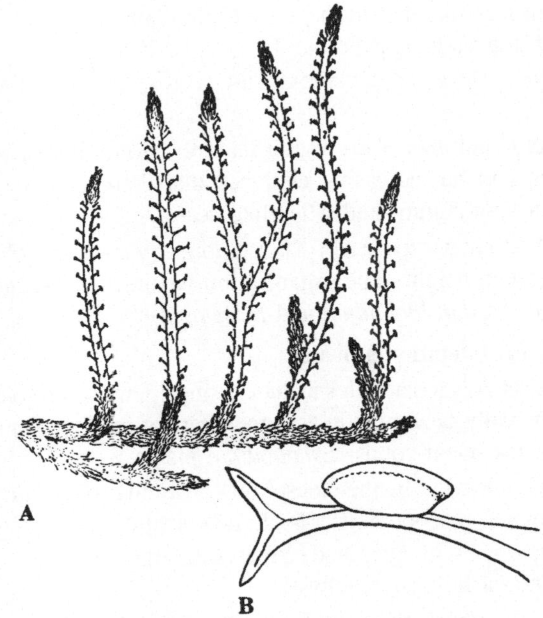

Figure 8.19: Protolepidodendron scharyanum.
A. Reconstruction of rhizome and aerial branches. B. Sporophyll.

fallen, the stem was covered with the raised, persistent bases. This feature is even more pronounced in another group of *Microphyllophyta* discussed below.

Another well-known member of the Protolepidodendrales is *Leclercqia*, described by Banks, Bonamo, and Grierson (1972). This herbaceous plant from the Upper Middle Devonian had dichotomously branched axes 3.5-7.0 mm in diameter, with some pieces reaching 46 cm in length.

Leaves were borne in great abundance in a tight helix, each divided near the middle into one elongate, recurved, median portion and two divided lateral segments. A ligule was borne on the upper side of the leaf, making *Leclercqia* the oldest ligulate microphyllophyte.

Globose-to-ellipsoidal sporangia were attached to the adaxial surfaces of leaves just proximal to the point of division of the leaf. The stele is very similar to that of *Protolepidodendron*, with a solid core of primary xylem with 14-18 protoxylem ridges. Tracheids have elongated bordered pits.

Order 3. Lycopodiales

Herbaceous, dichotomously branched plants with closely spaced leaves corresponding closely to the extant genus *Lycopodium* are known from rocks as far back as the Upper Devonian.

These fossils, which extend through the Cretaceous, are grouped under the name *Lycopodites*. Some specimens are fertile and indicate that the plants were homosporous.

Order 4. Lepidodendrales

The order Lepidodendrales includes giant, treelike members of the Microphyllophyta that were dominant components of late Paleozoic floras. The order is extinct, with repre sentatives ranging from the Upper Devonian to the Permian. *Lepidodendron* is the bestknown genus, with members Carboniferous and Permian in age.

Plants exceeded 50 m in height, with a tall trunk, unbranched for some distance and bearing a crown of branches at the top. Some of the more massive plants may have had trunks 2 m thick at the base. Leaves were linear and expanded into a swollen base at their points of attachment.

After abscission, an elevated leaf cushion was left on the stem surface, and impressions of *Lepidodendron* stems show these closely spaced, persistent leaf bases. Leaf size varied from species to species, and even on the same plant, with larger leaves borne in more proximal regions and smaller ones distally.

Some arborescent lepidodendralean leaves may have reached a meter in length. Strictly speaking, these are not "microphylls" so far as size is concerned, but traces to leaves do not produce leaf gaps in the stele of the stem, and most paleobotanists consider these long leaves as having originated phylogenetically from enations.

From the base toward the top of the unbranched trunk, the stele changed from an exarch protostele to an ectophloic siphonostele, with progressively larger pith. Steles in branches, however, were smaller than those in regions of the stem below the level of branching, and with each order of branching, the stele diminished in size so that ultimately, in the very tips, only tiny protosteles were present.

Secondary xylem is progressively less well developed in more distal regions, with none present at the stem tips. The massive trunk rested on dichotomously branching bases that are called *Stigmaria* (Gr. *stigma*, mark) (paleobotanical nomenclature involves assigning names to different parts of what might be the same kind of plant; these are called *organ genera*).

On these branching, underground axes are closely spaced, helically arranged, rootlike appendages. The internal organization of these appendages is quite similar to that of the roots of *Isoetes*. Terminating

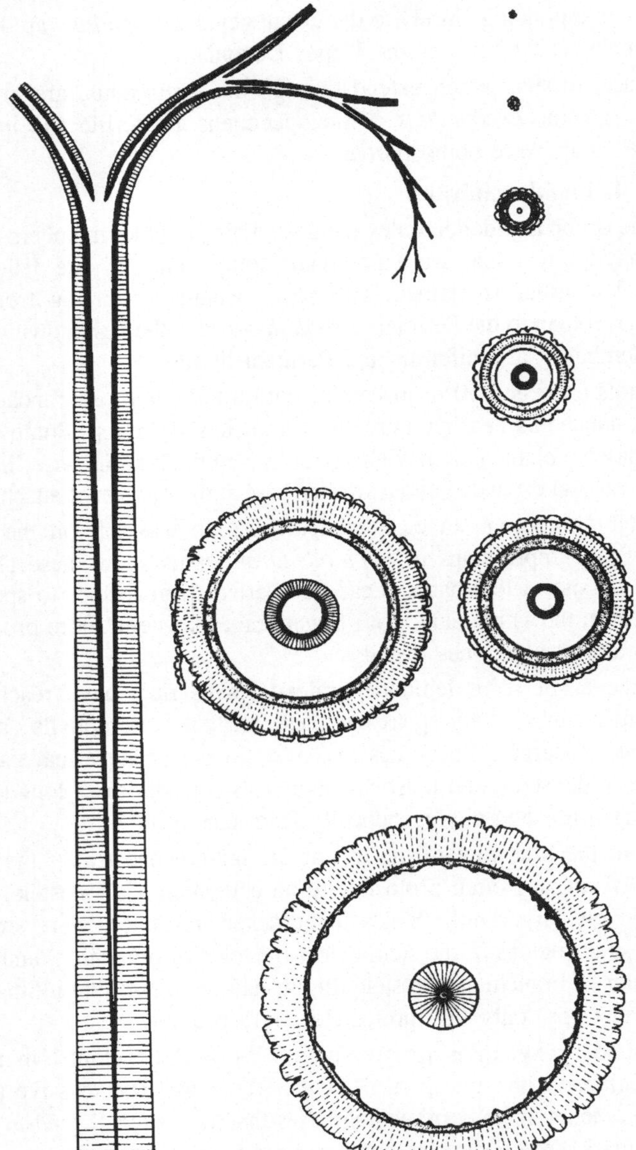

Figure 8.20: Diagram showing changes in structure of a Lepidodendron *stem at different levels. Diagram at left indicates pith (unshaded central region), primary xylem (shaded black), and secondary xylem (striped). Largest transverse section represents a level of the stem near the base; next larger section is near the top of the main trunk; and progressively smaller ones represent sections closer to the tips of the branches.*

some of the branches were elongated strobili, each consisting of an axis with closely spaced, helically arranged sporophylls. The proximal part of each sporophyll bore an elongated sporangium on the adaxial surface, and the distal part was bent abruptly toward the strobilar apex.

A ligule often occurred on the sporophyll just distal to the sporangium. Most strobili of *Lepidodendron* (placed in the organ genus *Lepidostrobus*) were heterosporous. In some instances, the number of functional megaspores per sporangium was reduced to one, the spore was not shed, the female gametophyte developed within the spore wall, and lateral margins of the sporophyll enveloped the sporangium, thus forming a seedlike body.

Sigillaria (*L. sigillum*, seal) is a genus closely related to *Lepidodendron*, but it differed in being unbranched or branched only once or twice. Its heterosporous strobili were borne along the stem surface interspersed among leaf bases.

Leaf bases, although arranged in a close helix, had the appearance of being aligned in vertical rows. *Lepidophloios* resembled *Lepidodendron* even more closely, but leaf bases were tangentially expanded. It bore strobili on short lateral branches.

Phytokneme (Gr. *phyton*, plant, + *kneme*, spoke of a wheel) *rhodona is* one of the earliest members of the Lepidodendrales, originating from the Upper Devonian of Kentucky. A sector of the transverse section of an exceedingly well-preserved specimen is illustrated in Figure elsewhere in this chapter and shows a central mass of primary xylem surrounded by a narrow zone of secondary xylem, probably a phloem, a broad "*middle cortex*," and an "*outer cortex*."

Order 5. Selaginellales

Selaginella-like plants are known as far back as the Carboniferous. Some of them exhibited anisophylly, a feature in many (but not all) extant species of *Selaginella. Selaginellites* is the generic name assigned to most of the fossil forms, but one fossil is so like the extant *Selaginella* it has been included within that genus.

Schlanker and Leisman (1969) reported on this Pennsylvanian plant and indicated that it bore a swollen basal root-bearing axis with a microphyll-bearing stem.

This stem had an exarch protostele, with the protoxylem borne along the ridges. Strobili were terminal, with microsporophylls and megasporophylls typical of those in *Selaginella.* Megaspores were borne near the base of the strobilus and microspores above.

Four megaspores were present in each megasporangium and were

800 μm in diameter. Each of the microspores that were abundant in microsporangia measured 80 μm.

Order 6. Pleuromeiales

Pleuromeia (Gr. *pleuron*, rib, + Gr. *meion*, fewer), the only genus in the order, was a Triassic plant about 2 m tall. The erect, stout stem was unbranched and had a crown of elongated linear leaves. The lower part of the stem was marked by scars left by fallen leaves.

The trunk rested on a swollen, stunted base with four upturned lobes, each bearing numerous, helically arranged roots. This basal structure has been considered to represent a very much reduced *Stigmaria* system.

A large, club-shaped strobilus terminated the stem. It bore rounded sporophylls, which had deeply embedded adaxial sporangia. *Pleuromeia* is regarded by many to be a derivative of the late Paleozoic arborescent Microphyllophyta.

Order 7. Isoetales

Nathorstiana (named for A. G. Nathorst, a Swedish paleobotanist), a Cretaceous member of the order Isoetales, was a small plant, about 20 cm tall, with a squat stem and quill-like terminal leaves.

The basal portion was ribbed, with closely spaced, helically arranged, rootlike appendages borne on it. This plant is thought to represent a further reduction in a line of plants that extends back to massive trees in the Paleozoic.

In fact, this reduction from arborescent microphyllophytes may have terminated in the extant *Isoetes*, which is also represented in the fossil record of the Cretaceous period. Some of these are included in the fossil genus *Isoetites*.

The history of Microphyllophytan plants extends from the Lower Devonian to the present, although many genera have become extinct, with only *Lycopodium*, *Selaginella*, *Isoetes*, and *Stylites* (if the last is to be regarded as distinct from *Isoetes*) having survived.

The first two probably represent persistently primitive types, having survived, with little modification, from the Carboniferous. The Isoetales, on the other hand, very possibly represent the end of a reduction series from arborescent ancestors.

Among the extinct genera, both ligulate and eligulate, homosporous and heterosporous, and herbaceous and arborescent types occurred. The last were striking plants, more than 50 m in height, and were abundant in Carboniferous forests.

Cambial activity (known only in the Isoetales among extant microphyllophytes) was a noteworthy attribute of the treelike forms, but the bulk of the secondary tissues was periderm rather than secondary xylem.

Although some forms had long leaves, all the fossil genera were clearly microphyllous, with no leaf gaps having formed in the stem steles. Sporangia were always adaxial, probably having been derived from the lateral sporangial attachment in the Zosterophyllophyta.

The Microphyllophyta are an ancient group of plants-probably the most ancient of all vascular plants living on the earth at the present time. Because of some of their unique characteristics, they seem not to have been the progenitors of other groups of vascular plants.

Classification

The genera of Microphyllophyta discussed above may be classified as follows:

Division Microphyllophyta
- Class 1. Aglossopsida
  - Order 1. Asteroxylales
    - Family 1. Asteroxylaceae
      - Genus: *Asteroxylon*
  - Order 2. Protolepidodendrales
    - Family 1. Protolepidodendraceae
      - Genera: *Baragwanathia*, *Protolep idodendron, Leclercqia*
  - Order 3. Lycopodiales
    - Family 1. Lycopodiaceae
      - Genera: *Lycopodium*, *Lycopodites*
- Class 2. Glossopsida
  - Order 4. Lepidodendrales
    - Family 1. Lepidodendraceae
      - Genera: *Lepidodendron*, *Stigmaria, Lepidostrobus, Sigillaria, Lepidophloios, Phytokneme*
  - Order 5. Selaginellales
    - Family 1. Selaginellaceae
      - Genera: *Selaginella*, *Selaginellites*

Order *6.* Pleuromeiales

Family 1. Pleuromeiaceae

Genus: *Pleuromeia* Order *7.* Isoetales

Family 1. Isoetaceae

Genera: *Nathorstiana*, *Isoetes*, *Isoetites*, *Stylites*

DIVISION ARTHROPHYTA

Although the history of the Arthrophyta parallels that of the Microphyllophyta quite closely, the beginning is somewhat more obscure. It is quite likely that their origin was during the Devonian period, and the division persisted to the present time, represented today only by the genus *Equisetum.*

Many fossil Arthrophyta are recognizable by their whorled branching, ribbed stems, and sporangia borne on reduced branches called sporangiophores. The ancestors of the Arthrophyta were probably forms such as those in the Trimerophytophyta, with a prominent principal axis and reduced laterals.

Subsequently, the sites of attachment of appendages became telescoped, with a number of them arising at a single level. Sporangium-bearing appendages became recurved.

That Arthrophyta could have had their origins among the Trimerophytophyta is shown by the recently described *Ibyka* (named for the Greek poet Ibykos) *amphikoma*, placed in the order Ibykales. The entire plant is not known, but the distal portions indicate a monopodial habit, with helically arranged appendages.

Reduced terminal appendages were dichotomous, with recurved tips. Obovoid sporangia were borne on the tips of some of these ultimate appendages. The Ibykales appear to be another instance where it is impossible to assign a group of plants into existing categories, but they are important in showing important evolutionary trends.

Following are selected orders of Arthrophyta:

Order 1. Hyeniales

Schweitzer (*1972*) is of the opinion that the Middle Devonian *Hyenia*, the type genus for the order, is more probably a fern than an arthrophyte, but because it has certain features like those of arthrophytes, it is included with them and, like *Ibyka*, indicates possible ancestry of the arthrophytes among the trimerophytophytes. The reconstruction of *Hyenia* shows a massive, horizontal rhizome system from which arise

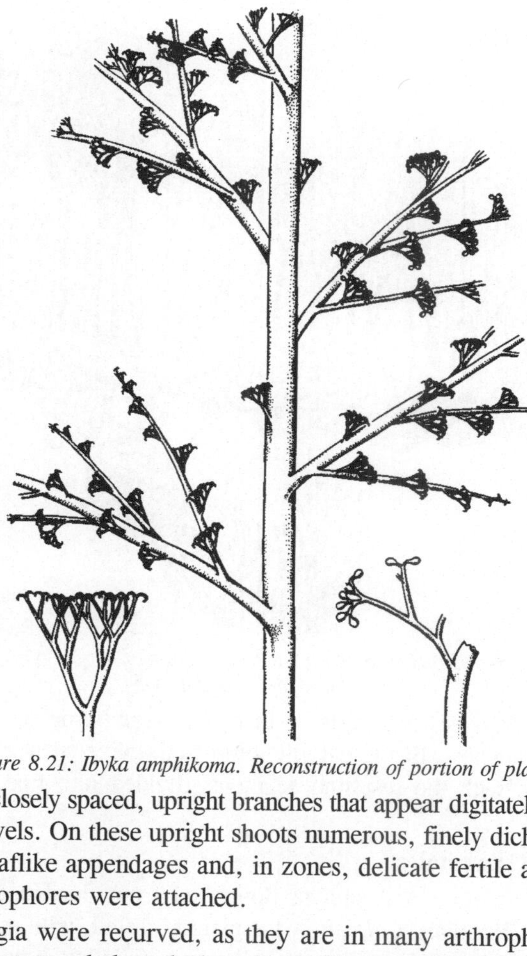

Figure 8.21: Ibyka amphikoma. Reconstruction of portion of plant.

numerous, closely spaced, upright branches that appear digitately branched at higher levels. On these upright shoots numerous, finely dichotomously branched leaflike appendages and, in zones, delicate fertile appendages or sporangiophores were attached.

Sporangia were recurved, as they are in many arthrophytes, with delicate dichotomously branched portions of the sporangiophores extending outward.

Appendages were not whorled as they are in typical arthrophytes, but the situation in *Hyenia* may easily be interpreted as one that had not yet reached the more highly organized pattern of arrangement of appendages in the Arthrophyta.

Order 2. Pseudoborniales

More typically arthrophytan than members of the Hyeniales is the genus *Pseudobornia* (Gr. *pseudes*, false, + *Bornia*, old generic name for arthrophyte foliage), from Upper Devonian strata. It was an upright tree, 15-20 m tall, with a jointed stem from which arose a small

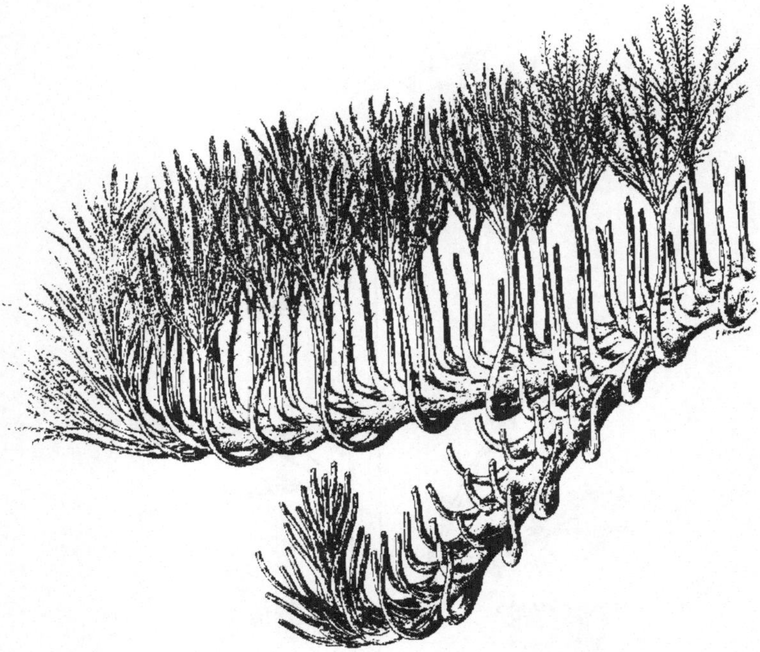

Figure 8.22: Hyenia elegans. Reconstruction of portion of plant. Scale in figure equals 10 cm.

number of branches in whorls. Four leaves were borne at each node on smaller branches. Each leaf dichotomized twice near the point of attachment, with the resulting segments divided into fine, featherlike laminae.

Order 3. Calamitales

Giant, treelike Arthrophyta flourished from the Upper Devonian through the Permian. *Calamites*, the giant horsetail, with many species, is abundant in strata ranging from Mississippian to Lower Permian. *Calamites* (Gr. *kalamos*, reed) was treelike in habit, in some instances probably having reached 20-30 m in height, with a trunk that may have been more than 40 cm in diameter.

The aerial portion of the plant arose from a large, horizontal underground rhizome, as in *Equisetum.* Stems were hollow, with the pith often having reached a considerable diameter. Primary xylem was in the form of a series of separate strands arranged in a cylinder about the pith; each primary xylem strand had a canal within it representing the disintegrated protoxylem.

Secondary xylem of considerable thickness was produced in larger

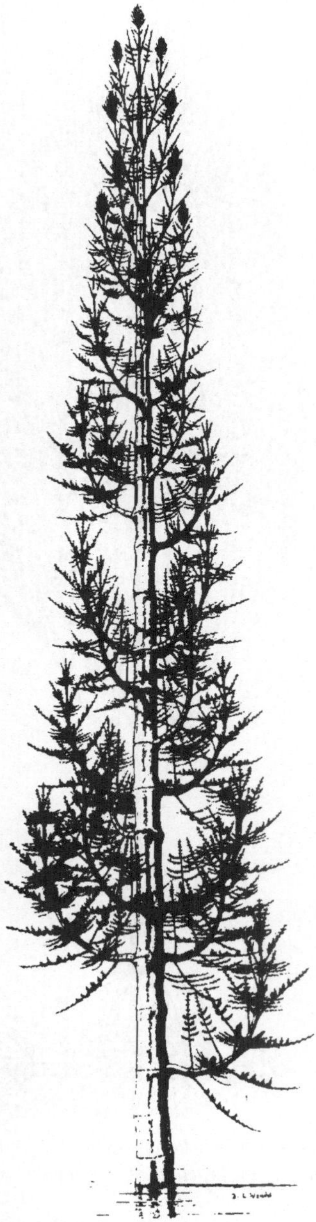

Figure 8.23: Pseudobornia ursina. Suggested reconstruction. Scale in figure equals 5 m.

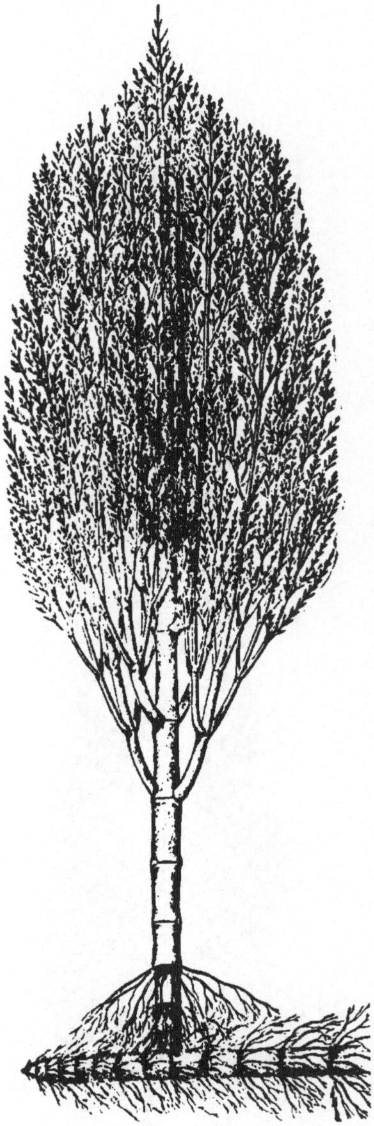

Figure 8.24: A. Calamites carinatus. Reconstruction; note rhizome, roots, and whorled aerial branches. B. Model reconstruction of a Calamites trunk (left) and leaf-bearing branch system (right).

axes by the vascular cambium. During the process of fossilization, pieces of *Calamites* stems may have been covered with sediment, which also washed into the hollow pith cavity.

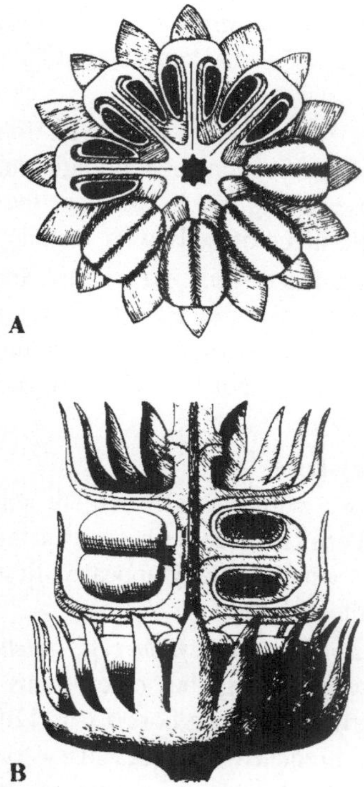

Figure 8.25: Calamostachys binneyana. A. Transverse section of strobilus; note bracts and sporangiophore whorls from above. B. Longitudinal section with alternating bract whorls and sporangiophore whorls.

Hardening of the sediment resulted in a "pith cast" that reflects the inner margin of the xylem. Grooves in the pith cast correspond to primary xylem strands, while the ridges represent projection of the sediment into the inner parts of major vascular rays between the primary xylem strands.

Horizontal lines were left by remains of pith diaphragms that occurred at nodes. Smaller branches departed from larger axes in whorls, and the ultimate branches, also whorled, were clothed with circles of slender leaves.

These leaves have been assigned to the organ genera *Annularia* (*L. annulus*, ring) and *Asterophyllites* (Gr. *aster*, star, + *phyllon*, leaf). As in arborescent fossil Microphyllophyta, daughter branches were smaller than parent axes, with less potential for growth.

They had a smaller pith, fewer primary xylem strands, fewer leaves per whorl, less secondary vascular tissue, and smaller leaves. Fertile appendages of *Calamites* were borne in compact strobili (some of which were called *Calamostachys-Gr. stachys*, ear of grain), each composed of a central axis that had alternating whorls of bracts and sporangiophores.

Sporangiophores were peltate, each with four sporangia directed toward the strobilar axis. Sections of sporangiophores indicate that they were much like those of *Equisetum* and that the sporangial wall was composed of a single layer of cells with annular thickenings.

Some species of cones of *Calamites* were heterosporous, and spores have been shown to have borne elaters. One strobilus, in the organ genus *Calamocarpon* (Gr. *karpon*, fruit), demonstrates an extreme manifestation of heterospory in that there is only one functional megaspore per sporangium.

Order 4. Sphenophyllales

Contemporaneous with the arborescent giant horsetails of the Carboniferous and Permian were herbaceous arthrophytes, members of the Sphenophyllales, which actually appeared first in the late Devonian and extended into the Triassic.

The slender stems of *Sphenophyllum* (Gr. *sphenos*, wedge, + *phyllon*, leaf) were ribbed when young, but older stems were cylindrical and covered with periderm. Each node bore a whorl of wedge-shaped leaves with dichotomously branched veins. Primary xylem of the stem was triangular in cross section and was exarch.

Older stems show evidence of secondary vascular tissue. The outline of the xylem in cross section in an older stem is circular. Roots were diarch and also may have had secondary vascular tissue.

Strobili were borne at the tips of certain branches. Each was composed of an axis bearing a whorl of fused bracts that subtended a whorl of sporangiophores.

Sporangiophores were variously branched in different species and were partially adnate to the bract whorl, and each branch of the sporangiophore bore a single, recurved sporangium. The most common kind of strobilus attributed to *Sphenophyllum* is the organ genus *Boum anites* (named after J. E. Bowman, the discoverer). All species appear to have been homosporous.

Order 5. Equisetales

Coexisting with extinct members of the Arthrophyta during late Paleozoic and Mesozoic times were herbaceous arthrophytes, many of which resemble the extant *Equisetum* quite closely. In fact, *Equisetum-like* fossils, often placed in the genus *Equisetites*, are so much like the extant genus that many workers place the fossils in *Equisetum*. *Equisetum* appeared first in the Triassic period and was an abundant component of Mesozoic floras. These Mesozoic plants were considerably more robust than present-day species, but it is quite likely that they had no secondary vascular tissues.

Other herbaceous arthrophytes in the Equisetales include the late Paleozoic-early Mesozoic genus *Phyllotheca* (Gr. *phyllon*, leaf, + *theca*, sheath), which was *Equisetum-like* except that the leaves were more conspicuous, arranged in a whorl that was fused near the point of attachment.

It is quite likely that members of the Equisetaceae were derived from arborescent *Calamites-like* ancestors by a progressive reduction in the amount of secondary vascular tissue, a reduction in size of leaves, and a reduction in numbers of branches.

In summary, it may be stated that the fossil record indicates that although currently represented in our flora only by a small number of *Equisetum* species, the Arthrophyta were formerly an important assemblage. Possible primitive arthrophytes are known from the Middle and Upper Devonian.

The whorled arrangement of appendages had not been fully established by that time, however. Arthrophytes, like members of the Microphyll-ophyta, were important components of Carboniferous and Permian forests. Both woody (arborescent) and herbaceous forms were present, and heterospory occurred in some of the members.

The occurrence of leaves with dichotomously branching veins in some fossil genera (*Sphenophyllum*) suggests that the leaves of *Equisetum*, with single, unbranched veins, have arisen from fossil forms with *Annularia*- or *Asterophyllites*-like leaves.

Classification

The members of the Arthrophyta treated in this chapter may be classified as follows:

Division Arthrophyta
- Order 1. Hyeniales
  - Family 1. Hyeniaceae
    - Genus: *Hyenia*
- Order 2. Pseudoborniales
  - Family 1. Pseudoborniaceae
    - Genus: *Pseudobornia*
- Order 3. Calamitales

Family 1. Calamitaceae
Genera: *Calamites*, *Calamostachys*, *Calamocarpon*, *Annularia*, *Asterophyllites*

Order 4. Sphenophyllales
Family 1. Sphenophyllaceae
Genera: *Sphenophyllum*, *Bowmanites*

Order 5. Equisetales
Family 1. Equisetaceae
Genera: *Equisetum*, *Equisetites*, *Phyllotheca*

DIVISION PTERIDOPHYTA

In addition to the rootless and leafless Rhyniophyta, Zosterophyllophyta, and Trimerophytophyta, and to the Microphyllophyta and Arthrophyta, ferns and their precursors were present on the earth during early Devonian times.

The Pteridophyta, or ferns, are held together by the fact that all are megaphyllous vascular cryptogams with foliar sporangia. Most likely the source of the ferns is the Trimerophytophyta, with most botanists believing that a lateral branch system of trimerophytophytes was the precursor of a megaphyll.

In fact, recent thought indicates that a megaphyll could have been derived from a branch system bearing microphylls, and that the megaphyll is a kind of compound structure composed of stems and leaves. The fossil record seems to offer some support to this idea.

Ferns and fernlike plants are represented in the fossil record in great abundance, especially in Carboniferous rocks. In fact, many paleobotanists refer to that period of geologic history as the "Age of Ferns."

A great many of the fernlike fossils are *form genera-that* is, they have superficially similar appearance but may actually belong to more than one natural group of plants. Unlike most modern ferns, in which the compound leaves are clearly two-dimensional appendages of well-differentiated trunks and/or rhizomes, this distinction between leaves and stems and the twodimensional organization of the former were absent in the earliest putative pteridophytan precursors.

CLASS 1. CLADOXYLOPSIDA

Order 1. Cladoxylales

Members of the class Cladoxylopsida are not typical fernlike plants in that it is difficult to recognize distinct fronds. Instead, branching of the stem system resulted in formation of smaller, lateral branches that bore minute, often dichotomously branched, appendages.

It is difficult to equate these small appendages with branching stem systems. More likely they represent modified enations and were, in a sense, microphylls. The distal branches with the microphylls may be regarded as precursors of large, compound fronds.

Although members of the Cladoxylopsida may vary in gross morphological characters, they have in common a stem structure in which, in transverse sections of the axes and larger branches, the xylem consists of radiating, sometimes branching, plates, often with their outer extremities enclosing nests of parenchyma cells.

Representatives of the Cladoxylales are found in strata ranging from Middle Devonian to Mississippian in age. *Cladoxylon scoparium* is a well-known species of the genus. The plant was branched with some of the distal branches bearing small, leaflike appendages and others bearing flattened, dichotomously branched, fan-shaped appendages with terminal, ovoid sporangia. Plants were homosporous.

Pseudosporochnus (Gr. *pseudes*, false, + *Sporochnus*, a genus of

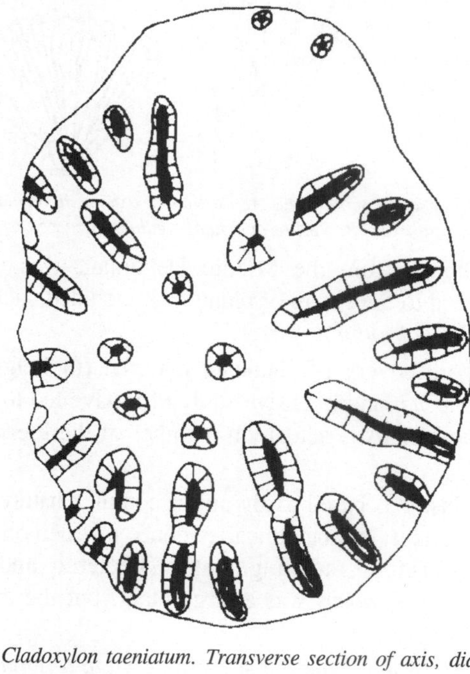

Figure 8.26: Cladoxylon taeniatum. Transverse section of axis, diagrammatic.

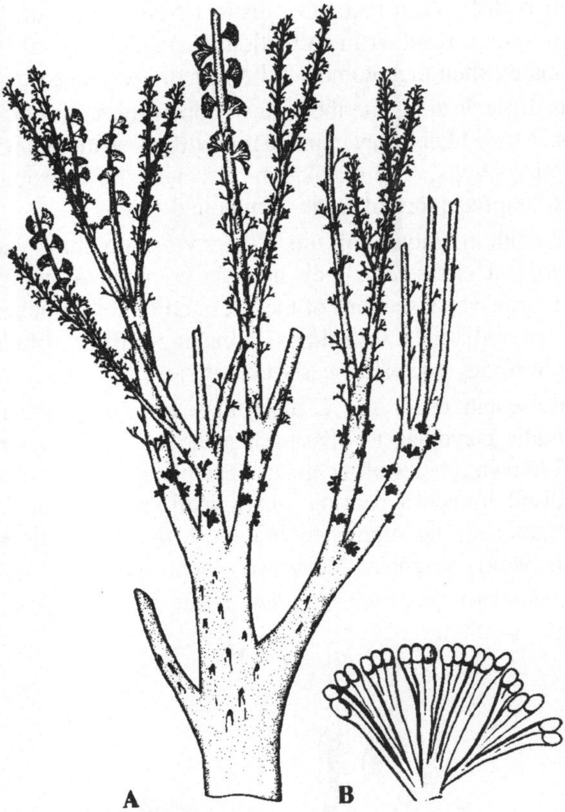

Figure 8.27: Cladoxylon scoparium. A. Portion of axis with vegetative and fanlike sporangium-bearing axes. B. Fertile appendage enlarged; note terminal sporangia.

Phaeophycophyta), from the Middle Devonian, was until relatively recently assigned to the group of plants that included such simple forms as *Rhynia* and *Cooksonia*.

However, discovery of abundant material (in Belgium) of a new species, *P. nodosus*, and intensive study of it have led to the conclusion that *Pseudosporochnus* is actually a member of the Pteridophyta, order Cladoxylales.

This conclusion is based partly on the complex nature of the "frond" and, more important, on anatomical evidence that demonstrates vascular tissue in the form of radiating plates (Leclercq and Lele, 1968). *Pseudosporochnus nodosus* was a large plant, but the overall height is not known.

At the base of the trunklike stem there were a number of principal roots bearing laterals helically. The main stem was unbranched for some distance, but at the apex was a crown of three-dimensional branches of two orders. The second-order branches bore dichotomizing sterile and/or fertile segments arbitrarily called "*fronds*.

Other ultimate branches were fertile, terminating in eight pedicellate, ovoid sporangia. Some fronds were mixed fertile and sterile. *Pseudosporochnus* differs from *Cladoxylon scoparium* in that the former has fertile branches that are not flattened into bladelike structures.

The Middle Devonian *Calamophyton* was classified earlier with the Arthrophyta on the basis of certain characters it seemed to have in common with *Hyenia*. More recent studies have resulted in its being assigned to the Cladoxylopsida because it has internal structure more like that of that class than that of the Arthrophyta. Stems of *C. bicephalum* had main axes at least 60 cm high.

Whether or not they arose from a rhizome has not been ascertained. These axes were digitately, monopodially, and dichotomously branched. The branchlets bore three-dimensional, terete appendages that branched two or three times (leaves).

Some of these appendages were somewhat more branched, with most of the tips recurved and bearing elongated sporangia; the distal parts extended outward and were sterile. Whether *Calamophyton* was homosporous or heterosporous is unknown.

The class Cladoxylopsida most likely represents an artificial group of plants held together principally by the fact that the stele consists of a series of radiating platelike masses of xylem and phloem.

Gross morphological features maybe quite different among the various genera, and there is no reason to assume that more than one group of plants could not have evolved such an anatomical pattern.

Further research based on additional collections may provide insight as to the significance of internal structure and importance of external form in classifying these organisms.

Class 2. Coenopteriodopsida

Order 1. Coenopteridales

Members of this class occur as fossils in strata extending from the Upper Devonian through the Permian, but are predominantly Carboniferous. The single order Coenopteridales may well represent an artificiall grouping of diverse organisms.

In fact, as more work progresses on plants that have been assigned to this order, it is becoming increasingly more apparent that some of them more appropriately may be assigned to other orders of ferns. Our knowledge of these plants is based principally on segments of fronds, petioles, rachises, pinna axes, and fertile regions.

In many of the coenopterid ferns it is difficult to distinguish between the rachis of a frond and a stem, and therefore the term *phyllophore* is used for a frondlike structure. The vascular pattern of the phyllophore is most frequently bilaterally symmetrical in either one or two planes and is often delicate and esthetically attractive.

Most of the stems were protostelic, and fronds were generally three-dimensional rather than constructed in one plane. The order may be divided, arbitrarily, into four families.

Stauropteris is the single genus in the Carboniferous family Stauropteridaceae and was characterized by a four-lobed protostele. Appendages were borne in pairs, with the two appendages at a given level arising on the side of the parent axis opposite the position of the two appendages below.

In this genus it is difficult to differentiate between stern and frond. Sporangia were borne terminally. One species of *Stauropteris is* heterosporous. The megasporangium is small, elongated, and composed of fleshy tissue proximally, with two large megaspores in a distal cavity.

The Botryopteridaceae include only the genus *Botryopteris* (Gr. *botrys*, grape, + L. *pteris*, fern) from the Lower Carboniferous to the Permian. Typically *Botryopteris* has protostelic stems with fronds containing vascular traces, the xylem of which in transverse section is curved, with three arms directed toward the stem.

Typical fern pinnules occurred at the distal parts, and some of the fronds bore massive, glohose clusters of tightly packed sporangia. In the Anachoropteridaceae, with a range from Carboniferous to Permian, plants were typically protostelic, with leaf traces Cshaped in transverse section.

The curvature of the "C" was abaxial, unlike the more common adaxial curvature seen in presentday ferns (e.g., *Osmunda*). *Anachoropteris* is the genus for which the family was named and often shows conspicuously curved petiole traces.

Internal structure of petioles in the family Zygopteridaceae (Upper DevonianPermian) generally involves petiolar xylem strands that were bilaterally symmetrical, with two planes of symmetry.

In transverse section some were elliptical (e.g., *Clepsydropsis* [Gr. *clepsydra*, water clock]), bow-tie-shaped (e.g., *Metaclepsydropsis*), or

H-shaped (*Zygopteris*). Pinnae were usually borne in pairs, with the plane of symmetry of a pinna at right angles to that of the rachis, in contrast to the situation in modern ferns in which all pinnae and the rachis are in one plane.

One genus of Zygopteridaceae, *Zygopteris* (Gr. *zygos*, yoke, + *L. pteris*), had secondary xylem, an unusual phenomenon among the Pteridophyta. Another, *Ankyropteris* (Gr. *ankyra*, anchor, + *L. pteris*), showed axillary branching, also not a typical pteridophytan feature.

Class 3. Filicopsida

Order 1. Marattiales

Among orders of extant ferns, the Marattiales, Filicales, and Salviniales are known also as fossils. Many examples of eusporangiate synangia are known as far back as the Carboniferous. These resemble very closely the sporangia of Marattiales. The order was also represented in the Paleozoic by the genus *Psaronius* (*NL.*, a precious stone), known from the Carboniferous and Permian.

In general habit *Psaronius* resembled certain extant tree ferns (members of the Filicales). Trunks exceeded 60 cm in diameter near the base and were probably more than 15 m tall. The bulk of the trunk, however, was actually composed of a thick root mantle surrounding a relatively slender stem.

These stems were exceedingly complex anatomically, containing a number of concentric dictyosteles. The stem increased in diameter and

Figure 8.28: Thamnopteris schlechtendalii. Transverse section of stem and leaf bases of a Permian osmundaceous fern.

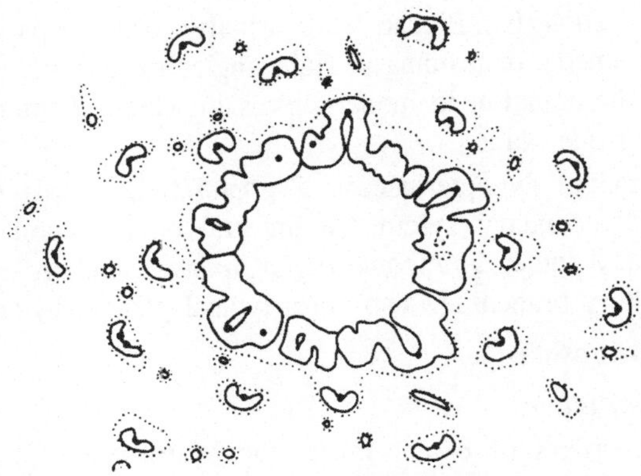

Figure 8.29: Palaeosmunda playfordii. Diagrammatic transverse section of stele and inner cortex.

in complexity from base to apex. The large fronds were pinnately compound with synangia borne on the abaxial surface of some of the pinnules.

The order Marattiales was represented in the Mesozoic era by various kinds of fronds with synangia resembling those, of certain extant genera.

Order 2. Filicales

Members of the Filicales are recognized as far back as the Carboniferous. Foliage with sporangia resembling those of the Schizaeaceae is placed in the gens *Senftenbergia. Oligocarpia* (Gr. *oligos*, few + *karpon*, fruit) is also Carboniferous and is the name given to foliage with sporangia similar to those of the Gleicheniaceae.

In both instances, however, similarity is confined to structure of the sporangia; the foliage is quite different from that of modern members of these two families, and there may be a question as to whether the families are actually that old.

There is no doubt about filicalean affinity, however. The Osmundaceae are probably the oldest family of living ferns, with the first ones appearing in the Permian period. *Thamnopteris* (Gr. *thamnos*, frequent, + *L. pteris*, fern) has a stem with structure like that of *Osmunda* - except that there is a protostele, with no leaf gaps. *Palaeosmunda* (Gr. *palaios*, old) is Upper Permian and more similar anatomically to *Osmunda.*

Other osmundaceous stems, often included in the genus *Osmundacaulis*, occur throughout the Mesozoic and Tertiary. Foliage, also thought to have been osmundaceous, was common in the Mesozoic era. The palmately constructed leaf of the Matoniaceae is distinctive, and the family is evident in the Mesozoic, as far back as the Triassic period. *Phlebopteris* (Gr. *phlebos*, vein, + *L. pteris*) has fertile fronds showing sporangial structure and arrangement that are like those in modem members.

Polypodiaceous ferns are known from the Jurassic, but really abundant and diversified remains did not occur until the Cenozoic era. For this reason, the Polypodiaceae are often called "the modem ferns." It is clear that because of their later origin, they could not have been in the ancestral lines that led to the other fem groups.

Order 3. Salviniales

Among the aquatic, heterosporous ferns, the Salviniales extend back into the Cretaceous period. The unusual microspore masses and megaspore apparatuses of both *Azolla* and *Salvinia* are known. Entire plants of these two genera are found in Tertiary rocks.

Classification

The representatives of the fossil Pteridophyta discussed above may be classified as follows:

Division Pteridophyta
- Class 1. Cladoxylopsida
  - Order 1. Cladoxylales
    - Family 1. Cladoxylaceae
      - Genus: *Cladoxylon*
    - Family 2. Pseudosporochnaceae
      - Genus: *Pseudosporochnus*
    - Family 3. Calamophytaceae
      - Genus: *Calamophyton*
- Class 2. Coenopteridopsida
  - Order 1. Coenopteridales
    - Family 1. Stauropteridaceae
      - Genus: *Stauropteris*
    - Family 2. Botryopteridaceae
      - Genus: *Botryopteris*
    - Family 3. Anachoropteridaceae
      - Genus: *Anachoropteris*
    - Family 4: Zygopteridaceae
      - Genera: *Clepsydropsis, Metaclepsydropsis, Zygopteris, Ankyropteris*

Class 3. Filicopsida
Order 1. Marattiales
Family 1. Psaroniaceae
Genus: *Anachoropteris*
Order 2. Filicales
Family 1. Schizaeaceae
Genus: *Senftenbergia*
Family 2. Gleicheniaceae
Genus: *Oligocarpia*
Family 3. Osmundaceae
Genera: *Thamnopteris*, *Osmunda*, *Palaeosmunda*, *Osmundacaulis*
Family 4. Matoniaceae
Genus: *Phlebopteris*
Family 5. Polypodiaceae
Genera: *Woodwardia*, *Dennstaedtiopsis*
Order 3. Salviniales
Family 1. Salviniaceae
Genera: *Azolla*, *Salvinia*

DIVISION PROGYMNOSPERMOPHYTA

Although not ferns, the progymnosperms are included here because the plants were cryptogamous. For many years they were interpreted to be highly specialized ferns because some of the forms had lateral appendages that superficially resemble fern fronds.

The progymnosperms occupy an interesting position in the plant kingdom because they combine characters of vascular cryptogams (sporangia that shed spores) with those of gymnospermous seed plants (e.g., eusteles without leaf gaps; secondary xylem, often with circular bordered pits; and simple leaves derived from flattened branch systems).

Beck first recognized the existence of such a group based on his work with the Upper Devonian *Archaeopteris* (Gr. *archaio*, ancient, + Gr. *pteris*, fern) and the contemporaneous *Callixylon* (Gr. *kalli*, beautiful, + Gr. *xylon*, wood). *Archaeopteris* was a tree, with flattened branch systems bearing wedge-shaped leaves.

These flattened branches had the appearance of fern fronds (hence the name *Archaeopteris*). Replacing certain leaves were elongated, branched axes bearing slender sporangia. At least two species of *Archaeopteris* were heterosporous.

Callixylon had been thought to represent the trunks of gymnospermous trees because anatomically, with a eustele and compact secondary xylem bearing circular bordered pits, it resembled the stems of conifers quite closely.

Beck showed that sections of the axes of *Archaeopteris* that bore leaves showed an internal structure like that of *Callixylon*. The latter genus is readily recognizable in radial section because of the peculiar and characteristic grouping of pits in radial files.

The Upper Devonian *Tetraxylopteris is* another progymnosperm with stems bearing helically arranged branches. These laterals, in turn, bore decussate branches. Some of these axes were fertile and bore sporangial clusters in a decussate pattern.

Primary xylem in the larger axes was cruciform in cross section, with secondary xylem eventually having produced a cylindrical outline to the xylem cylinder. *Rellimia* (perhaps better known by its former name, *Protopteridium*), from the Middle Devonian, differed only slightly from *Tetraxylopteris*.

It was a shrub or a low arborescent plant with main axes dichotomously or pseudomonopodially branched. Leaf-bearing branch systems were helically arranged and bore leaves that were bifurcated two or

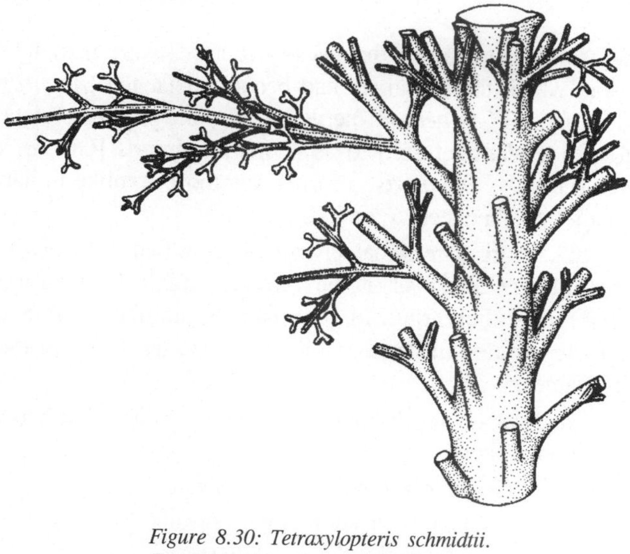

Figure 8.30: Tetraxylopteris schmidtii. Reconstruction of a portion of a plant.

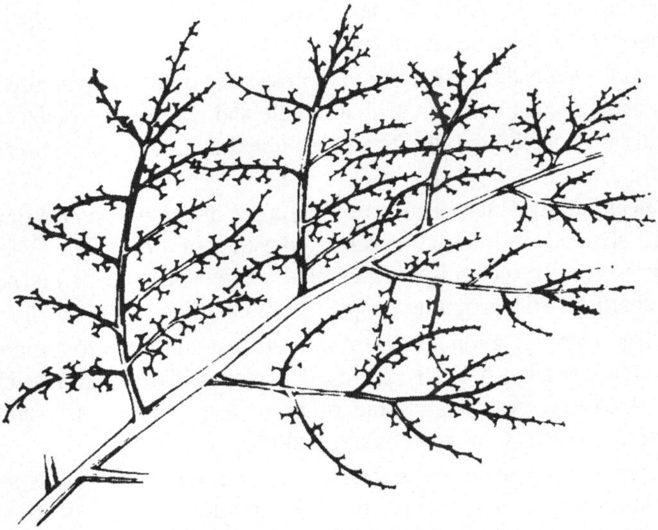

Figure 8.31: Aneurophyton germanicum. Part of branch system.

three times. Fertile branches were also helically placed and bore pinnately divided sporangium-bearing structures.

Earlier work reported that this plant had ultimate sterile portions that were pinnately divided and apparently bladelike. These were interpreted as representing the initiation of fern fronds in a phyletic sense.

It has since been shown that these structures were actually fertile organs from which the sporangia had become detached. *Aneurophyton* (Gr. *a*, lacking, + Gr. *neuron*, nerve, + *phyton*, plant) (thought to be identical with a plant referred to as *Eospermatopteris* [Gr. *eo*, dawn, + *sperms*, seed,' + Gr. *pteris*, a fern]) was more fernlike in habit and was a small tree, between 6 and 12 m tall.

The trunks bore a terminal crown of frondlike branches, 1-2 m long. The ultimate divisions of the "fronds" might be interpreted as leaves that were dichotomized and lacked laminae. Some of the appendages terminated in large, ovoid sporangia up to 6 mm long and 3 mm in diameter.

Representatives of the Progymnospermophyta discussed above may be classified as follows:

Division Progymnospermophyta

Class 1. Progymnospermopsida

Order 1. Aneurophytales

Family 1. Archaeopteridaceae
Genera: *Archaeopteris*, *Callixylon*
Family 2. Aneurophytaceae
Genera: *Tetraxylopteris*, *Rellimia,* *Aneurophyton*, *Eospermatopteris*

CONCLUSION

From this brief account of representative fossil vascular cryptogams, several conclusions may be drawn. In the first place, vascular land plants first appeared in the late Silurian.

During the following Devonian period, which lasted approximately 50 million years, relatively rapid diversification occurred, since representatives of major groups of vascular cryptogams (Rhyniophyta, Zosterophyllophyta, Trimerophytophyta, Microphyllophyta, Arthrophyta, Pteridophyta, and Progymnospermophyta) made their appearance.

Of these, representatives of only three (Microphyllophyta, Arthrophyta, and Pteridophyta) have survived. Descendents of the Progymnospermophyta exist at the present time in the form of gymnospermous plants. As the fossil record becomes still better known, a greater diversity of these ancient spore-bearing plants will probably be revealed.

The discovery of seeds in Devonian strata is significant and pushes back the geologic history of the seed plants. It will, no doubt, stimulate and intensify the search for more fossil plants that will shed light on the actual transition from the sporebearing to the seed-bearing habit.

9

Introduction to Seed Plants: Divsion Cycadophyta

The members of the plant kingdom discussed as representative morphological types in Chapters elsewhere in this book all are seedless plants, the *supposedly obscure* (in the eighteenth century!) reproductive organs and life cycle of which suggested to Linnaeus the name Cryptogamia (Gr. *kryptos*, hidden, + Gr. *gamos*, marriage).

The seed plants were later called Phanerogamae (Gr. *phaneros*, visible, + Gr. *gamos*), an allusion to the prominence of their supposed sexual organs, which in fact are spore-bearing organs. The seed plants are vascular plants usually containing abundant xylem and phloem, except in secondarily reduced aquatics.

This attribute they share with the vascular cryptogams, with which they sometimes are ' grouped in a single division, Tracheophyta (inside back cover). This category has not been adopted in the present text, because in the authors' opinion such a grouping places too much weight on one attribute.

The habit of producing seeds formerly was considered to be such an important indication of relationship that all seed-bearing plants were once classified in a single division, Spermatophyta (inside back cover). Paradoxically, however, this division has been replaced in many modern classifications by a still more inclusive taxon, the Pteropsida, under the division Tracheophyta.

In spite of its lower rank, the Pteropsida includes a wider assemblage of plants, namely, the megaphyllous ferns as well as the seed plants. This arrangement reflects the views of those who see in the extinct seed ferns a possible bridge between the ferns and the living seed plants.

In some systems of classification, the seed plants in which the seeds are not enclosed in a sporophyll are usually grouped in a taxon, Gymnospermae (inside back cover).

This is not done in this text because it is considered that this practice also places too much emphasis on a single attribute. The formal taxonomic designation "Gymnospermae" (Gr. *gymnos*, naked, + Gr, *sperma*, seed) and the informal term "gymnosperm" refer to the lack of enclosure of the seeds of certain plants. By contrast, the terms "Angiospermae" (Gr. diversities apparent among the plants formerly included in the Gymnospermae.

The production of seeds is considered to occur in plants of several *divisions:* The Cycadophyta, *angeion*, a vessel, + Gr. sperma) and "angiosperm" signify that in other seed plants the seeds are enclosed in a structure variously known as the *carpel* or carpels, *pistil*, or *megasporophyll*.

Angiosperms, the division Anthophyta, comprise the "flowering plants," to be discussed in other chapters of this book. Such topics as the origin and evolution of the seed and the origin and relationships of the seed plants are deferred to Chapter elsewhere in this book, a point by which, it is hoped, the reader will have assimilated adequate basic information to profit from such a discussion.

The classification of the seed plants used in the present text recognizes the important the Ginkgophyta, the Coniferophyta, and the Gnetophyta (all four gymnospermous) and the Anthophyta (angiospermous).

DIVISION CYCADOPHYTA

The Cycadophyta, perhaps an unnatural group, include both extinct and extant gymnospermous seed plants with complex, fernlike foliage. Three classes-the Pteridospermopsida, the Cycadeoidopsida (cycadeoids), and the Cycadopsida (cycads)-formerly constituted the division.

However, the first and second classes, known only as fossils, have herein been elevated to divisional status. The remaining class, Cycadophyta, in addition to fossil members, includes a single order (Cycadales) with living genera.

Because of their familiarity and availability, the living Cycadales

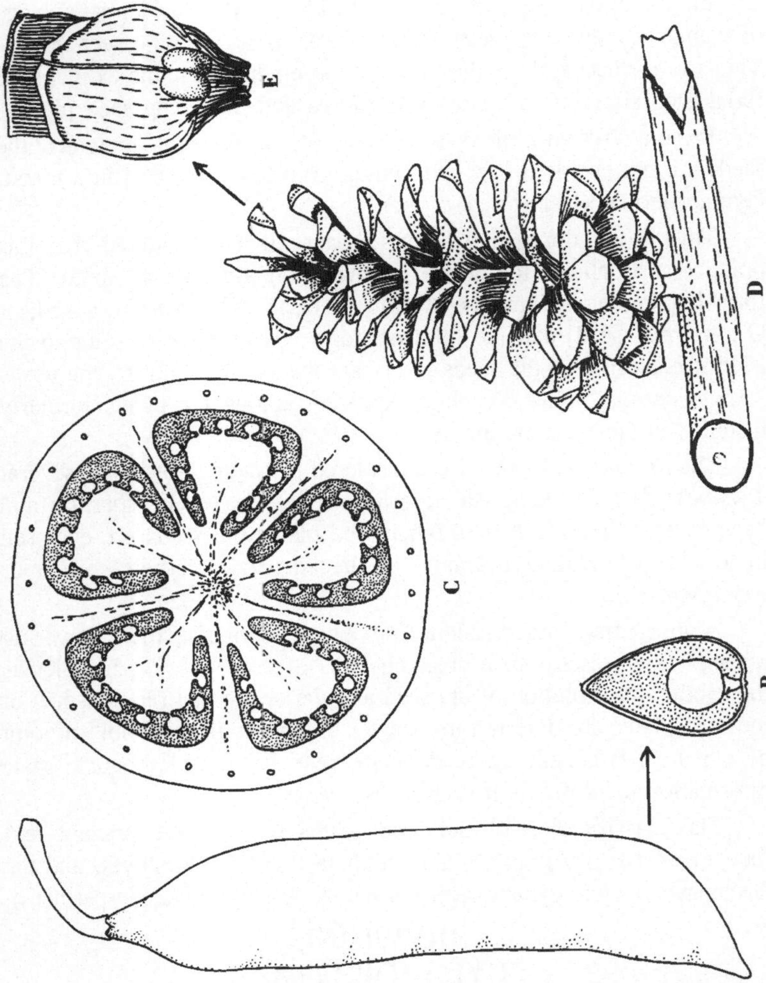

Figure 9.1: Location of the seeds of seed plants. A-C. Angiospermy. A. Fruit (pod) of garden pea. B. Transection of the preceding showing enclosed seed. C. Transection of the tomato fruit with enclosed seeds. D, E. Gymnospermy. D. Seed cone or strobilus of pine. E. Adaxial view of one of the ovuliferous scales of the preceding showing unenclosed, winged seeds.

will be discussed first in introducing the seed plants. Treatment of the fossil Cycadophyta is deferred to other chapter anywhere else in this book.

Class1. Cycadopsida

The Cycadopsida include the single order Cycadales, with three families, discussed together in the following account.

General Features

The Cycadales, commonly called the cycads, include a small group of nine or ten genera and 100 species of tropical plants that superficially suggest both ferns and palms insofar as the general form of the plant body is concerned.

Formerly included in a single family, the ten genera of cycads are now classified in three families: Cycadaceae, with the single genus *Cycas;* Stangeriaceae, which includes only *Stangeria;* and the Zamiaceae, to which *Zamia*, *Microcycas*, *Macrozamia*, *Lepidozamia*, *Encephalartos*, *Bowenia*, *Ceratozamia*, and *Dioon* belong.

The Cycads are sometimes regarded as "living fossils," and it has been predicted that they will be extinct in the future. There is good evidence, indeed, that one of the genera, *Microcycas*, endemic to Cuba, is rapidly approaching extinction at present.

Once widely distributed and important components of the earth's vegetation, they now are reduced in number of genera, species, and individuals. Only one genus, *Zamia* (*L. zamiae*, erroneous reading in Pliny for *azaniae*, pine nuts), is represented in the flora of the United States (in Florida), although the other genera are cultivated in conservatories and tropical gardens.

In addition to *Zamia*, other cycads of Mexico and the West Indies are the genera *Dioon* (Gr. *dis*, two, + Gr. *oion*, egg), *Ceratozamia* (Gr. *keras*, horn, + *Zamia*), and *Microcycas* (Gr. *mikros*, small, + *Cycas*).

In the Southern Hemisphere, cycads occur especially in Australia and Africa. *Stangeria* (after Dr. Stanger) (originally described as and considered to be a fern until it produced strobili!) and *Encephalartos* (Gr. *encephalos*, brain, + Gr. *artos*, bread) are native to South Africa.

Bowenia (after G. T. Bowen'), *Macrozamia* (Gr. *makros*, long, + *Zamia*), and *Cycas* occur in Australia. *Cycas* (Gr. *kykos*, a palm) occurs in India and extends to southern Japan; one species grows natively in Madagascar.

Cycas is widely planted as an ornamental in warmer portions of the United States in the southern portions of states bordering on the Gulf of Mexico, but *Zamia* is emphasized as representative of the cycads in this book because it is usually to be found in university greenhouses or may be obtained readily.

Furthermore, the small stature of the plants, usually less than 4 ft tall, makes it feasible to maintain a supply of fruiting specimens in limited space. Two or more species of *Zamia* occur in Florida. Of these, *Z. integrifolia* and *Z. umbrosa* have been studied with respect to reproduction. *Zamia* is widely distributed in the West Indies, Mexico, and northern South America to Chile.

Vegetative Morphology

The plant body of *Zamia* consists of a relatively short, vertical, approximately conical stem, which tapers toward the base; the base bears a number of fleshy roots. Remains of leaves of former seasons are visible on the upper portions of the tuberous stem, and the apex supports a crown of spirally arranged, leathery, dark-green leaves.

The latter are pinnately compound and decidedly fernlike in appearance. The leaves of *Cycas* are even more fernlike because of the circinate vernation of the young pinnae. In *Ceratozamia*, moreover, the entire young fronds are circinately vernate.

As in the Pteridophyta, the leaves of a majority of the cycads are the most striking and dominant organs of the plant. They are arranged spirally on the axis, and under usual greenhouse conditions both *Zamia* and *Cycas* produce a new crown of leaves annually.

Leaf crowns of preceding seasons may persist, but they finally become reflexed and abscised. The veins run in a direction parallel to the long axes of the pinnae; they arise from basal dichotomies in *Zamia;* the pinnae of *Cycas* have a single midvein and lack laterals.

The leaflets of *Zamia* display histological features usually associated with xerophytism. The epidermis of both surfaces is thickened heavily on the outer walls. Stomata are present only on the lower surface of the pinnae and are sunken.

A thick-walled hypodermis, an additional protective layer, lies beneath the upper epidermis. The mesophyll is differentiated into palisade and spongy zones. The apex of the cycad stem is occupied by a dome of meristematic cells rather than by the single apical initial that is characteristic of so many vascular cryptogams.

The meristematic zone differentiates into permanent tissues during the formation of strobili, and new apical meristems arise successively from subapical meristematic cells lateral to the original meristem. A transverse section of the mature stem of *Zamia* reveals a surprising paucity of xylem.

The latter is composed largely of scalariform-pitted tracheids. A large part of the stem is occupied by the central pith and the extensive cortex, the cells of which are full of stored metabolites. The stem surface is protected by an impermeable periderm layer.

Mucilage canals are abundant in the cortex and pith. The cortex is traversed by leaf traces, which have an unusual path. Each leaf of *Zamia* receives from seven to nine traces, which depart from different points in the stele and girdle it, rising slightly as they approach the leaf base, which may be 180° from the point of origin of some of the traces.

Although a cambium is present between the xylem and phloem, it is relatively inactive, so that the amount of vascular tissue remains small, and clearly defined growth rings are absent from the xylem of *Zamia*. The roots of cycads are fleshy, although considerable secondary xylem is produced.

In some genera, *Cycas*, for example, certain root branches are apogeotropic, growing on and above the soil. It is postulated that they serve as vehicles for gaseous interchange. Such roots develop tubercular nodules, which contain the blue-green algae *Anabaena* (or *Nostoc*?).

The alga lives in the intercellular spaces between the epidermal cells and forms a distinct layer, which is buried by an extension of the root cap (Wittmann, Bergersen, and Kennedy, 1965). Grilli (1974) and Grilli-Caola (*1975*) have investigated the blue-green algae in the roots of *Macrozamia* and *Encephalartos* and in culture.

The alga fixes gaseous nitrogen. Storey (1968) has reported that in seven species of cycads he studied, somatic reduction in chromosome number occurs regularly in the algal zone of the apogeotropic roots.

Reproduction: the sporophyte

In *Zamia* and other cycads, and in all seed plants, two kinds of spores, with respect to function, are produced: One type is genetically conditioned to produce male gametophytes, and the other, female gametophytes.

This obligate dioecism differs from that in *Marchantia* and *Polytrichum*, however, in that all four spores arising from one sporocyte in the seed plants grow into either male or female gametophytes.

Furthermore, in seed plants, the spores that produce male gametophytes arise in sporangia different from those in which female gametophyte-producing spores develop. It will be recalled that in the vascular cryptogams *Selaginella*, *Isoetes*, *Marsilea*, *Azolla*, and *Salvinia,* a similar dichotomy of spore function prevails, but in those genera it is associated with a dimorphism in the spores themselves, a phenomenon known as heterospory.

Now careful measurements of the two kinds of spores in seed plants reveal little significant size difference between the male and female gametophyte-producing spores. Accordingly, it has been suggested that seed plants are homosporous. It is clear, however, that such so-called homospory differs profoundly from that of other homosporous plants, as noted above.

In current usage, as in this text, the two kinds of spores of seed plants are considered to be *functionally* heterosporous, in spite of the absence of marked differences in their size. It has been suggested that the permanent retention of the female gametophyte-producing spore within its sporangium in seed plants accounts for diminution of its size.

As a matter of fact, this spore in seed plants *ultimately* (during gametogenesis) achieves much greater size than the microspore. The time of its increase in size is later than in heterosporous cryptogams.

Those who are unwilling to accept this broader usage of heterospory have suggested the terms "androspores" and "gynospores" for the spores of seed plants. The assignment to spores of prefixes denoting sex cannot be supported, in the writers' opinion.

After due consideration of these points, the spores that develop into male gametophytes are called *microspores* and those that develop into female gametophytes are designated *megaspores* in the present volume, on the basis of their homology with those of vascular cryptogams and in light of the *ultimate* increase in size of the megaspore.

The microsporangia and megasporangia of *Zamia* are segregated in different strobili, which are produced by different individuals. This segregation is known as *dioecism* (Gr. *dis*, two, + Gr. *oikos*, house). The cytological basis for this has been reported for *Cycas revoluta*.

Plants that produce megaspores have 20 somatic chromosomes and an XX pair, while microstrobilate plants have 20 somatic chromosomes and an XY (heteromorphic) pair. Marchant, however, was unable to find convincing evidence of chromosomal differences in dioecious cycads.

The microstrobili are borne among the leaves at the stem apex in *Zamia*. They appear in summer (July) at first as small, conical emergences and gradually enlarge, finally becoming as long as 10 cm.

They are brown, rather fleshy throughout development, and are composed of a central axis to which the spirally arranged microsporophylls are attached. There are between 28 and 50 microsporangia attached to the abaxial surface of each microsporophyll. They may show some evidence of being arranged in clusters.

Each microsporangium is supported by a short thick stalk and has a several-layered wall. The number of spores is large, and the sporangial wall is composed of several layers.

A tapetum functions in nutrition during microsporogenesis, the cells disintegrating to form a tapetal plasmodium. The microsporocytes undergo, meiosis, each giving rise to a tetrad of microspores, which finally separate from each other.

The walls of mature microspores are composed of several layers. The megastrobili, which appear among the leaves of plants other than those that bear the microstrobili, are massive in construction. The megasporophylls are dark brown, peltate structures attached to the axis of the strobilus by stipes.

Each megasporophyll bears two white ovoidal bodies, the ovules, which are attached to the adaxial surface of the megasporophyll by extremely short stalks. A median longitudinal section of a young ovule shortly after the appearance of the megastrobilus is shown in Figure elsewhere in this chpater.

The central cells of the young ovule contain dense protoplasmic contents. These cells constitute the young megasporangium, in which the megasporocyte has not yet differentiated. The megasporangial tissue is surrounded by a multicellular covering, the *integument*, which is incompletely closed, leaving a minute passageway, the *micropyle.*

The integument is free from the megasporangial apex in the cycads. This is at the pole opposite the point of attachment of the ovule. The *ovule* of *Zamia* and of other seed plants is an indehiscent megasporangium surrounded by an integumentary layer or layers.

In the cycads, six to nine vascular bundles arranged in a circle run vertically through the integument. This may indicate a phylogenetic union of previously distinct entities. The ovule of *Zamia* is about 10 cm long at the time of pollination. Ovules occur only in seed plants. Their possible origin is discussed anywhere else in this book.

Somewhat later in its development; one of the deeper cells of the megasporangium enlarges, functions as a megasporocyte, and undergoes two successive nuclear and cell divisions, during which meiosis takes place. The products of these divisions are arranged in linear fashion.

They are interpreted usually as four megaspores arranged as a linear tetrad. The cell that gives rise to the linear tetrad is known as the megasporocyte.

As noted above, the name megaspore has been assigned to the cells of the linear tetrad on the basis of comparison with the heterosporous cryptogams, in which the megaspores are markedly larger than the microspores.

Soon after the formation of the linear tetrad, three of the four

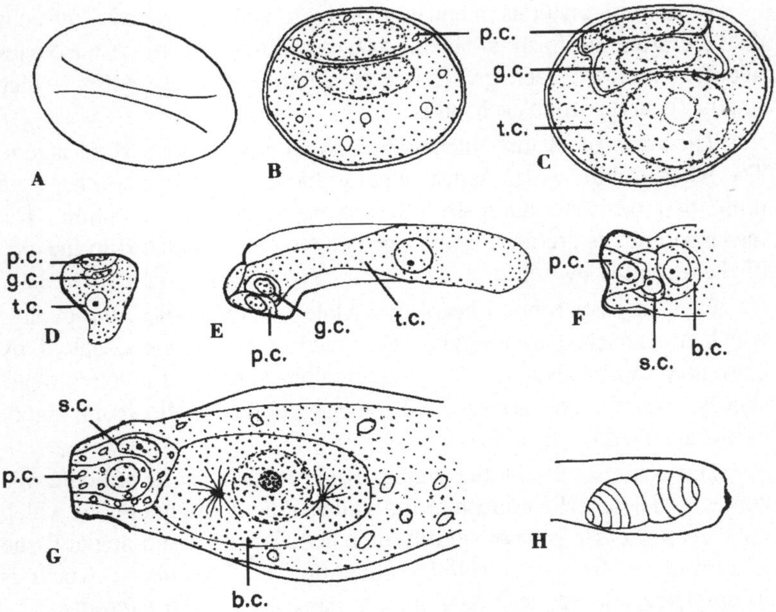

Figure 9.2: Zamia sp. Development of gametophyte. A. Surface view of microspore. B. Sectional view of microspore showing prothallial cell. C. Sectional view of microspore (pollen grain) at shedding stage; note immature d gametophyte, consisting of prothallial cell, generative cell, and tube cell. D, E. Germination of pollen grain with development of the tubelike haustorial protuberance; note migration of tube nucleus. F. Pollen-grain end of d gametophyte some time after pollination; note prothallial cell, stalk cell, and body cell. G. Pollen-grain end of d gametophyte; note prothallial cell, stalk cell, and body-cell nucleus in prophase. H. Two sperm cells in pollen tube. b.c., body cell; g.c., generative cell; p.c., prothallial cell; s.c., stalk cell; t, c. , tube cell. A-C. X 1030. D-H.

megaspores degenerate. The survivor, usually the one farthest from the micropyle, hence the *chalazal* one, appears to appropriate the products of the degeneration of the nonfunctional megaspores, and it increases in size as a result.

This increase in size also depends on the transfer of nutriment from the fleshy megasporangial tissues to the megaspore. The latter never contains large amounts of stored metabolites, as do the megaspores of the heterosporous cryptogams. This surviving megaspore, which gives rise to the female gametophyte, is known as the *functional megaspore*.

Reproduction: the gametophytes. As in many species of *Selaginella*, the microspores begin their development into male gametophytes, and the megaspores their development into female gametophytes, while still enclosed by their respective sporangia.

The early stages of the male gametophytes are also intrasporal, and those of the female gametophyte are permanently so in seed plants. When the microspore separates from the tetrad, it is uninucleate. A single nuclear division and cytokinesis then take place within the microspore.

This results in the formation of a small *prothallial cell* and a larger cell. The male gametophyte is considered to consist of a single vegetative cell, the prothallial cell, and an antheridial remnant. A second nuclear cell division in the large cell forms a small *generative cell* and a large *tube cell*.

When the male gametophytes have attained this stage of development, the microsporophylls separate slightly, apparently by elongation of the internodes of the axis of the microstrobilus, thus exposing the microsporangia to the air.

During microsporogenesis and subsequently, the surface cells of the microsporangium thicken, except for a vertical belt over the summit. When the microsporangia are exposed, drying effects their bivalvelike rupture along a vertical line of dehiscence.

The microspore walls containing the immature male gametophyte thus are shed from the microsporangium in the three-celled stage. They are known as pollen grains at the time of shedding. In the vicinity of Miami, Florida, this occurs between December and February each year.

A *pollen* grain is a microspore containing an immature male gametophyte. The wall of the pollen grain consists of several layers. Changes now take place in the megastrobili and the ovules within them.

A slight elongation of the internodes, beginning at the base of the megastrobilus and extending gradually to the higher nodes, separates the hitherto contiguous sporophylls by 0.3- to 0.6-cm crevices. It is through the latter that the windborne pollen grains sift into the megastrobilus.

During this period, the cells at the apex of the megasporangium disintegrate, and a droplet of colloidal material known as the *pollination droplet is* secreted. The breakdown of these cells results in the formation of a small depression, the *pollen chamber*, at the apex of the megasporangium.

A number of pollen grains come to rest in the pollination droplet when it protrudes through the micropyle, the latter a tubular passageway through the integument. As the pollination droplet dries, it contracts, carrying the pollen grains into the pollen chamber.

The actual transfer of the pollen grains from the microsporangia to the micropyle of the ovule is known as *pollination*. When the pollen grains have come to rest on the walls and base of the pollen chambers, their protoplasts protrude from the pointed pole through the portion of their wall that lacks an outer layer, and they form tubelike haustoria into which the tube nuclei migrate in each case.

These pollen tubes digest their way through the sterile tissue of the megasporangium, at first in a radial direction but then curving toward the apex of the developing female gametophyte. That they accumulate some of the substance digested from the megasporangium tissue is indicated by the appearance of starch grains in the elongating pollen tubes.

The tubes are unbranched or sparingly branched. As many as 14 pollen tubes may be present within the apical tissues of a single ovule. The tubes may attain a length of 2-4 mm. Shortly after the pollen tube has been initiated, about a week after pollination, the generative cell divides to form a stalk *cell* and a *body cell*; the former name is based on the supposed homology with an antheridial stalk, while the latter refers to the antheridium itself.

It has recently been suggested that the stalk cell is a sterile spermatogenous cell, while the body cell is, of course, a fertile one. Hence, the stalk cell is sometimes referred to as the sterile cell and the body cell as the spermatogenous cell. The body cell enlarges gradually as the pollen tube lengthens.

The prothallial, stalk, and body cells all remain at the pollen-grain end of the elongating pollen tube. Meanwhile, the thin-walled functional megaspore within the megasporangium has begun to enlarge. The tissue immediately surrounding it becomes vacuolated, forming a so-called spongy layer.

The latter seems to function like a tapetum, its protoplasmic contents contributing to the enlargement and subsequent development of the functional megaspore. The nucleus of the megaspore now begins a period of repeated free-nuclear divisions. This results, at first, in the formation of a number of nuclei that lie in a peripheral layer of cytoplasm just within the cell wall of the original megaspore; the center of the latter is occupied by a large vacuole.

As free-nuclear divisions continue, however, additional cytoplasm is synthesized, so that the vacuole is obliterated gradually, and the megaspore lumen, which has been increasing constantly by absorption of the surrounding megasporangial tissues, is ultimately filled with large numbers of nuclei and watery cytoplasm. As the female gametophyte matures, it is surrounded by two layers.

The innermost, contiguous to the female gemetophyte, is the true *megaspore wall*. On this is deposited a layer of material derived from the degenerated sterile tissue of the megasporangium, sometimes called the "tapetum"; this deposition is called the *tapetal membrane*.

Since the megaspore is never discharged from the megasporangium, this augmentation of the megaspore wall by the tapetal membrane is sometimes considered a vestigial attribute persisting from free-spored precursors.

Pettitt (1977b) has investigated ultrastructurally the wall of the megaspore of several cycads. He found that the detritus deposited on the wall (to form the tapetal membrane) contains lipids and sporopollenin. He emphasized that there are many similarities in the organization of the megaspore and pollen grain surfaces.

Pettitt (1977c) investigated chemically the pollen and ovules of several cycads. He found that enzymatic proteins were present in the walls of pollen grains and suggested that these may be involved in penetration of the megasporangium.

He reported further the probability that a lectin was present in the female gametophyte and megaspore wall and suggested that this substance may be involved in discrimination between two sperms at the time of fertilization.

Cell-wall formation is then initiated in the free-nuclear female gametophyte, at first between the peripheral nuclei, and it continues in a centripetal direction until the female gametophyte is entirely cellular.

The details of the formation of the cellular female gametophyte from its freenuclear precursor have not been satisfactorily elucidated for any gymnosperm. Four (sometimes fewer) cells of the micropylar pole of the female gametophyte now function as archegonial initials.

Each of them, by cell and nuclear division, forms an extremely large archegonium consisting of four neck cells and a large central cell. Just before maturation, the nucleus of each central cell undergoes mitosis, forming the egg and ventral canal nuclei, which usually are not separated by cytokinesis.

The vegetative cells of the female gametophyte that surround each archegonium form a *jacket* layer, the cells of which presumably function in the transfer of nutriments to the developing egg and proembryo. The egg cytoplasm projects into these cells through small pitlike apertures. The egg cell may attain dimensions of 3.0 by 1.5 mm and is readily visible to the naked eye.

The egg nucleus may attain a diameter of 550 μm. Megasporogenesis and the maturation of the female gametophyte occupy about 5 months in *Zamia integrifolia*. During this period, all the component tissues of the ovule increase greatly by cell division, as do the megasporophylls and the strobilus axis.

It has been demonstrated that the epidermis of the integument of the ovule has stomata, and that stomata also may be present on the surface of the megasporangium. Median sections of ovules containing mature female gametophytes are shown in figures elsewhere in this chapter.

During the development of the female gametophyte, the haustorial pollen tubes progressively digest the tissues of the megasporangium. As the archegonia mature, subapical cells of the female gametophyte increase slightly in size and number, so that the group of archegonia comes to lie in a slight depression, the *archegonial chamber*, sometimes called the *fertilization chamber*, which is about 2 mm in diameter and 1 mm deep.

Soon after this, the pollen tubes complete digestion of the megasporangium, and the pollen and archegonial chambers then become continuous. Just prior to this, usually late in May, the body cell divides to form two sperm cells. These contain very large nuclei invested with a delicate layer of cytoplasm.

During the enlargement of the body cell and its nuclear division, two centrosomelike bodies, currently called *blepharoplasts*, with astral radiations appear in the body cell, and one becomes associated with each sperm. These blepharoplasts are about 10 p.m in diameter.

Electron microscopy reveals that each has a single surface layer of about 20,000 procentrioles; these apparently become the centrioles, or basal bodies, of the numerous flagella (cilia) of the sperm.

The flagella are arranged in a spiral pattern. Each of these spirals ultimately generates a great many short flagella or cilia. The mature sperms now are liberated from the body cell, become motile, and swim actively within the pollen tube.

The sperms of Z. *integrifolia* may attain a length of 300μm; those of Z. *chigua* reach 400μm, the largest known in the plant kingdom. The pollen tubes are extremely turgid, probably because of the high osmotic value of the substances that have been digested and absorbed.

This is evidenced by the fact that the sperms continue their motility

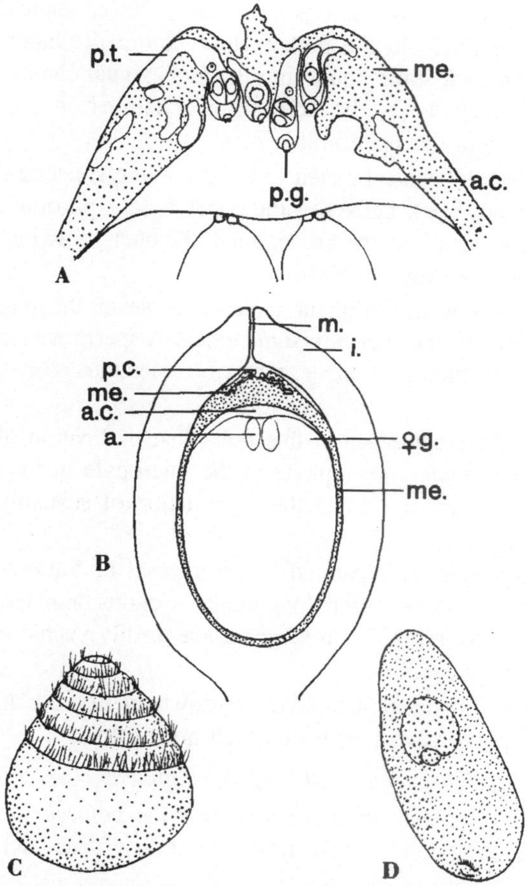

Figure 9.3: Zamia *sp. A. Longitudinal section of apex of megasporangium; note four maturing pollen tubes, elongating at their pollen-grain ends and protruding into archegonial chamber; clear spaces in megasporangium are segments of other pollen tubes. B. Median longitudinal section of ovule before fertilization. C. Single sperm cell. D. Egg cell at karyogamy; remains of flagellar band near apex. a., archegonium; a.c., archegonial chamber; 4 g., 9 gametophyte; i., integument; m., micropyle; me., megasporangium; p.c., pollen chamber; p, g. , pollen-grain end; p, t. , pollen tube.*

in a 20% solution of cane sugar. The pollen tubes finally burst and discharge the sperm.

Plants with pollen tubes are said to be *siphonogamous;* this means that the male gametes are conveyed by a tube to the egg cells. Strictly speaking, this does not occur in the cycads or *Ginkgo*, but it does in *Pinus*, *Ephedra*, and in *Anthophyta*; in the cycads and *Ginkgo* the sperms are discharged into the archegonial chamber from the pollen-grain end of the pollen tube. Observations of living material indicate that the sperms swim actively in the pollen tubes before the latter burst and discharge them with some liquid into the archegonial chamber; that the sperms swim actively in the archegonial chamber in the fluid that gathers there from the open pollen tube.

This fluid has been estimated to have a solute concentration of 0.6 M; that the four neck cells separate; and that a portion of the egg cytoplasm protrudes into the archegonial chamber, drawing the sperm or sperms into the egg cytoplasm.

This process is of sufficient violence to sever the flagellar band from the surface of the sperm in some cases. A sperm nucleus migrates to the vicinity of the egg nucleus, now of tremendous size, and nuclear union occurs.

It should be emphasized at this point that pollination (the transfer of the immature male gametophyte to the micropyle of the ovule) and fertilization (nuclear union and the culmination of sexuality) are very different processes.

In *Zamia*, they are separated by an interval of 5 months. Figures 20-16 and 20-17B show median longitudinal sections of an ovule at about the time of fertilization. The archegonia are readily visible by the unaided eye at this stage.

When the female gametophyte is grown in tissue culture, it can develop roots and leaves, both of which are haploid.

Reproduction: embryogeny and seed development

In the development of the zygote into the embryo in *Zamia* and other cycads, the zygote nucleus enters a period of free nuclear mitoses

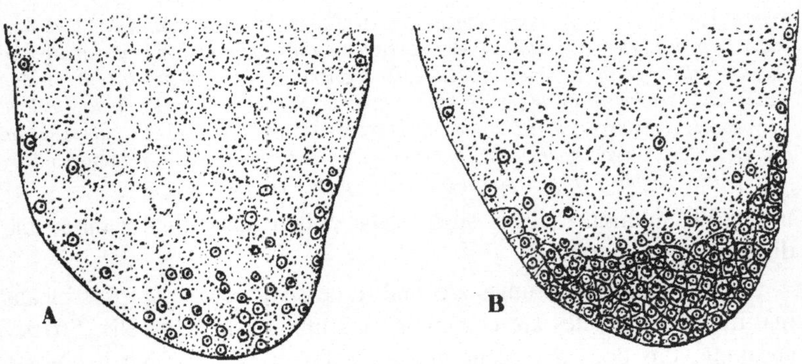

Figure 9.4: Zamia umbrosa. Early embryogeny. A. Base of archegonium with free nuclei of proembryo. B. Cellular proembryo.

that is variable in extent. In *Zamia*, approximately 256 nuclei are formed in the egg cell.

Development of the embryonic sporophyte has recently been studied in *Z. umbrosa*. Wall formation here is initiated among the free nuclei near the base of each archegonium and extends gradually toward the neck end.

Some free nuclei may remain unenclosed by walls. The lowermost cells of this intra-archegonial proembryo function as a meristematic zone, which is covered by a caplike layer.

An intermediate layer of meristematic cells toward the neck region of the archegonium ceases to divide; its component cells increase in length and force the basal meristematic cells and their cap out through the base of the egg cell into the vegetative tissues of the female gametophyte.

This elongating zone of the *proembryo*, the former called the *suspensor*, is augmented from the meristematic zone below. Although the zygotes of all the archegonia of one female gametophyte may initiate embryo formation (the phenomenon of *polyembryony*), only one embryo normally is present in the maturing seed, the others having aborted.

The embryo grows at the expense of the female gametophytic tissues, which are gradually digested. The uppermost cells (those nearest the archegonial neck) of the proembryo function as a sort of buffer zone that resists the pressure of the elongating suspensor sufficiently to cause the latter to become coiled.

The terminal, embryo-forming cells of the proembryo organize two *cotyledons*, between which is a minute terminal bud, the *plumule*. The axis of the embryo consists of a hypocotyl, which extends from

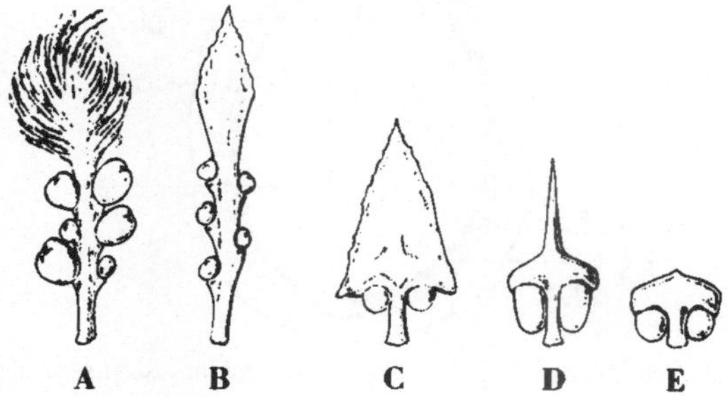

Figure 9.5: Scheme deriving Zamia type (E) of megasporophyll from that of Cycas. A. Cycas revoluta. B. C. media. C. Dioon. D. Macrozamia.

the cotyledonary node to the *radicle*, the embryonic root. The latter is covered with a special sheath, the *coleorhiza*.

During development of the female gametophyte, fertilization, and embryogeny, the entire ovule increases in size, and changes occur in the massive integument, in which three layers are more clearly differentiated. The outermost of these becomes fleshy and bright yellow-orange.

The middle layer is hard and stony, and the innermost remains soft. A median longitudinal section of the mature ovule, now the *seed*, reveals that it contains an embryonic sporophyte embedded in vegetative tissue of the female gametophyte, the latter surrounded by the remains of the megasporangium and an integument.

This statement regarding the seed of *Zamia* will serve to define seed structure in all gymnosperms. As the seeds ripen, the megasporophylls separate and the seeds are abscised. Mature seed-bearing cones are 10-12 cm long. Germination may follow immediately, and no fixed dormant period occurs, except as it may be evoked by the environment.

Germination of the seed may be hastened by carefully removing the fleshy and stony layers of the seed coat and then planting the seed on the surface of moist vermiculite.

The first manifestation of germination is the protrusion of the coleorhiza and enclosed root through the micropyle. The coleorhiza soon grows downward and is penetrated by the enclosed primary root.

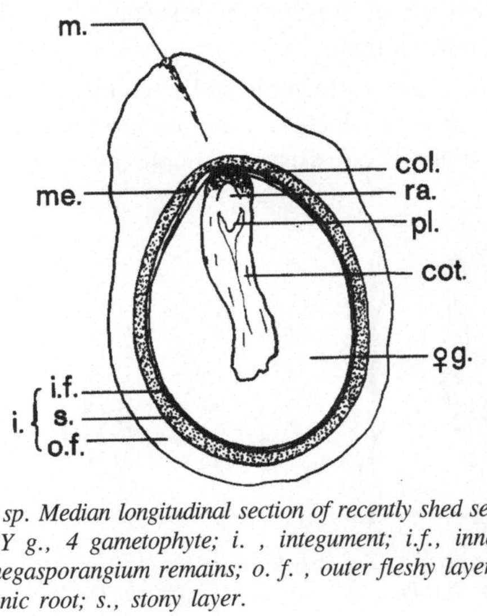

Figure 9.6: Zamia sp. Median longitudinal section of recently shed seed. Col., coleorhiza; cot., cotyledons; Y g., 4 gametophyte; i. , integument; i.f., inner fleshy layer; m., micropyle; me., megasporangium remains; o. f. , outer fleshy layer; p1., plumule; ra., radicle or embryonic root; s., stony layer.

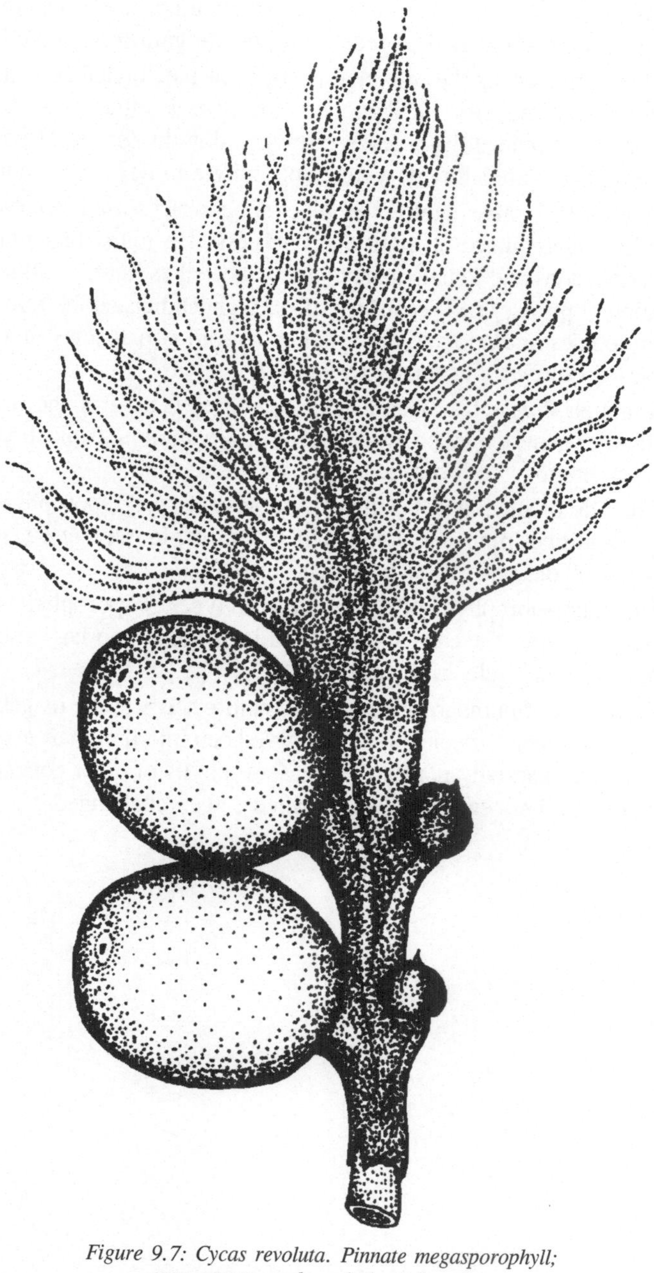

Figure 9.7: Cycas revoluta. Pinnate megasporophyll; note mature seeds and aborted ovules.

The tips of the cotyledons remain embedded within the seed, where they function in absorbing food stored in the female gametophyte cells.

After some weeks the proximal portions of the cotyledons emerge, and ultimately the first foliage leaf appears. Further growth and development of other foliage leaves are very slow in *Zamia*. More than 10 years are required for the young sporophyte to develop strobili.

Webb (1977) investigated the development of excised embryos of *Zamia* in axenic culture in light and darkness. He found that removal of the cotyledons and female gametophyte, as well as light, inhibited the elongation of primary and secondary roots: Light stimulated the formation of root nodules and apogeotropic root growth in two species of *Zamia* and one of *Bowenia* but not in *Dioon*.

Although *Zamia* has been chosen as representative of the cycads, several other genera may be available for observation in tropical regions or in conservatory collections.

Cycas is of phylogenetic interest because its megasporophylls are woolly, modified, pinnately compound structures, loosely aggregated at the crown of the plant, and not borne in strobili.

The microsporophylls of *Cycas* and both types of sporophylls in the remaining genera of cycads are localized in strobili. Rao has described the reproductive cycle in *C. circinalis*.

Variations of number of ovules and mature seeds in the megasporophylls of the several species of *Cycas* have been interpreted as evidence as to how the markedly nonfoliar megasporophylls of other genera may have evolved. This evidence has, however, been challenged.

10

Transport of Material

The movement of materials into and out of plants, and from place to place within the plant, was often mentioned in previous chapters without reference to the manner of movement or to the energy necessary for it.

The reason for this omission will soon be apparent. Energy is always necessary for the movement of material from one position to another. The immediate source of this energy may be in the moving object, or it may be in the environment of the object.

For a clear concept of the movement of materials into, out of, and within a plant it is necessary, therefore, that one distinguish whether the source of the energy which causes the movement is within the moving material, within the plant, or in some other external agency.

It will be much easier to attempt this distinction now by viewing in retrospect some of the processes already discussed and considering some additional ones. It is sometimes difficult, even impossible today, to make this distinction; but the major source of energy in many plant processes is not difficult to recognize.

Intrinsic and extrinsic sources of energy. Perhaps a crude analogy may clarify this problem of recognizing different sources of energy. The movement of a floating log in a river is dependent upon a source of energy obviously outside the log. The movement of a man swimming in the river results from a combination of the energy that moves the log plus a source of energy within the man.

By utilizing this second source of energy the man may move upstream. The movement of a boat in the river may be traced to the same source of energy we think of when explaining the movement of the log, plus another external source of energy that may be traced to the motor attached to it, or to the man rowing it.

The movement of materials into, out of, and within plants, like that of the objects in the river, depends upon several diverse sources of energy. The plant may have no active part in the movement. We must not be misled into thinking that the plant, being alive, can take in substances, move them where they are needed, and throw off those that are not needed.

The active agent may be the moving substance itself, and the energy that impels it may be external to the plant. Obviously such movements should be described not by terms implying that the plant "takes up," "takes in," and "gives off" the materials, but by terms implying that the materials are moving into, or out of, the plant.

The latter terms focus one's attention upon the really active agent, while the former imply that the passive medium (the plant) is the active agent. By common agreement the term absorption is used merely to indicate that a substance enters the plant, without reference to the manner of its entrance or the energy that moves it.

Movements of materials and the water medium within plants. In addition to recognizing the energy relations of moving substances, it is also important to visualize the water within the plant, since this water is the medium in which substances move.

We have already seen that leaves are composed of cells. In each living cell of the leaf a central vacuole filled with water and dissolved substances is surrounded by a thin film of protoplasm, which is in turn enclosed by a cell wall composed of cellulose and pectic compounds and sometimes of other substances also.

Similarly, all other organs of a plant are composed of cells. Water not only fills the vacuoles of the cells, but it also surrounds and is between most of the minute particles of which the protoplasm and cell walls are composed. Cell walls become much thinner when the water in them disappears by evaporation, just as a wet cardboard becomes thinner as it dries.

By weight, about 80 per cent of a growing corn plant in midsummer consists of water. We may therefore think of a corn plant as a branched column of water held in place by exceedingly thin films of protoplasm and cell walls. Substances that move into and within the plant are moving mainly in solution in this water.

Substances that move out of the plant are moving out of this water. The water also moves. These movements may be inhibited or retarded by layers of cork and by cell walls that are highly cutinized because the fat-like particles in these walls may not be embedded in water.

Movement of materials into and out of cells may be impeded also by the film of protoplasm in each cell. This fact may seem strange because of the large amount of water in protoplasm, but it is probably due in part to a greater accumulation of fat-like substances in the outer surface layer of the protoplasm.

For the present, however, we may accept and use the fact without accounting for all the intricate physico-chemical conditions of which it is a consequence. For many years students of plants have been trying to explain the movement of materials into, out of, and within plants.

Not all the questions raised have been satisfactorily answered, but enough has been learned for botanists to conclude that these movements are dependent upon the same physical processes that occur in non-living systems. Most of them have already been imitated in experiments by means of laboratory apparatus.

These movements will now be considered in more detail in relation to some of the physical processes involved. Mass movements. The flow of water in a stream and the movement of a current of air (wind) along the street are familiar examples of what is meant by mass movement. Frequently it is a flowing movement or current.

Mass movements of materials may occur in plants. If you put your finger in water and then withdraw it, a film of water adheres to it because of the cohesion of the molecules of water, and the adhesion of the molecules of the water and those of the skin.

These cohesive and adhesive forces between molecules at the surfaces of objects may result in tensions, called *surface tension.* Surface tension may cause the movement of water for short distances, and any substances dissolved or dispersed therein move with the water.

For instance, if two microscope slides are held closely together and one end is placed in a shallow dish containing a dye dissolved in water, a small mass of the solution quickly moves up between the two slides.

This is a familiar phenomenon to anyone who has frequently washed slides or dishes. Similarly, water may move into the small spaces between the fibers of a blotter, a piece of wood, or a plant, or into the pores of the soil. This movement of water into small spaces as a result of surface tension is often referred to as *capillarity*.

We have already seen that protoplasm may move about within a cell by flowing movements (protoplasmic streaming). Substances, such as food and salts, that are in the protoplasm are of course carried along in the same manner that a log is carried in a stream.

There may even be some movement of materials in this way between cells when strands of protoplasm extend from cell to cell through minute pores in the cell walls. Surface tension is one of the forces which cause protoplasmic streaming.

There is also a streaming, or mass movement, of water up the conductive tissues of a plant from the roots to the leaves. This movement is discussed in a later chapter.

In other chapter of this book we mentioned the fact that one of the results of oxidation-reduction processes in living cells is a small electrical difference between the parts of a cell and between the tip and base of a plant organ.

These electrical differences are mentioned here merely because they may affect the mass movements mentioned above and also some of the diffusion phenomena described below. For example, electrical polarity is thought to be an important factor in axial as well as lateral movement of certain substances in plants.

DIFFUSION

All soluble materials that move into, out of, or within plants move wholly or in part by diffusion. Plants may wither and become dry. Water placed in an open dish slowly disappears. We cannot see the water moving from the dish or from the plant, because it is moving in the form of free molecules that have separated from the liquid mass.

It is diffusing from them into the air, and what we see is the result of this diffusion. Later we shall see some of the results of the diffusion of water into a plant, and from cell to cell within it. Instead of water we may place some aromatic liquid, such as peppermint oil, in the open dish.

In a short time the presence of this oil in all parts of the room may be detected by its odor. Neither the oil nor the water has been destroyed, but the molecules of each have become widely dispersed in the air of the room. That is, they are now scattered among the molecules of oxygen, nitrogen, and other gases in the air.

Similarly, the odor of flowers and fruits is the result of the diffusion of some substance from them that we detect by our sense of smell. From these examples it is perhaps clear that we are using the term *diffusion* to refer to the *dispersion of material by molecular movement.*

Although we can neither see nor smell oxygen and carbon dioxide, there are ways of proving that they also move into, within, and out of plants by diffusion. If a water-soluble colored salt, such as potassium permanganate, is placed at the base of a column of water in a glass J-tube, changes in depth of color become apparent as molecules of the salt move among the molecules of the water.

These color changes accompany the slow diffusion of the salt upward in the column of water. Even the force of gravity does not prevent the upward movement of the molecules of a salt in the water. Similarly, any substance that is soluble in the water of the plant may move into the plant and from cell to cell within the plant by diffusion.

As we shall see later, some substances do not pass through the layer of protoplasm in the cells as readily as others. The accumulation of water in the vacuole by the process of osmosis and the swelling of cell walls or of a piece of wood by the process of *imbibition,* are merely processes of diffusion under special conditions with special results.

Even the mass movement of a stream of water up the conductive tissues of a plant is indirectly dependent upon the energy of diffusion. An understanding of all these processes evidently depends upon a fairly clear concept of the process of diffusion. One may begin by thinking of all solids, colloids, solutions, liquids, and gases as composed of molecules always in motion.

Anyone who has used a microscope has probably observed that the smallest visible particles mounted in a drop of waterfor example, chalk dust-are constantly in motion as the result of being bombarded from all sides by the molecules of the water. This is called *Brownian movement* after Robert Brown, an English botanist who first described it.

The smaller the particles of a given substance the more rapidly they move. While watching them one needs only to imagine more and more rapid movement of smaller and still smaller particles to form a mental image of molecular motion.

Diffusion is the result of molecular motion. Consequently the energy involved in all diffusion processes can be traced to the energy of molecular motion of the diffusing substances themselves. Each substance diffuses independently of the diffusion of other substances, except for the interference caused by one molecule colliding with another.

A substance will diffuse more rapidly into a vacuum than into air because of the fewer collisions with other molecules. Likewise, a gas, such as oxygen or carbon dioxide, will diffuse more rapidly in air than in water.

The energy of molecular motion is correlated with heat and is directly proportional to the absolute temperature. Apparently at minus

273° C. there would be no molecular motion and no diffusion. One may therefore think of the heat energy of the environment as being the source of energy of the movement of materials into, within, and out of plants by diffusion.

The heat energy liberated in the plant, by respiration would be an additional source of energy in this process, but a rather insignificant one. The radiation of energy from the sun is the principal source of the heat energy of the earth's surface, and this in turn becomes the source of the energy of molecular motion in plants and all other objects on the surface of the earth.

When a soluble dye is placed in the bottom of a slender glass tube filled with water, the greater concentration of the dye in the bottom of the tube at the beginning of the demonstration is evident by the deeper color there. Gradually, however, the color of the dye becomes evident farther and farther up the tube, and after many months the color is uniform throughout the tube.

The dye is now equally concentrated throughout the entire column of water. That is, the number of molecules of dye in comparison to the number of molecules of water would be the same in a cubic centimeter of the solution taken from any part of the tube.

Evidently for several months before the concentration of the dye became uniform a greater number of molecules of dye moved upward than downward in the tube. Since more molecules of dye are moving in any direction in the region where its concentration is greatest, the dye will diffuse from regions where it is more concentrated toward regions where it is less concentrated.

When the concentration of the dye becomes uniform, as many of its molecules will be moving in any direction in any part of the tube as in any other. When the above facts are fully appreciated it will be easy to see why carbon dioxide and oxygen diffuse into the green parts of a plant at one time and out of them at another time.

Each gas diffuses independently of the other, and solely in relation to its own concentration inside and outside the plant. The same principle holds for the diffusion of water, of a salt, or of any other substance dissolved in the water.

For instance, if carbon dioxide is used in photosynthesis in a particular cell, its concentration within that cell becomes lower than it is outside the cell. Then, according to the laws of diffusion, a greater number of molecules of carbon dioxide will move into that cell than out of it, until its effective concentration is again equalized.

If we gauge our language by our knowledge, we will no longer say that the plant "takes in" and "gives off" carbon dioxide; we will use expressions that imply that the carbon dioxide passes into and out of the plant. To be specific, we may say that it diffuses into and out of the plant. The movement of other materials should be similarly analyzed.

As our knowledge increases, it becomes more and more evident that a plant is a, complex system of materials and processes surrounded by another system of materials and processes that we call the environment; and that the same natural laws are operating in both systems.

Processes follow one another as a consequence of their dependent relations in these systems. To explain why a particular process occurs we must be able to show that it is a consequence of preceding processes.

Diffusion under special conditions. When the basic facts of diffusion are clearly understood they may be used in interpreting complicated processes in which diffusion plays a part. Among these processes are imbibition, osmosis, and transpiration.

IMBIBITION

We have already seen that a piece of wood is composed of cell walls. Even more familiar is the fact that when a piece of dry wood is placed in water or in a moist atmosphere it swells, or increases in volume and weight. Before the discovery of explosives stone was quarried by pouring water upon pieces of dry wood that had been wedged into holes drilled in the rock.

Even at the present time this method is used in quarrying marble and granite for special purposes. The swelling of wood is the result of the entrance of water between the particles of which the *cell walls* are composed. The entering water pushes these particles farther apart and increases the size of each cell wall.

This fact is easily demonstrated by placing a flat piece of dry gelatin, or agar, in water for a few minutes. Any of the solid or colloidal parts of a plant may increase in size in the same manner, but the swelling of cell walls, protoplasm, and mucilages are the most conspicuous examples.

The entrance of water into solids or colloids and the resultant swelling have long been referred to as *imbibition*. Evidently the energy of diffusion is involved in imbibition. The concentration of water is greater outside than inside the piece of dry gelatin or the dry cell walls of the piece of wood.

But the water also adheres to the smaller particles of the wall and forms thin films around them. The cohesion of the wall particles is overcome by the pressure of diffusion and by the adhesion of the water to them. They are forced farther apart by the entering water and the walls swell.

When a piece of dry wood is placed in water the water first enters the intercellular spaces, pores, and open vessels, forcing out the contained air. This movement is the result of surface tension (capillarity). It rapidly distributes the water into some of the xylem tubes and intercellular spaces in the wood block, but it does not result in increasing (swelling) the volume of the block.

OSMOSIS

The term osmosis is sometimes used synonymously with diffusion. It has been used also to refer to the diffusion of anything through any membrane. These uses are not acceptable, because there is no need for the word if it is a synonym of diffusion, and because the term is needed to designate diffusion through a particular kind of membrane under special conditions with special results.

There are certain conditions in plant cells under which the number of molecules of water moving from outside the cell through the film of protoplasm into the vacuole is greater than the number moving outward from the vacuole.

As a result, the water in the vacuole increases in volume and thereby presses against the protoplasm and cell wall. These structures become stretched and extended, and the whole cell becomes larger and firmer, or turgid.

When the enlarging cells occur in masses as in plant organs and press against each other, the mutual pressure among all the cells causes the whole plant to become rigid or turgid. When these processes and conditions become reversed, the plant wilts.

If there is any advantage in adding the word osmosis to our consideration of diffusion in plants, it lies in limiting its use to the diffusion of water through certain kinds of membranes, such as protoplasm, when certain other conditions exist. What are these conditions, and what is peculiar about these membranes?

The concentration of water in the vacuole is a factor in osmosis. When the diffusion of water is inward through protoplasm into the vacuole, one may infer from the general laws of diffusion that the *water* inside the vacuole is less concentrated than the *water* outside the cell.

This condition actually occurs when the concentration of dissolved substances (sugars, salts, organic acids) in the water enclosed in the vacuole exceeds the concentration of dissolved substances in the water surrounding the cell.

At room temperature (20° C.) there is a definite number of molecules of water in each cubic centimeter of pure water. If some sugar is added, the water then appears to occupy more than a cubic centimeter of space.

The reader will undoubtedly explain this increase in volume by visualizing the molecules of sugar as diffusing or moving among the molecules of water and jostling them farther apart. Molecules of sugar now occupy spaces formerly occupied by some of the molecules of water, and there are fewer molecules of water in a cubic centimeter of this solution than there are in a cubic centimeter of pure water.

The presence of the sugar molecules decreases the concentration of the water. Obviously the more sugar present the more dilute the water will be. In solutions of this sort the water is said to be the *solvent,* and the sugar the *solute.*

Many other conditions related in one way or another to the concentration of water sometimes appreciably affect osmosis in plant cells, but seldom need be considered in problems discussed in general botany. Four of these conditions will be mentioned briefly.

In a solution of water and sugar several molecules of water become chemically attached to each molecule of sugar; this is equivalent in effect to decreasing the concentration of freely moving molecules of water in the solution.

Furthermore there is a well-known law in physical chemistry from which we may infer that the concentration of molecules of sugar in the surface of the drop of water in a vacuole is relatively greater than it is in the interior of the drop, thus further decreasing the relative number of freely moving molecules of water in contact with the protoplasmic membrane.

In certain problems it is necessary also to realize that an increase in molecular motion of molecules of water in the vacuole caused by a rise of temperature in the cell beyond that of the external medium is equivalent in effect to increasing the concentration of water in the vacuole. Likewise an increase in turgor pressure in the cell is equivalent in effect to an increase in the concentration of water in the vacuole.

Differentially permeable membranes are factors in osmosis. The nature of the membrane, however, is as important in osmosis in plant cells as is the concentration of water. This fact may be demonstrated with a simple physical apparatus and also with living plant cells.

Membranes such as filter paper and cellulose cell walls are very permeable to both water and the solutes in water. This is only another way of saying that water and solutes can diffuse readily through these membranes. Such membranes are of no importance in osmosis in plant cells.

There are, however, certain kinds of membranes through which water can diffuse readily, but through which certain solutes in the water do not diffuse so readily. These are the membranes that are important in osmosis in plant cells. Protoplasm is an excellent example of this type of membrane. It differs in its permeability to different substances.

It is very permeable to water but under most conditions it is practically impermeable to the anthocyanin and some of the other substances in solution in the water in the vacuole. Membranes of this type are said to be *differentially permeable!*

There is a second type of differentially permeable membrane which is more permeable to certain solutes than to water: Sheets of rubber and cutinized cell walls are more permeable to carbon dioxide than they are to water.

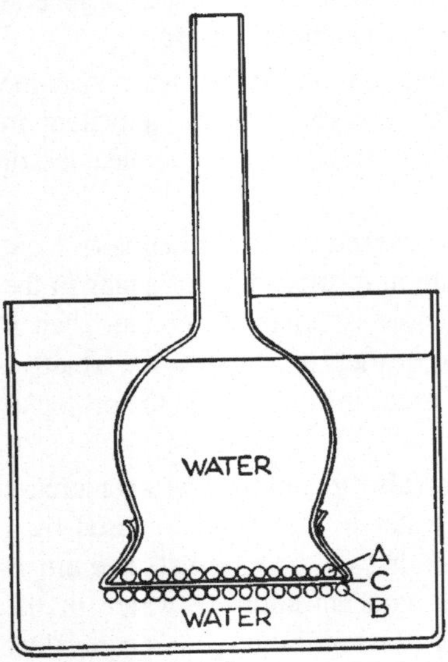

A

Figure 10.1: Diagram to illustrate the passage of water through a membrane.

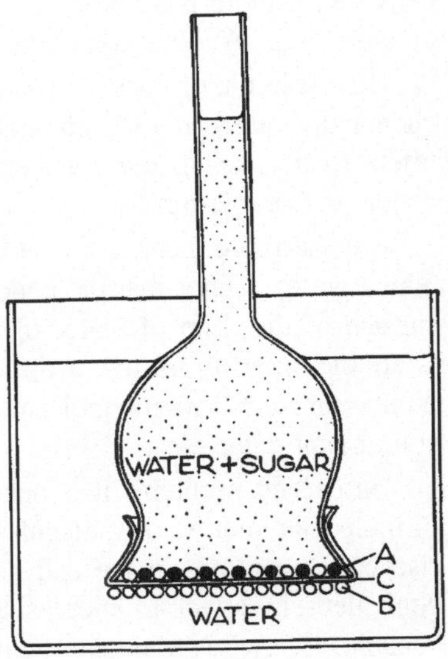

B

Figure 10.2: Diagram to illustrate osmosis.

Such membranes are of no importance in osmosis in plant cells, but they are useful in demonstrating certain principles of osmosis and permeability. Molecules of oxygen and nitrogen are smaller than those of carbon dioxide, but sheets of rubber are much more permeable to carbon dioxide than to the other two gases.

Consequently, if one ties a knot in the neck of a rubber balloon filled with ordinary air and then places it in a bottle of carbon dioxide, the balloon will gradually increase in size. Outside the balloon there is pure carbon dioxide.

In the air inside the balloon there are about 3 parts of carbon dioxide in 10,000. At the beginning of the demonstration, therefore, there must be about 3000 molecules of carbon dioxide entering the balloon for every one that leaves it.

Obviously both the swelling of the balloon and the pressure inside that stretches it result from the entrance of carbon dioxide. The entrance of carbon dioxide and the pressure on the walls of the balloon are consequences of the energy of molecular motion.

For a demonstration of the osmosis of water in a non-living system one *-nay* use the apparatus represented in figures elsewhere in this book. Various kinds of membranes and solutes may be tested by this means.

The thistle tube with attached membrane is first placed in a vessel of water as in figure elsewhere in this book to see if the membrane is permeable to water. The solute may then be added to the water in the thistle tube.

If there is a definite continued rise of water in the thistle tube the membrane is more permeable to water than to the solute. A temporary rise that soon subsides, such as one obtains with a membrane of filter paper, is due merely to the fact that the molecular motion of water molecules is more rapid than that of the molecules of the solute.

One may also tie the membrane across the mouth of a bottle filled with a solution and then immerse the bottle in water; or one may convert the membrane into a small bag.

Demonstrations that are even more instructive may be made directly with living plant cells. In a series of small glass dishes or hollow groundglass slides we may place distilled water containing different amounts of sugar varying all the way from none at all on one end of the series to as much as 20 per cent on the opposite end.

We may now place living plant cells in these different solutions and with a microscope watch what happens. At one end of the series where there is little or no sugar in the external water, the plant cells may become larger; a little farther along in the series the cells appear to remain unchanged in size and shape; still farther along they will decrease slightly in size. Toward the end of the series the protoplasm is partly separated from the cell wall, and in the last of the series the protoplasm has become a small mass in the cell, since the vacuole has entirely disappeared.

That is, the water that was formerly in the vacuole has diffused out of it. All these observations may be interpreted on the basis of the laws of diffusion and the differential permeability of membranes.

Perhaps it is sufficient to add here that where the protoplasm just began to separate from the wall the concentration of the water in the vacuole was practically the same as that of the water in the dish if the temperature was the same; where the cells became larger the concentration of the water in the vacuoles was originally lower than that in the dish; and where the protoplasm was separated from the wall the concentration of the water in the vacuole was originally higher than that of the water in the dish.

Since the protoplasm separated from the cell wall, it is the differentially permeable membrane of the cell. The bounding surfaces of plastids and nuclei within the protoplasm are also differentially permeable.

Instead of single cells, pieces of plant tissue may be placed in the series of solutions and the relative changes in turgidity and size of the tissue may be observed. When fresh-water plants are placed in salt lakes, water diffuses out of them into the lake because the concentration of the water in the lake is less than it is inside the plant cells.

Such conditions are sometimes referred to as *physiological drought*. There is an abundance of water outside the plant but its concentration is too low. A whole lake full of salt water may be as dry as a desert to a plant.

PLASMOLYSIS AND TURGOR

When the protoplasm of a cell separates from the wall because water is diffusing out of the vacuole, the cell is said to be *plasmolyzed*, and the process is referred to as *plasmolysis*. The shrunken cell is *flaccid,* and conversely the swollen cell is *turgid*.

Cell turgor may result from the entrance of water by imbibition or osmosis, or both. Other conditions being equivalent, turgor becomes greatest in the cells with the least extensible walls and in which the volume changes least.

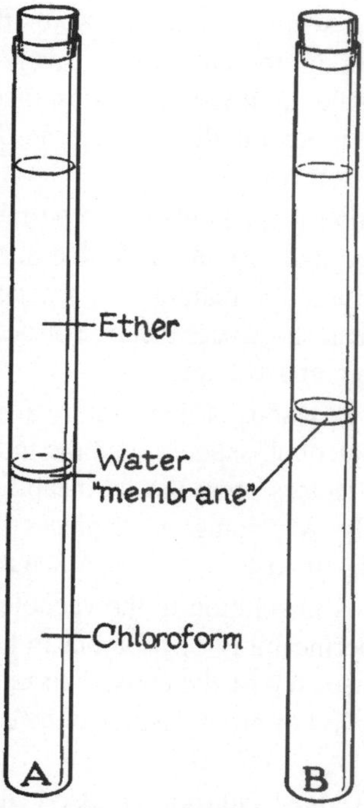

Figure 10.3: Diagram of apparatus used to demonstrate the differential permeability of water to ether and chloroform: A, when first set up; B, several days later.

Permeability

Permeability is a property of membranes that affects the movement of materials into and through them. At the present time it appears to be due to a number of qualities; we shall mention only the simplest ones here.

A differentially permeable membrane should not always be visualized as a crude sort of sieve through which particles can or cannot pass according, to their size. This fact is illustrated by the differential permeability of rubber membranes, through which the larger molecules of carbon dioxide pass more readily than the smaller molecules of water, oxygen, and nitrogen.

One of the features of premeability appears to be illustrated by a simple demonstration in which the membrane consists only of water. Ether diffuses through a water membrane more rapidly than chloroform: Since ether is much more soluble in water than chloroform, this demonstration is cited to indicate that the solubility of the diffusing substance in the membrane is one of the factors of permeability.

Solubility in turn seems to depend upon the relative attraction between the molecules of the substances involved. If the membrane were equally permeable to these two substances, ether would still diffuse through it the more rapidly because its diffusion rate is about 1.6 times that of chloroform.

The most interesting features about the permeability of protoplasm are (1) its variability, and (2) the fact that the continuation of life depends upon its variation remaining within certain limits. A great number of conditions and substances increase or decrease the permeability of protoplasm to water and solutes.

Among them are variations of temperature and light, or the presence of chloroform, ether, alcohol, saponin, and the ions of various salts. The influence of external factors upon the permeability of protoplasm may be demonstrated easily by placing small pieces of the red garden beet in water and exposing them to any one of a number of factors.

The anthocyanin is in solution in the vacuoles of the cells. If some factor increases the permeability of protoplasm beyond a certain point, this red pigment diffuses out of the cells. The influence of a factor that increases the permeability of protoplasm may be counteracted by another factor that decreases it.

For instance, if sodium chloride is added, the red pigment begins to diffuse out of the cells; but if a little calcium chloride is also added the influence of sodium chloride is annulled. The permeability of protoplasm at any instant in a living cell is apparently an equilibrium dependent upon the interaction of many factors.

The movement of materials into, out of, and within plants occurs by various combinations of physical processes. All investigations indicate that these processes occur, not because plants exert some peculiar vital force, but because these processes are universal properties of matter.

Their interactions in simple physical systems may be accurately measured, but the plant is such a complex system of structures and processes that it is difficult to detect these interactions in all their details.

We begin by recognizing the forces involved and then try to relate them to our present knowledge of plants. Among these forces we must recognize the mutual attractions among molecules of gases, liquids, and solids; surface tension; molecular motion and diffusion; and electrical forces.

Certainly we shall no longer think that substances move into and out of plants because they are good or bad for the plant, or because the plant needs or does not need them. Also we shall be less inclined to think and say that the plant "takes in" and "gives off" these substances.

The movement of materials into, out of, and within plants by diffusion is much easier to perceive and is better understood than movement by other means. Moreover, several of the common observable results of this diffusion are not difficult to analyze. We have therefore given most attention to diffusion.

A substance diffuses from regions where it is more concentrated toward regions where it is less concentrated, regardless of the concentration or the diffusion of any other substance with which it may be mixed.

This is the result merely of the relative number of moving molecules. There are many more molecules of a substance moving in all directions where the substance is most concentrated. Water may be diffusing out of a cell, while the solutes in the water are diffusing into the cell or vice versa.

The factors that influence diffusion most are temperature in relation to the rate of molecular motion, the concentration of the diffusing substance, and the nature of the medium into which it is diffusing. Diffusion under certain special conditions may be distinguished as imbibition and osmosis. Imbibition results in the swelling of colloidal membranes and cell walls.

Osmosis results in the enlargement of vacuoles. In the following chapter we shall note how diffusion that is called osmosis underlies certain plant behavior familiar to all of us. In later chapters we shall see how energy of diffusion is the force underlying some of the mass movement of materials within a plant.

11

Effects of Transpiration

Transpiration is essentially the evaporation of water from within plants. It includes both the vaporization of water at all cell surfaces exposed to the air and the subsequent diffusion of the vapor into the atmosphere surrounding the plant. In the chapters immediately preceding it was apparent that the diffusion of water molecules is a primary process in imbibition and osmosis.

It is also a primary process in transpiration. Transpiration is the most generally recognized of all processes in plants. Among the common practices based on this recognition are the daily watering of house plants; the elaborate systems of overhead and underground irrigation of gardens; the wrapping of cut flowers and freshly dug plants in waxed paper or other waterproof containers; the packing of nursery stock in moist sphagnum moss for long shipments; the enclosing of fruit and vegetables in oiled cloth or covered dishes in electric refrigerators; the periodic sprinkling of the floor and crates in the low-temperature storage of apples; and the placing of glass or paper covers over newly transplanted seedlings in the garden.

These and many other practices are attempts to reduce the more harmful effects of evaporation of water from plants or isolated parts of plants. Transpiration not limited to leaves. Transpiration may occur from the surface of any plant organ. Even the bark of trees does not prevent it entirely. "Sun-scald" of trees that have been transplanted from nurseries where their stems were shaded is the result of heating and drying by direct sunlight.

Mature potato tubers, in spite of a cork covering, lose noticeable amounts of water and shrivel in the course of time. The evaporation of water from roots in dry soil, or from roots during the process of transplanting may result in serious injury or death.

Transpiration from fruits in drought periods may result in shrinkage. The tips of tomato fruits may die as a result of excessive transpiration. The subsequent decay of these dead portions of the fruit is referred to as "blossomend rot."

After removal from the plant such fruits as prunes and grapes are often artificially exposed to warm dry air to hasten the loss of water vapor from them, so that they may be safely stored for future use. The harvesting of many seeds, grains, and hay involves the drying, or the acceleration of transpiration, under natural or artificial conditions.

High transpiration may result in the death of young flowers and in the cessation of sexual reproduction. Of the various plant organs the thin blades of the leaves of most plants have the largest evaporation surface exposed to the atmosphere, and it is in them that the greatest amount of transpiration occurs in the growing plant.

Cactuses are notable exceptions. The bulk of the growing parts of plants is water. As we learned earlier, all the living cells of a plant contain protoplasm and a vacuole filled with water in which various substances are dissolved.

Young tissues of plants may contain as much as 95 per cent water by weight, and older parts 60 to 75 per cent. When the water content of the active cells of plants is gradually decreased they become less and less active until a point is reached where injury or death results.

The leaves of most plants, therefore, with their high water content (60-85 per cent), their relatively large areas, and their exposure to an atmosphere that is usually only 10 to 75 per cent saturated, constitute the most important surface of water loss from plants.

Discussion in this chapter, therefore, will be confined largely to the processes and factors that influence transpiration as it occurs in leaves. Circumstances of water loss from leaves. In other chapter of this book the organization of water-conducting tissues and their distribution among the mesophyll cells are described.

Attention was called to the air spaces among these myriad cells and also to the epidermis which encloses the mesophyll cells, air spaces, and veins. The upper epidermis of the leaves in many species of plants is an unbroken layer of cells. Its outer cellulose walls may be thick and have a cutinized outer layer which is commonly called the cuticle. The lower epidermis, and frequently the upper, have stomates distributed among the epidermal cells.

Hence when the stomates are open the epidermis of the leaf contains many thousands of minute passages through which bases may diffuse into the labyrinth of air passages among the mesophyll cells, or diffuse out of them. Any gas may do this, and its diffusion is quite independent of the diffusion of other gases or vapors.

Molecular motion and consequently evaporation are accelerated by a rise in temperature. When the surface molecules of the water acquire sufficient momentum to overcome the cohesion by which they are held in the liquid state, they diffuse into the surrounding air.

The same is true of the evaporation of water that is dispersed among the particles of a cell wall. In the diagram of the diffusion of water from the vessels of the stem to the veins and cells of the leaf, and finally into the atmosphere, the paths of the diffusion of liquid water and of water vapor are indicated by arrows.

From this diagram it should be clear that there are two surfaces where evaporation of water occurs: first, the outer surface of the epidermis, and, second, the cell wall surfaces of the mesophyll.

The diffusion of water vapor from the outer surface is comparatively simple and is discussed under "cuticular transpiration"; that from the internal surfaces of the leaf is complicated by certain structural and physical factors and will be discussed under "stomatal transpiration."

CUTICULAR TRANSPIRATION

Let us now have another look at a leaf-first the outside. The epidermis of the leaf is composed of living cells all containing water and having more or less saturated cell walls. Some of the water molecules continually acquire sufficient energy to break the mutual bonds of cohesion and also of adhesion of the water to the wall molecules, and pass into the atmosphere.

The cuticle, which is the outer layer of the epidermal walls, reduces this evaporation to an extent which depends upon its thickness and its fat or wax content. The cutin simply decreases the number of water molecules that reach the epidermal surface since water molecules do not pass readily into fat-like and waxlike substances.

Nevertheless the cuticle is not wholly impervious and some water reaches the surface, vaporizes, and diffuses into the air. This water-vapor loss from the surface of the epidermis is termed *cuticular transpiration*. It occurs at all times, but less rapidly from leaves coated with cutin and wax than from leaves with little or no cutin. Cuticular transpiration amounts to only 5 to 15 per cent of the total water-vapor less from the leaves of most plants. The epidermis of many plants has small unicellular or multicellular outgrowths known as hairs and glands.

Some of these remain alive as long as the leaf or stem on which they grow; others die early and become filled with air. All living hairs and glandular outgrowths increase the cuticular surface of the leaf and also increase the cuticular transpiration.

Leaves of pumpkin and squash, nettles, tobacco, cultivated geraniums, and petunias have long-lived hair-like epidermal appendages. Dead hairs are common on leaves and stems of most plants. The mullein has a dense covering of much-branched dead hairs on all exposed surfaces, and on the leaves the felt-like layer on either side may be thicker than the blade itself.

Other examples of plants with hairy leaves are velvet grass, silky willow, Labrador tea, Shepherdia, Spanish moss, some species of sage, goldenrod, and aster. When the rates of transpiration in plants of equal leaf area were measured it was discovered that the rate of water-vapor loss from mullein is about the same as that from tobacco, which has very similar leaves but lacks the dense hairy coverings.

Mullein leaves are often mentioned as examples of leaves that conserve water allegedly because "the hairs cut down sunlight and wind." Further experiments with mullein show that these effects are quite unimportant and that the hairs do not reduce stomatal transpiration at all. They may decrease cuticular transpiration slightly in the dark and in still air.

Mullein plants with hairs removed from the upper leaf surfaces, mullein plants with hairs removed from both surfaces, and mullein plants with hairs intact, under the same conditions lost water at nearly identical rates.

Whether the shield-shaped hairs of such plants as Shepherdia are effective in reducing transpiration is unknown. But it is a safe assumption that hairy coverings are of no importance in "protecting" the plant from excessive transpiration in dry situations and in enabling them to survive in dry habitats.

Anyone who digs down to the very end of the taproot of mullein will be able to explain why this plant survives in dry habitats as well as in moist ones. This is deeper than many care to dig.

Of the numerous differences among leaves, such as those mentioned in other chaptrers of this book, a few may influence the rate of transpiration one way or the other, but a casual inspection of leaf differences is not a reliable means of discovering their influence on transpiration rates.

Very thick cuticles, waxy layers, and resinous layers on leaves and stems undoubtedly decrease cuticular transpiration; but their effectiveness in curbing stomatal transpiration of any plant cannot be judged by appearances. It can be ascertained only by carefully planned experiments.

STOMATAL TRANSPIRATION

Transpiration from mesophyll cells is similar to that from epidermal cells, but there are a few important differences. Let us first consider conditions on a spring morning when the soil is moist and the whole plant is turgid with water. The sun is up and the air is clear.

Under these conditions the stomates are fully open. The water-conducting tissues of the veins are filled with water slightly diluted by inorganic salts or other substances. The vacuoles, the cytoplasm, and the walls of the mesophyll cells are nearly saturated with water, and likewise the walls on the inner side of the epidermal cells.

This internal moist surface is 6 to 30 times that of the cuticular surface and bounds the labyrinthine intercellular air passages. The energy from the sun increases the molecular energy of the water molecules and their rate of movement is speeded up.

They leave the cell surfaces more rapidly and diffuse in all directions in the intercellular spaces, from which they diffuse through the stomates into the atmosphere. Outside the leaf, the atmosphere has a lower humidity and a lower concentration of water molecules.

Consequently the diffusion of water vapor will be outward through the stomates. This loss of water vapor from the mesophyll cells is far greater than the evaporation of water from the epidermal cells. Quantitatively it amounts to 85 to 95 per cent of the water that passes into the atmosphere from plants.

Evaporation of water from cell walls inside the leaf and the subsequent diffusion of water vapor through the stomates is called *stomatal transpiration*. When the leaf only is considered, it might also be called mesophyll transpiration.

The number of stomates is so great, they are so evenly spaced among the epidermal cells, and the individual pores are so small that diffusion of gases and vapor molecules from the interior of the leaf may be almost as great when the pores are open as if there were no epidermis on the leaf. Later in the day as the stomates gradually close, the stomatal transpiration is also reduced, but not much until the stomates are nearly closed, because the rate of diffusion through the stomates is dependent not upon their area, but upon the perimeter of the pore.

During the daylight period both stomatal and cuticular transpiration occur. At night there is usually only cuticular transpiration. This difference plus the effects of the higher day temperatures are shown in the following table in which the relative amounts of the total transpiration from certain plants during daylight and darkness under field conditions are stated in percentages.

Plant	*Daylight*	*Darkness*
Wheat	96%	4%
Oats	94%	6%
Alfalfa	97%	3%
Pigweed	97%	3%

Opening and closing of stomates. The opening and closing of stomates are obviously matters of first importance in modifying transpiration. The relation of stomates to the movement of guard cells was discussed in other chapter of this book.

The stomates on a plant are not opened or closed simultaneously, because conditions are not identical in all parts of a leaf or in the different leaves on the same stem. Consequently, when we say that the stomates are gradually closed, we mean that some are closed quickly, some are closed slowly, and others scarcely at all.

When we say that the stomates are closed, we mean that almost all are closed and the remainder nearly so. We learned earlier that oxygen and carbon dioxide, gases important in respiration and photosynthesis, diffuse into and out of the leaf largely through the stomates.

Here we are emphasizing water-vapor loss through stomates. In this connection it is well to remember that stomates do not open to promote photosynthesis and do not close to conserve water. During droughts they may open most inopportunely and allow further water losses.

In late summer they may close early in the daytime and restrict photosynthesis when all other conditions appear to be favorable. The turgor movements of guard cells are conditioned neither by photosynthesis nor by transpiration, but by a series of changes in these cells.

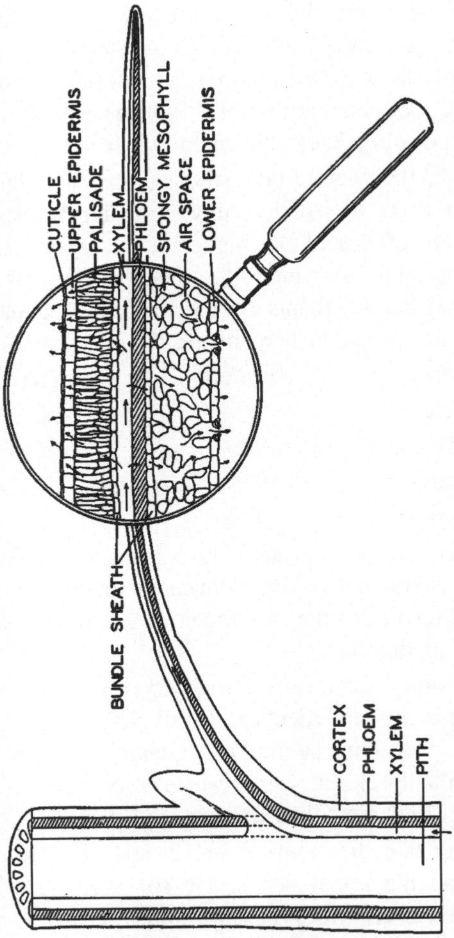

Figure 11.1: Diagrammatic section of a stem and leaf. Arrows indicate paths of movement of water molecules.

These are slight changes in acidity which influence the activity of enzymes and also the change from starch to sugar, or sugar to starch. Increase in sugar content leads to diffusion of water into the guard cells, and greater turgor. The stomates are opened.

Change of sugar to starch in the guard cells results in closing the stomates. Movement of water from veins to mesophyll cells. Let us, however, again turn our attention to the mesophyll cells. During the morning the sugar content of these cells increases.

They also contain salts, acids, and other soluble compounds that dilute the water. As water molecules leave the walls and diffuse into the intercellular spaces, other water molecules are pulled into their places by the forces of cohesion and surface tension. This cohesion of the molecules of water in closed tubes is so great that the pull extends all the way down the veins and vessels of the leaves and stems.

For example, when the cut ends of stems in a bouquet are placed in a vase of water, transpiration from the leaves results in a movement of water from the vase and up the veins of the stems to the leaves and flowers exposed to the air.

The removal of water from the cells of the leaf increases the concentration of the sugar and other solutes and decreases the concentration of the water. The water becomes less concentrated in the mesophyll cells than it is in the xylem of the veins.

Water molecules, therefore, diffuse osmotically from the vessels into the adjoining mesophyll cells, and finally into the epidermal cells, in both of which the concentration of water has been lowered by transpiration.

The lifting power of evaporation may be demonstrated by evaporation from a porous porcelain cup suitably mounted on a long glass tube, both of which have been *completely* filled with freshly boiled water. The lower end of the tube dips into a vessel of water and mercury.' When the porous cup is exposed to the air, evaporation occurs at the surface of the cup.

This develops a tension which is transinitted through the water column in the tube to the mercury, and the mercury is pulled upward. If the apparatus is carefully constructed and all air removed from the water, the mercury column may be readily pulled to a height of 120 to 130 cm.

When the cups were coated with gelatin and the size of the pores was thus reduced, a height of 226.6 cm. was attained. Mercury is 13.6 times as heavy as water, and when evaporation of water lifts mercury 226.6 centimeters it is equivalent to lifting water 100 feet. The height to which the mercury is lifted in such experiments is limited by the entrance of air into the cup or tube through minute pores.

The tensile strength of water enclosed in tubes is equivalent to at least 150 atmospheres, and the energy of molecular motion is sufficient to lift columns of water many times the height of the tallest trees.

When twigs of arbor vitae, red cedar, or box elder are used in place of the porous cup, transpiration may raise mercury columns 90 to 101 cm. in height before enough air enters the tube to terminate the demonstration. This is equivalent to a column of water 40 to 50 feet in height.

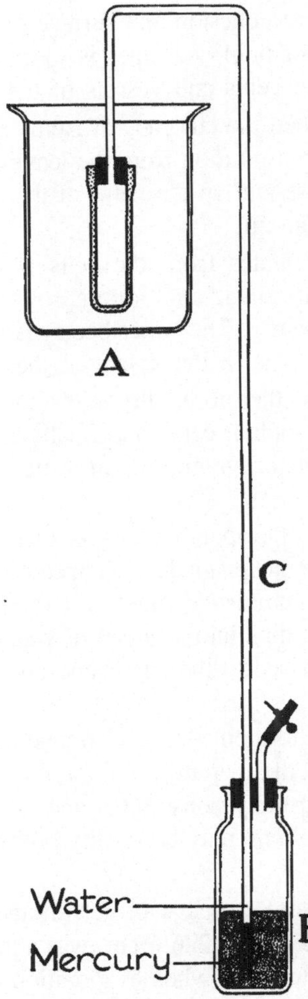

Figure 11.2: Diagram of apparatus used to demon strate the lifting power of evaporation.

During the experiments from which the above figures were obtained the height of the barometer varied from 73 to 75 cm. of mercury. Is barometric pressure the cause of the rise of water in these experiments?

Water-Vapor Gradient

Next to the opening and closing of the stomates, the most important factor influencing transpiration is the condition of the water vapor inside and outside the leaf. If the concentration of water vapor inside the intercellular spaces of the mesophyll is greater than it is outside the leaf, there will be a gradient in the diffusion of vapor from the cells of the leaf to the outer atmosphere. This gradient is augmented by the relative rates of molecular motion whenever the temperature of the leaf is higher than that of the atmosphere.

The gradient may be steep if the air outside is very dry and the air inside nearly saturated, and the temperatures of the leaf and the air are the same.

Under these conditions the concentration of water molecules is much greater in the air spaces of the leaf than in the atmosphere. If the temperature of the leaf becomes higher than that of the atmosphere the gradient will be increased because within the air spaces the number of free molecules is increased as well as their rate of movement.

If the temperature of the leaf becomes lower than that of the atmosphere the gradient will be reduced because the number of free molecules within the air spaces and their rate of movement are decreased. Let us assume that during the course of a clear warm morning in summer the temperatures of both the atmosphere and the leaf are gradually raised from 68° F. to 86° F.

The concentration of water vapor in the atmosphere changes very little, because the volume of air is so enormous and the air is continually moved by currents. Inside the leaf the same rise in temperature results in rapid increase in water-vapor content, because the volume of the intercellular spaces is very small compared with the evaporation surface.

Calculations indicate that the vapor diffusion gradient between the inside of the leaf and the atmosphere has increased 2.5 times. If now the internal temperature of the leaf rises an additional 9° above that of the air, the gradient is increased to 4 times what it was in the early morning.

Assuming that there is an abundant supply of water within the plant and the stomates are open, the rate of transpiration would be about 4 times as great. Guard cells may open and close stomates and thus accelerate or stop stomatal transpiration.

But when the stomates are even partially open the most important factor is the water-vapor gradient from inside the leaf to the air outside. Intensity of sunlight and transpiration. Under good growing conditions light intensities naturally occurring in daytime are sufficient to result in the opening of the stomates, except on extremely cloudy days and when the plants are densely shaded. Sunlight thus indirectly accelerates transpiration.

Furthermore, the radiant energy of sunlight directly increases transpiration in humid climates, because it raises the internal temperatures of exposed leaves above that of the air, sometimes as much as 5° to 10° F.

This in midsummer is enough to double or treble the vapor diffusion gradient between the inside of the leaf and the atmosphere. In the shade, leaf temperatures are about the same as those of the air, or lower. When the atmosphere is very dry, leaf temperatures in the shade may be several degrees cooler than air temperature.

SOIL WATER AND TRANSPIRATION

Another factor that greatly influences transpiration is the water content of the soil. Even though the stomates are open and other conditions favor high transpiration, if the water supply in the soil becomes low, transpiration may be markedly decreased.

If the soil water in immediate contact with the roots is soon exhausted, water in the xylem vessels of the stem and roots fails to diffuse into the leaf cells as rapidly as it evaporates from them.

There is an increase of tension in the water in the veins and vessels of the leaf, the stem, and finally of the root; the mesophyll cell walls become less and less saturated hence fewer water molecules leave the cell surfaces. The percentage of water in leaves during dry periods has been found to be 5 to 10 per cent less in early afternoon than in similar leaves at night.

Under moist conditions the daily fluctuations may be only 1 to 5 per cent. Obviously even if the stomates are open the rate of transpiration is reduced, since the mesophyll walls are drier by midday than they were in the early morning.

A dandelion plant rooted in a shaded ravine bottom may lose 5 to 10 times as much water as a similar plant living near the top of the southfacing slope of the same ravine. The lower plant has a constant soilwater supply; the upper plant has a very limited supply.

A corn plant in a moist region may lose more water in a season than a similar plant in a dry region, simply because there is more water available. If the corn plants in the dry region were growing in irrigated fields, they would lose more whiter than the plants in moist regions.

If the soil is dry and little water passes into the plant, transpiration from the leaf and stem surfaces may lead to wilting and finally to the death of the cells of the leaves, the stem, and the roots. This is death by desiccation. The lower or older leaves usually dry out first and the younger leaves last.

Water-holding substances. Another effective factor that may retard transpiration is the presence within the plant tissues of colloidal gels such as pectic compounds, mucilages, and gums. When saturated, these compounds, like saturated jelly, have little effect on the rate of evaporation of water from them; but as their water content decreases, the force by which the remaining water is held increases.

Many succulents contain these compounds. Cacti, which contain mucilages and are highly cutinized, may retain sufficient water for life and renewal of growth for a year or more.

Even such thin leaves as those of tobacco, when removed from the plant, may retain sufficient water to keep them pliable for weeks in a room where most other leaves become desiccated and brittle.

Wind. Moderate air currents may accelerate transpiration by the removal of more or less saturated layers of air from the immediate surfaces of the plant. When these layers have been removed further increase in wind velocity has little or no effect on the rate of transpiration.

The Pull of Transpiration

One of the consequences of transpiration that extends throughout the plant is the movement of water to the leaves from other organs. The net result of all the diffusions of water molecules in leaves from vessels to mesophyll and epidermal cells is that water, because of the cohesion of its molecules when confined in small tubes, is pulled forward in the veins of the leaf and the vessels of the stem.

It is this pull upon the continuous water columns in the xylem vessels of stems that accelerates the movement of water to the leaves at the tops of trees. If during rapid transpiration the upward movement of water is stopped by compressing the stern or by severing the stem from the roots, the water in the veins of the leaf and in the vessels of the stem is soon depleted.

No more water passes to the mesophyll cells and the epidermis. Transpiration continues and leads to the loss of turgor of the mesophyll and epidermal cells. The stomates are closed by the loss of turgor of the guard cells, and the rigidity of the leaf declines-the leaf is "wilting."

On a clear warm day in midsummer the same sort of thing happens in an intact plant, but it does not always proceed so far. If the rate of transpiration is more rapid than the rate at which water enters from the soil and is drawn up the stem into the leaf, turgor decreases and stomates gradually close.

Cuticular transpiration alone continues, and the transpiration rate is greatly reduced. Water continues to move up from the roots through the stem and into the leaf cells; and after a time the water content of all cells is restored, and the cells become turgid. Under the conditions assumed in this paragraph the leaves may not regain their customary rigidity before evening.

The stomates, however, may remain closed until after sunrise the following morning. During dry periods in summer, water may move to the leaves from nearby fleshy fruits on a tree, and as a result the fruits become shriveled. The water is kept from the fruits by the pull of transpiration from the leaves.

TRANSPIRATION AFFECTS PLANT DEVELOPMENT AND DISTRIBUTION

Environmental factors that affect the rates of transpiration, photosynthesis, or respiration often limit the development and distribution of plants. In green plants both photosynthesis and respiration are essential processes. Without them these plants neither grow nor survive very long.

When respiration continuously exceeds photosynthesis green plants die of starvation. Although transpiration, unlike respiration and photosynthesis, is not known to be essential to plants, its harmful effects become apparent when water loss exceeds absorption and results in wilting, desiccation, and even death.

Excessive transpiration may profoundly affect food synthesis, growth, and the formation of flowers, fruits, and seeds. It is often an effective factor in limiting the geographic distribution of individual plants and of plant communities. Because of its effects on the qualities and yields of crop plants, transpiration has been an ever-present influence in the regional allocation of crops in the United States.

Throughout human history it has been one of the primary factors that limited the population of various geographic regions. Tissue development in the growing regions of plants depends upon an adequate water content in the cells. The enlargement of cells and tissues ceases when transpiration exceeds the water supply.

During hot dry weather in summer a plant exposed to full sunlight may be actually smaller in the evening that it was in the early morning. Tree trunks may be measurably smaller in diameter in late afternoon than they were in early morning.

Each spring we may observe the opening of buds and the growth of new leaves on trees and shrubs. There is little cell division after the leaves are one-fourth grown, and further expansion is the result of the growth of cell walls and the osmotic absorption of water in the cells of the leaf.

During warm moist weather the volume of a young growing leaf may become doubled during one night. When transpiration exceeds absorption there will be no further enlargement. Likewise, any increase in size of other parts of a plant occurs by cell division and enlargement or by the enlargement of cells previously formed.

Consequently, the growth of all plant organs may be affected by transpiration. Furthermore, the rates of chemical processes (oxidation-reduction, hydrolysis, and condensation) may vary as the water content of the cells fluctuates, and result in changing the chemical compounds formed in these cells.

Some of the effects of drought upon the growth of the epidermis and mesophyll of leaves are illustrated in other chapter of this book. The effects of low water content in plants are most pronounced during those occasional short or prolonged periods of drought, of high temperature, or of low humidity, when transpiration greatly exceeds water absorption in many species of plants.

If a number of different species are exposed to these extreme environmental conditions, the effects OD their individual rates of transpiration, their photosynthesis, their growth, and their survival are usually different.

The vegetative tissues of certain fungi, mosses, ferns, and a few seed plants may become dry and brittle without being killed. They may survive in this condition for days or weeks, and resume growth when water becomes available. The vegetative tissues of most plants, however, die from the effects of excessive water loss long before they become air dry.

A deficiency of water within the cells of plants is sometimes referred to as "internal drought." Transpiration from seeds, bulbs, tubers, and other dormant organs is slow, and these are the only organs of many plants that survive prolonged periods of drought.

The *very* slow-growing and succulent species of desert regions and other extremely dry habitats may survive, grow, and reproduce in surroundings in which other species wither and die in a short time. Experiments have shown that some of these succulents, when detached from the soil and placed on a window ledge or table, not only survive for months, but may even bloom and bear fruit several months later. The extremely slow rate of transpiration from these plants in a hot desert climate is almost incredible.

Some of the differences in rates of transpiration among a variety of species of plants growing in diverse environments, are summarized in Tables elsewhere in this chapter.

Table 11.1: Rates of water loss per day in midsummer:

A single plant of corn may lose 3 to 4 quarts
A single plant of giant ragweed 6 to 7 quarts
A single young 10-foot apple tree 10 to 20 quarts
A 12-foot columnar cactus 0.02 quart
A coconut palm in the moist tropics 70 to 80 quarts
A date palm in a Sahara desert oasis 400-500 quarts

On an average day in the growing season a mature corn plant may lose the equivalent of 100 per cent of the water contained in it. On the same basis a date palm may lose 90 per cent and a columnar cactus .04 per cent.

Table 11.2: The water losses from single plants during a growing season estimated from experimental data.

Plant	*Length of season in days*	*Water loss*
Tomato	100	30 gallons
Corn	100	50 gallons
Sunflower	90	125 gallons
Giant ragweed	90	140 gallons
Mature apple tree	188	1,800 gallons
Coconut palm, Philippines, moist tropics	365	4,200 gallons
Date palm, Sahara desert oasis	365	35,000 gallons

Effects of Excessive Water Loss

When rains are frequent and well spaced throughout the growing season and the soil contains a favorable supply of water, the enormous losses of water vapor by individual plants, or by plant communities, are of little importance in the survival of the plants.

However, if transpiration in excess of water absorption leads to a reduced water content in tissues, photosynthesis is decreased and growth is retarded or stopped. If this retardation of processes takes place during the early life of many species of plants, the plants may not fully recover from these effects when subsequently supplied with an abundance of water.

Irrigation and dry farming are methods of balancing transpiration with soil water. The former is a method of conveying water to fields, and the latter of conserving water that enters the soil from natural sources during the years crops are not planted.

Irrigation

Long before the earliest historical records man cultivated plants in deserts and semi-deserts by irrigating gardens and fields with water from streams, lakes, and artesian springs. Egypt, for example, has practically no rainfall, but the government had organized irrigation projects along the Nile River as early as 4000 B.c.

Later it became the granary of the Roman Empire. The high transpiration rates of most crop plants can be sustained if the soil water is renewed at all times. Today more than 7 million acres in Egypt are irrigated and 2 or 3 crops of cotton, cereals, beans, sugar cane, and vegetables grow and mature each year.

At the present time more than 25 per cent of the land surface of the earth is too deficient in rainfall for crop plants without irrigation, and only a very small fraction of this land can be irrigated.

The half-buried cities discovered in some of the deserts of Asia are evidences of the former existence there of large human populations. As a result of shifts in rainfall patterns in these regions irrigation long ago become impossible and the inhabitants migrated elsewhere.

When the Aztecs established their capital in 1325 A.D. where Mexico City now stands, they built floating gardens in the nearby lake in which maize, beans, tomatoes, and vegetables were raised for the community. Seeds were planted in soil on large mats of interwoven branches which were moored in shallow water.

This scheme of irrigation brought the plants to the water instead of the water to the plants. Irrigation has long been practiced in our southwestern deserts, first by the Indians and more recently by the white settlers.

These irrigation projects made possible the cultivation of tropical and subtropical fruits and vegetables wherever irrigation water was available. At first these gardens were mostly of local importance; but with the introduction of better methods of harvesting, better refrigeration, and more rapid transportation, the desert gardens became big business, and the fruits and vegetables now enrich the markets of the eastern states.

Irrigation and Crop Yields

How directly crop yields are correlated with the available water in regions of high evaporation may be seen in the following results of experiments with corn at the Utah Experiment Station:

Acre-inches Water Added	*Yield in Bushels per Acre*
0.00	26.00
15.00	53.00
20.00	63.00
37.00	76.00

Similar results were obtained in experiments with wheat:

Acre-inches of Water Added	*Yield in Bushels per Acre*
4.60	4.50
8.90	11.30
17.50	15.30
30.00	9.6.60

Even in the eastern states where irrigation is usually considered unnecessary, market gardeners and orchardists have found it quite profitable to supplement the water in the soil from rains. During drought periods this practice has often led to profitable yields when nearby unirrigated crops were a total failure.

Geographic Allocation of Crops

During the early migration of settlers westward from the eastern seaboard into the great central valley, the selection of crop plants suitable for cultivation was gradually altered by trial and error. Temperature effects led to the early separation of crops profitable in the southern, middle, and northern states.

When new generations of pioneers invaded the grasslands beyond the forest border a new group of factors set limits to crop production. Not only does the rainfall gradually decrease westward to about one-half that at the forest border, but the rains usually occur in the spring and early summer.

Moreover both the amount of rainfall and its distribution are very irregular in successive years. The atmosphere is drier, and in late summer hot winds move in from the southwest and cause wilting, arrest of growth, or desiccation of immature crop plants which mature regularly in the same latitudes eastward.

To stabilize agriculture in the grasslands new crops or varieties were needed that could withstand high temperatures, that mature earlier, and that have smaller tops in proportion to the root system. Sorghums were introduced by the Department of Agriculture from the dry regions of Asia and Africa that met the above specifications.

Sweet sorghums were widely planted in the southern and mid-western states as a source of syrup and fodder. The shorter grain sorghums, especially Milo and Kaffir, are more dependable than corn. Still another sorghum called Sudan grass was proved to be a better source of forage in the southern half of the plains region.

Short-lived millets were likewise introduced from the Old World. South of Nebraska the yield of hard winter wheats was found to he more consistent than that of soft red winter wheats from the eastern states.

Northward hard spring wheats and durum wheats are profitable even as far west as the mountains of Montana. As a result of hybridization and selection at the experiment stations, many new varieties of all these plants have been made available.

They are higher yielding, less susceptible to injury by certain fungi and insects, and better fitted to the various local temperature, moisture, and soil conditions in the plains country.

DISTRIBUTION OF LOCAL PLANT COMMUNITIES

The differences among the native plant communities that develop in ponds, marshes, shrub swamps, swamp forests, and the adjoining upland are so marked that almost everyone can recall the distinctive appearance of both the plants and the communities.

In the pond are wholly submerged "pond weeds," some rooted and others not. On the surface may be floating algae or duckweeds, and extending above the water surface are water plantain, arrowhead, water smartweed, and many others.

The marshes are characterized by bul- rushes, cattails, sedges, and grasses; the shrub swamps by certain dogwoods, buttonbush, alders, and shrubby willows. The swamp forest is dominated by species of sycamore, elm, ash, maple, hickory, and oak.

There are also scattered small trees and shrubs beneath the forest canopy, and certain characteristic herbaceous plants form a ground cover. An undisturbed upland forest in the same region consists of another group of tree species such as the upland oaks, hickories, maples, beech, walnut, and linden.

It also has several layers of undergrowth-small trees, shrubs, and herbs. In the chapters on photosynthesis attention was called to the manner by which certain kinds of plants may exclude others in a forest by overshading them.

Likewise the discussion of respiration included the fact that only certain species of plants can grow submerged in water, or where the soil is saturated with water and deficient in free oxygen. Transpiration is a third factor in the elimination of species, and is most effective in upland forests.

Here high transpiration rates may cause wilting and death during periods of drought. Again the plants most affected are the seedlings with their limited root systems. But in very prolonged droughts certain species of trees in the swamp forest may be injured to a greater extent than the upland trees because they have shallow root systems.

In the complex forest communities the largest plants, while shading and reducing the transpiration of the plants beneath them, also have far more extensive root systems.

Consequently transpiration of the larger plants may decrease the water content of the soil so much during certain seasons that the herbaceous and woody plants beneath with small or shallow root systems die.

Another example of the effectiveness of transpiration may be illustrated by the vegetation in gorges. On the sides of the gorge are rock cliffs above long talus slopes. A narrow flood plain borders the stream. To picture the extreme conditions we may consider a section of a valley extending in an east and west direction.

On top of the cliffs the upland hard pines are the only trees that have survived. On the south-facing talus slope the mixed oak forest predominates, with scattered pines and hickories. On the steep north-facing talus, hemlock, beech, birch, maple, and tulip are dominant.

In the upland surrounding this gorge the vegetation is oak, hickory, and pine. Beech, hemlock, and birch have not survived above or on the south-facing slope. Evaporation is several times as great there as on the shaded, humid side of the gorge, and the water supply in the upper layers of the soil is exhausted much sooner.

Similar gorges where the upland climate is too dry for trees such as beech, hemlock, tulip, and birch may be found in many parts of the eastern United States. The trees in the gorges are living in a humid "microclimate" where drought rarely becomes sufficiently excessive to inhibit their development. The undergrowth in such situations is just as different from that on the south slope and the upland as are the dominant tree species.

MAJOR VEGETATION TYPES AND TRANSPIRATION

Transpiration when studied in the laboratory and greenhouse is often compared with evaporation from a wet surface. Under the experimental conditions the curves representing the rates of evaporation and transpiration are frequently very similar.

One may therefore be led to the conclusion that where the rate of evaporation of water is high in nature, the transpiration will also be high. This reasoning overlooks the matter of water supply upon which all transpiration is dependent.

Forests, prairies, steppes, semi-deserts, and deserts occur in regions of successively increasing drought and increasing evaporation from water surfaces. The annual evaporation may be 50 times as great from an open pan of water in the desert as from a similar pan in some wet forest region.

The annual transpiration from desert plants, however, is very slight when compared with that of plants in a wet forested region. Transpiration in nature decreases as one goes from forest to prairie, to steppe, to semi-desert, and to desert for the obvious reason that the plants in these formations have successively decreasing amounts of water available.

Their periods of greatest loss of water are more and more limited to moist periods instead of throughout the year. The date palm mentioned earlier in this chapter illustrates how great transpiration may become in some plants when there is an unlimited water supply.

The cactus exemplifies how low it may be when the water supply is reduced to a minimum. An acre of forest may lose 10 to 25 acre-inches of water in moist temperate regions, while an acre of prairie grass in Nebraska loses about 2 acre-inches.

If transpiration of trees were as effectively checked as in certain cacti without interfering with photosynthesis and respiration, the whole landscape east of the Rockies would be dominated by forests.

Is transpiration an essential process? Transpiration is an inescapable physical process in most species of plants. Is it merely neutral, or harmful, or is it an essential process comparable to photosynthesis and respiration? This question has often been discussed pro and con in botanical literature, and it is frequently answered without a clear analysis of the problem. In the case of a green alga or a flowering plant growing submerged in water, transpiration certainly is not an essential process.

If the plant is removed from the water and placed in the air, transpiration occurs only as an unavoidable process and its effects soon cause death. Transpiration goes on whether its effects are harmful or beneficial, just as water evaporates from a wet towel or any other saturated object exposed to the air.

Consequently if transpiration is an essential process in plants, it must be limited to those in which some part or the whole plant is exposed to the atmosphere.

One should be clear whether the term "essential" is applied to the survival of the plant, or merely to some particular quantitative difference in its development. We have already seen that leaves are thicker, have a thicker cuticle, more layers of palisade cells, and a greater amount of woody cells when they develop in dry air where transpiration is high than when they develop in moist air where transpiration is low.

Transpiration may be essential to many such quantitative differences among plants, without being essential to the survival of the plant. These differences are merely the ultimate effects of transpiration on development.

Among the claims that transpiration is an essential process are:

(1) that it is necessary to cool the plant on hot summer days,

(2) that it is necessary in the absorption and conduction of salts from the soil to the leaves,

(3) that it increases the water supply of the plant,

(4) that it regulates the water content of the plant,

(5) that it maintains the water supply of leaf cells, and

(6) that it would not occur in plants if it were not of some value to them.

The fallacies implied in the last four statements should be so obvious from data discussed in previous chapters as to make further discussion unnecessary here. Some additional data may help to evaluate the first two statements.

The cooling effect of transpiration is most frequently cited as its essential feature. It is claimed that if transpiration did not occur, the temperature of leaves in full sunshine on a hot summer day would rise to 150 °F. or more; this rise is sufficient to kill protoplasm.

The wellknown fact that the evaporation of water lowers the

temperature of the mass from which it is evaporating is sufficient evidence that transpiration has a cooling effect on the plant, but it is not sufficient evidence that it is essential, or that it prevents the temperature of a leaf from rising to 150° F. every day in summer.

When one compares the enormous differences in the rate of transpiration in the date palm, coconut palm, and cactus in the tropics he might expect them to differ greatly in their internal temperature. It is known, however, that the temperature of all plants corresponds fairly closely to that of the atmosphere in which they are growing.

The daily evaporation of water from the columnar cactus mentioned earlier in this chapter would lower its temperature less than 1/1000 of a degree, yet it daily absorbs sufficient radiant energy from the sun to raise the temperature and kill the protoplasm if there were no other way by which heat passed from the plant to the surrounding air.

A hot stove loses heat by radiation and convection. A plant warmer than the surrounding air also loses heat by radiation and convection. When the temperature of a plant is more than a few degrees above that of the surrounding air the loss of heat from the plant by radiation and convection usually exceeds the amount lost by transpiration.

The greater the difference between the temperature of the plant and that of the surrounding air, the less important is the loss of heat by transpiration in comparison to that lost by radiation and convection. The relation of transpiration to salt absorption and conduction is an indirect one.

The date palm mentioned earlier absorbs and loses 40,000 times as much water as the cactus plant cited in the same table. The roots of the coconut palm grow in both brackish and fresh water. If the absorption of salts depended upon the absorption and transpiration of water, one would expect to find corresponding differences in the salt content of these plants.

No such differences occur. Salts enter the roots of plants as molecules and ions by diffusion. This diffusion of salts is undoubtedly influenced by electrical charges, but, as we have already seen, it is independent of the diffusion of water into the cells.

After the salts have entered the plant, their movement within the plant is brought about by further diffusion accompanied by flow in the xylem tubes and by protoplasmic streaming. Transpiration may indirectly influence the total amount of salts absorbed by plants through its effects upon several other processes.

Two plots of bean plants were placed under experimental conditions so that the plants in one plot grew in a saturated atmosphere, the others in an atmosphere having only 25 per cent humidity. Transpiration was much greater in the plants exposed to the drier atmosphere.

These plants were not as tall as those that grew in the saturated atmosphere. Their root systems were larger in proportion to the leaves and stems above ground, and both their dry weight and salt content were greater.

That is, there was a greater amount of photosynthesis in the plants in the drier air, a greater amount of assimilation of foods, and a greater amount of salts absorbed. Here again is evidence of quantitative variations in plant development due in part to differences in transpiration, but such facts are not evidence that transpiration is essential to the plant.

One may say, however, that it is essential to certain differences in development, provided that these same differences cannot be obtained by changing some other process.

From the experimental data available it appears that the most efficient leaves are those that develop when the roots of land plants are well supplied with water and transpiration rates are moderately high during the periods when the leaves are growing.

The number of layers of mesophyll cells is greater and the mesophyll surface exposed to the air in the intercellular spaces per leaf area is at a maximum. As a result a greater amount of sugar may be made throughout the life of the leaves.

All these favorable effects of transpiration may be partially annulled by such conditions as an overabundance of nitrates, or by a deficiency of light or of certain ions of inorganic salts-for example, a deficiency of magnesium ions.

Most plant physiologists have come to the conclusion that wet cell walls, exposed directly either to the atmosphere or to the intercellular spaces, necessarily lose water to the surrounding air by evaporation. Through a long process of evolution stomates have become an hereditary structure in all the larger land plants.

The opening and closing of these structures have a marked effect upon the inward and outward diffusion of CO_2, O_2, and water vapor. When stomates are closed there is nothing to prevent the slow diffusion of water through all plant surface walls even though the walls contain cutin and suberin.

When stomates are open there is nothing to prevent the rapid diffusion of water vapor from the mesophyll cell walls through the intercellular spaces and the stomates to the atmosphere. This rate is greatly increased in full sunlight when leaf temperatures rise above that of the atmosphere.

If in the course of plant history a cell wall substance permeable to oxygen and carbon dioxide but impermeable to water vapor had developed, the present daily waste of water in transpiration from plants might have been eliminated.

12

The Main Transport Machinery

Several facts about stems have already been considered. We have seen that leaves and axillary buds appear on the nodes of stems in a definite arrangement, and that stems of shrubs branch at or near the surface of the ground, in contrast to stems of trees. Foods may accumulate in any stem, but a greater amount accumulates in some stems than in others.

The green stems of cacti and many herbs and the numerous young twigs of both shrubs and trees contain chlorophyll, and hence photosynthesis may occur in them.

In many processes previously discussed it was evident that sugar made in the leaves moves through the stems to the roots; that water and inorganic salts after diffusing into the roots move to the leaves through the stems, and that processes characteristic of all living cells occur in living cells of stems.

Some stems are shortlived; others remain alive and increase in both height and diameter for centuries. We have already seen that the direction and rate of stem growth are affected by gravity, light, moisture, and other environmental factors. In many sections of the country where deciduous forests prevail, the principal features of the forested landscape from late autumn until the early spring are stems.

What is a Stem?

The cylindrical, erect, aerial stems of most plants are readily distinguishable from leaves and roots. Many stems, however, are flattened leaf-like organs; others are succulent, and still others are so short that they are nearly obscured by leafy scales or rosettes of leaves. Many stems are entirely underground.

What, then, are the distinguishing characteristics of stems? A stem develops from the plumule (bud) of the embryo, usually bears leaves and flowers, and has certain other characteristic features, both external and internal. Examination of several kinds of stems will help us recognize these features.

Woody Stems

Stems 1 to 2 feet long of such plants as hickory, horsechestnut, or maple consist of several yearly increments of growth. The most prominent features of woody stems in winter are the dormant buds, leaf scars, terminal bud scars, and lenticels.

Leaves and branches usually occur only at certain places on the stem called *nodes.* The part of the stem segment between two nodes is the *internode.* The length of a twig or branch and the height of the plant depend upon the amount of elongation of the internodes.

We noted in an earlier chapter that deciduous trees lose their leaves annually and that the scar on the stem left by the abscised leaf is called the *leaf scar.* Within the leaf scar are smaller scars. These small scars are the severed ends of vascular bundles that extended from the leaf into the stem, and are known as *bundle scars* or *vein scars.*

The age of the twig may often be ascertained by counting the ring-like markings, the *terminal bud scale scars,* found at intervals along the stem. These rings may be used as a means of locating the position of a dormant terminal bud of some previous year.

The distance between two successive terminal bud scale scars is a measure of the growth in length of the stem during one year. This length may be used to compare the annual growth of stems of different plants, as well as the variations in growth from year to year on the same plant.

Scattered over the surface of the internodes are numerous small, roundish or elongated structures, the *lenticels.* When young, these are made up of loosely arranged cells through which gases pass into or out of the bark of the twig. Stomates are often present in very young stems, and the formation of a lenticel may be initiated by the division of cells immediately beneath a stomate.

Later cork develops beneath the lenticel. Owing to the peculiar growth of the bark of such trees as birch and cherry, the lenticels become greatly elongated and partly encircle the stem. Conspicuous external features of stems during dormant periods are the *buds.*

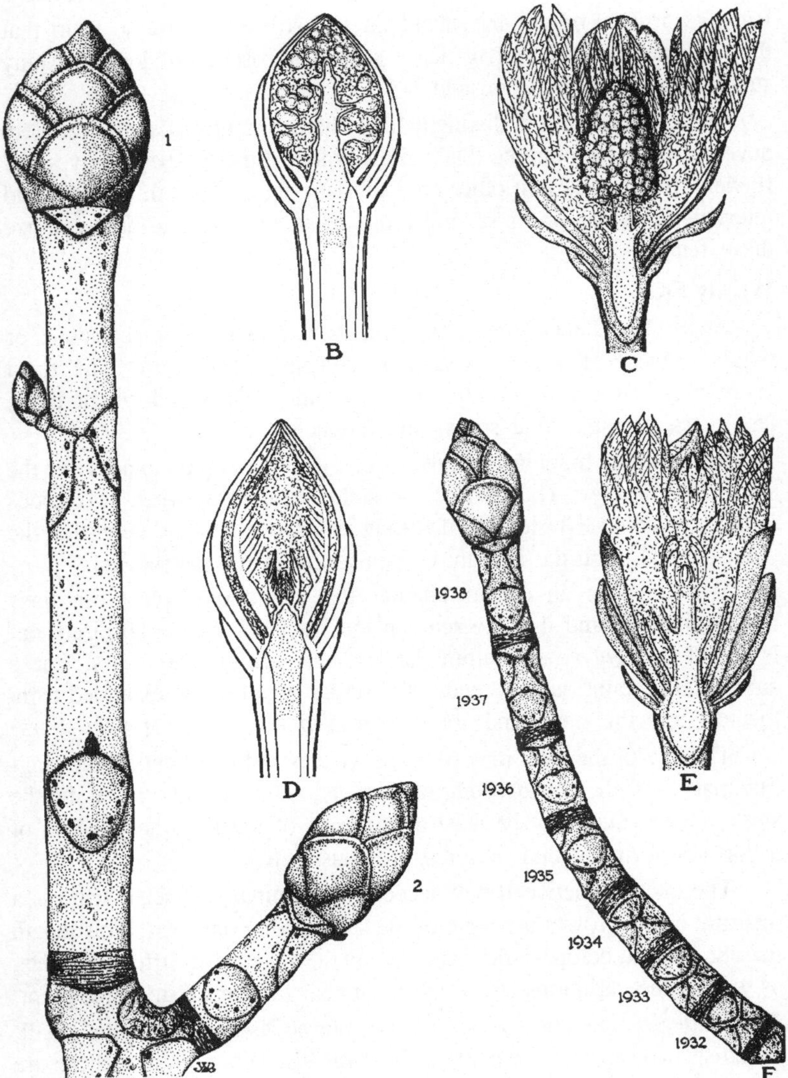

Figure 12.1: External features of stems and composition of buds of horse chestnut (Aesculus hippocastanum). A, twig bearing a terminal reproductive bud (1), and a lateral branch bearing a terminal vegetative bud (2) ; nodes, internodes, leaf scars, vascular bundle scars, terminal bud scale scars, lenticels, and the lateral axillary buds are also represented. B-C, longitudinal sections of reproductive buds: B, dormant in winter; C, unfolding in spring. D-E, longitudinal sections of vegetative buds: D, dormant in winter; E, unfolding in spring. F, terminal bud scale scars and other external features on a 7-year-old branch in which there was comparatively little elongation of internodes each season.

There may be only one bud at a node, as on most stems with alternate leaves. Where the leaves are opposite there are two buds at each node. On the stems of other species of plants there may be several buds at each node either arranged in a whorl about the node or grouped about the primary axillary bud.

In species of soft maple and forsythia these *accessory* buds are usually flower buds. The bud at the apical end of the stem is the *terminal bud;* all others are *lateral buds.* The terminal buds of some plants, such as willow, elm, hackberry, linden, and ailanthus, die and drop off in the spring of the year before the elongation of the internodes of the new stem segment is completed.

The last lateral bud formed on twigs of these plants appears to be terminal in position, if only a casual observation is made.

Bud Scales

The buds of most trees and shrubs of the temperate zones have external leaf-like scales, which are usually hard and fibrous as are those in the buds of oak, elm, maple, and buckeye. Less frequently, the buds are enclosed by stipules as are those of the tulip tree, magnolia, and some viburnums.

The scales are often hairy or sometimes covered with wax and resins. These scales decrease transpiration from the tissues in the bud but do not "protect" them from freezing.

In some plants there is a gradual transition from the bud scales on the outside to true leaves on the inside of the bud. Nearly everyone has witnessed the opening of buds on shrubs and trees in spring. Sometimes the hard scales on the outside of the bud are pushed off by the enlargement of the inner scales and young leaves.

In other buds the scales may elongate somewhat, but in a short time abscise and fall off.

Composition of Scaly Buds

The composition of a scaly bud may be recognized easily by removing the scales and other structures, or by examining longitudinal sections of the bud, or, better still, by studying unfolding buds in spring.

Each bud contains a *stem tip;* in most buds leaves have begun to develop on the stem tips. Such buds are *vegetative buds* (also called *branch buds* and *leaf buds)* and from them develop the leaf-bearing segments of the stems of the current season.

From a careful examination of perennial woody stems one may learn that the number of young leaves in the bud corresponds with the number of leaf scars on each annual segment of stem growth. What inference may be drawn? What exceptions have you seen? Are all the leaves of a herbaceous plant, such as coleus, present in the terminal bud at a given time?

A similar examination of some buds of elm, forsythia, cherry, peach, or soft maple will reveal a stem tip bearing young flowers, but no leaves. These are the *reproductive buds,* which are also called *flower buds* and *fruit buds*. Subsequent growth of these structures results in flowers and fruits.

In other buds, such as those of horse-chestnut, lilac, apple, and catalpa, both flower clusters and leaves are present. Such buds may be termed *mixed buds*.

Composition of Non-scaly Buds

If we examine actively growing herbaceous plants, we find that the buds are less conspicuous because of their small size and the usual absence of bud scales. The leaves near the growing stem tip are small; the youngest ones are folded about the stem tip just as they are in scaly buds.

A longitudinal section of a coleus stem tip under the microscope

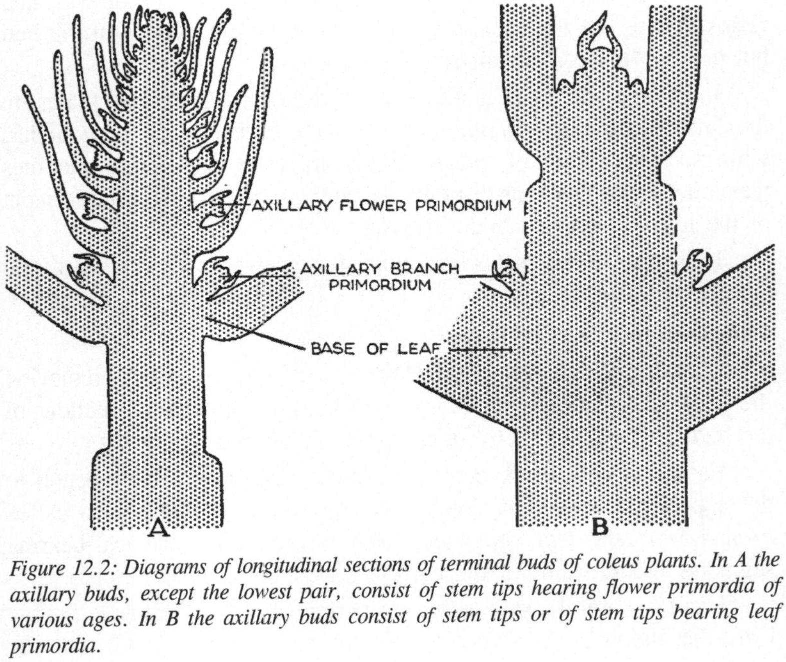

Figure 12.2: Diagrams of longitudinal sections of terminal buds of coleus plants. In A the axillary buds, except the lowest pair, consist of stem tips hearing flower primordia of various ages. In B the axillary buds consist of stem tips or of stem tips bearing leaf primordia.

is seen to have all the structures found in scaly buds except the scales. In addition to the stem tip there are young leaves, with additional buds in their axils.

These small axillary buds within the larger bud may consist either of stem tips bearing leaf primordia or of stem tips bearing flower primordia, depending on whether the plant is continuing vegetative growth or is changing to flower formation.

This change to a reproductive state in coleus is accompanied by a change in the shape of the terminal bud and the upper pair of leaves. The youngest bud primordia consist only of stem tips. Buds of many embryos and those in the "eyes" of potato tubers often consist only of stem tips.

Apical growth is particularly characteristic of stems and roots. A bud then may be defined as a stem tip having extremely short internodes and bearing young leaves or flowers, or both. It may or may not be enclosed by bud scales.

Stem segments bear leaves but once, and all the leaves of a tree or shrub may have been present in some stage of development within the dormant buds of the preceding season.

Adventitious Buds

Branches usually develop from buds in the axils of leaves and may be referred to as axillary branches. Branch buds may., however, develop from internodes of young stems, from roots, and even from leaves. These are *adventitious buds.*

Their occurrence on the internodes of stems is often a result of some interference with the growth of the tissues, as injury or disease. New branches from trunks of trees several years old, and sprouts from the base of stumps were formerly thought to develop solely from adventitious buds, but recent investigations have shown that some of them develop from lateral buds that survive in the bark of the tree for many years.

Others start from adventitious buds. Pollarding (Fig. 85) results in the growth of many new lateral branches from the decapitated stumps of former branches. Perhaps all or nearly all of these new branches in pollarded trees start from latent lateral buds similar to those illustrated in Figure elsewhere in this chapter.

APICAL DOMINANCE

When the terminal bud of a twig is cut off, branches develop from lateral buds that would otherwise have remained dormant or died.

Moreover, such branches usually grow from the uppermost lateral buds. This inhibiting influence of the buds nearest the apex over the buds lower down the stem is known as *apical dominance.*

From present experimental data it appears to be the effect of one or more hormones, one of which is made in the young leaves. If this hormone is artificially applied to the cut ends of decapitated stems it checks the growth of the lateral buds.

Apical dominance, through its influence on the relative growth of different parts of the plant, is one of the primary factors determining the form of a plant.

BUDS AND STEM TYPES

Many trees and shrubs may be recognized at considerable distances by the form of the plant and the type of branching. Such features are often obscured by the effects of environmental factors or by repeated pruning.

Plants of the same species may be far from identical in appearance when growing in dense forests and in the open, or along water courses and on dry uplands. The appearance of ornamental shrubs may be changed markedly by the removal of certain dominant buds, thus allowing for the growth of other buds as noted in the paragraph above.

By comparing a palm, a spruce, and an elm, three types of tree crowns may be distinguished with reference to the mode of branching. Branches usually do not grow from the lateral buds of the palm, and the growth of the terminal bud alone results in an unbranched stem or trunk with a crown of leaves at its summit.

Such a stem is said to he *columnar*. A dominant terminal bud is present in spruce. Each year the main stem increases in length, and from the lateral buds branches grow outward, forming a whorl at the apex of the previous year's growth.

The type of branching which results in a prominent main stem that extends beyond the smaller lateral branches is referred to as *excurrent* branching.

In contrast to the spruce, the terminal buds of the elm are temporary. Since all branches of an elm develop from lateral buds, the main stem appears to be repeatedly divided and subdivided until it is lost in the crown of the tree.

The tree trunk is ultimately terminated by innumerable branchlets, and from this fact the name, *deliquescent* branching was proposed. Although these types of branching are readily distinguishable, all gradations among them occur. The form of a plant is thus seen to depend on the relative development of terminal and lateral buds.

As indicated above, advantage is taken of this knowledge by florists, gardeners, and orchardists. Various ornamental effects in lawn trees and shrubs may be obtained by removing the terminal buds that inhibit the growth of the lateral buds.

Fruit trees and grape vines are "pruned" to regulate the shape of crowns as well as the number and spacing of the branches.

Fruit Spurs

It was indicated earlier that the age of a twig could be discovered by counting the number of scars left in successive years by the terminal

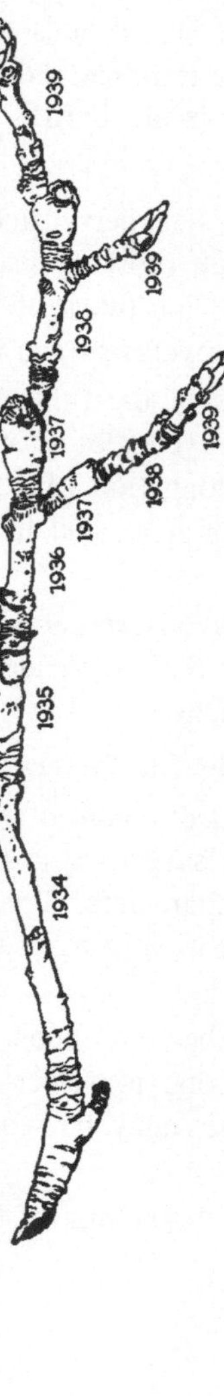

Figure 12.3: Drawing of fruit spur of apple. Fruits were borne every other year. The fruit scars are present only on the annual stem segments formed during oddnumbered years.

bud scales. The distance between two such scars may be indicative of the favorable or unfavorable conditions under which the plant grew in a particular year, or it may be indicative of local internal conditions resulting from the growth of flowers and fruits.

On fruit trees such as apple and pear, the flower buds often occur at the ends of short stems known as "spurs." When the terminal bud is a flower bud, subsequent elongation of the spur is dependent on a lateral bud.

Frequently the spurs bear flowers only in alternate years, and the fruit scars are found only on alternate annual segments of the spur. The spurs usually continue to bear flowers and fruits for many years and grow much more slowly than the vegetative branches.

Successive development of lateral buds results in a crooked spur. The interval between successive terminal bud scale scars is exceedingly short during the years that fruits are borne.

Saint John's Shoots

Some trees, such as elms, hackberry, and certain oaks, have two periods of stem elongation each growing season: one in early spring and another in early summer. The twigs of citrus trees in California have three such intra-seasonal cycles of growth.

The twigs on young trees of the rubber plant *(Hevea)* in Brazil may have as many as eight cycles of growth in one year. In the latitude of Ohio, a second elongation of shoots on elms is usually evident during the latter half of June, and frequently a third extension appears in August.

In Europe these shoots have been called "St. John's shoots" and "Lammas shoots" because of their coincidence with the festivals of St. John's Day and Lammas Day.

Recognition of Trees by Twig Characters

To those of us who are in the habit of recognizing common trees by leaf characters, it is at first surprising to find that identification can be just as certain with twig characters. Trees may be recognized by types of branching, which are usually more obvious in the absence of leaves.

A critical comparison of the bark, buds, lenticels, and pith of our common trees soon enables one to select a few simple distinctive characters by which these trees may be readily identified during the winter.

The prevailingly opposite branching of the younger twigs of ash,

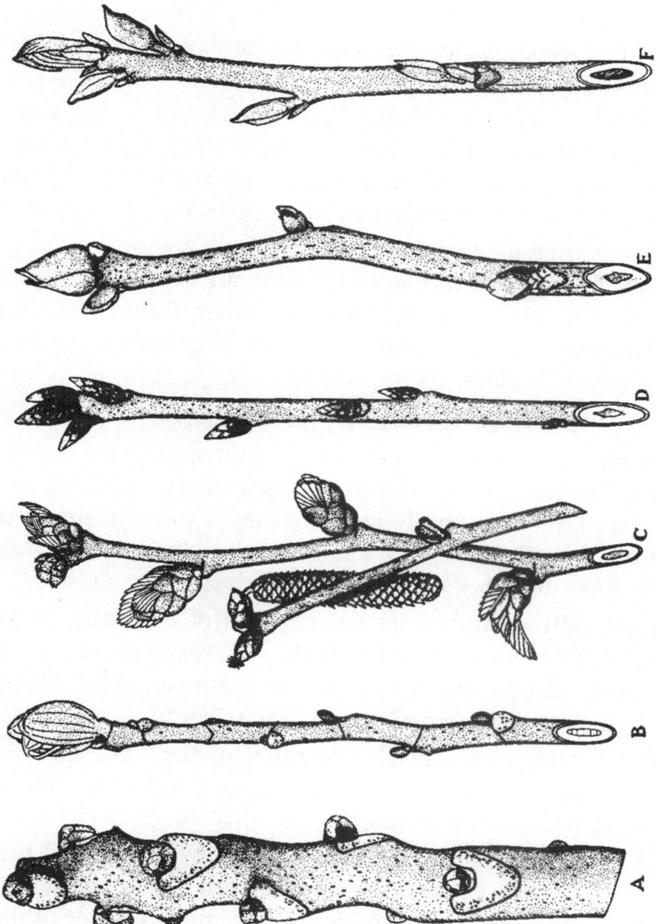

Figure 12.4: Bud and twig characters of a few woody plants: A, tree of heaven (Ailanthus); B, tulip tree (Liriodendron); C, hazel (Corylus); D, red oak (Quercus); E, white heart hickory (Carya alba); F, bitternut hickory (Carya cordif ormis) .

maple, and buckeye; the innumerable and slender ultimate branches of the elm; the papery bark and elongated lenticels of some birches and cherries; the resinous buds of horse-chestnut; the star-shaped pith visible in cross sections of oak twigs; and the chambered pith of walnut and hackberry are a few examples of distinguishing characters that may be selected. Such characters may be used as a basis for making a key for the ready identification of woody plants.

Herbaceous Aerial Stems

Stems of herbs are usually readily distinguished from those of trees and shrubs by the comparatively smaller amounts of woody tissues. Some annual stems, such as those of sunflower, giant ragweed, and a few asters, become woody at maturity in certain habitats, but they are classed with herbaceous plants. It is really a matter of opinion whether certain semi-woody plants should be called herbs.

Many herbs are annuals or biennials, in contrast to trees and shrubs which are generally perennials. Many herbaceous plants have perennial underground stems some of which are very hard and woody; but the annual aerial shoots that develop from these stems are herbaceous.

Herbaceous stems are frequently green and have stomates. Although many external features common to woody stems are absent, herbaceous plants are nevertheless often identified by certain features of their stems, such as shape, color, amount of hairy covering, and the presence of certain types of prickles, thorns, and tendrils.

RHIZOMES AND RUNNERS

A common type of underground stem is represented by the *rhizome* of bluegrass, Johnson grass, cord grass, Canada thistle, and Solomon's seal. Rhizomes grow horizontally at some depth below the surface of the soil, have scale-like, non-green leaves, and axillary lateral buds from which aerial branches develop at certain seasons of the year.

Roots generally appear on the ventral sides of a rhizome at the nodes. The rhizome may be thick and fleshy, or slender and woody as in many grasses. Slender, prostrate stems, such as occur in strawberry and some ferns, are often termed *runners* or *stolons.*

These prostrate stems and all underground stems are excellent means of vegetative propagation. They are distinguished from roots by the presence of nodes and internodes.

The "turf" of lawns and meadows is a shallow layer of soil held together by an interwoven mass of rhizomes and the accompanying roots. Many of these structures are illustrated in other chapter of this book.

TUBERS, CORMS, AND BULBS

An underground stem familiar to everyone is that of the Irish potato. The slender rhizomes of the potato enlarge terminally into thickened structures known as *tubers.* In each eye of the tuber there is a cluster of rudimentary buds.

When the tuber is planted, an aerial branch develops from a bud in one or more of the eyes, depending upon the degree of apical dominance. Large quantities of starch accumulate in the potato tuber, and it has become an important source of food, even replacing bread made from cereals in some countries.

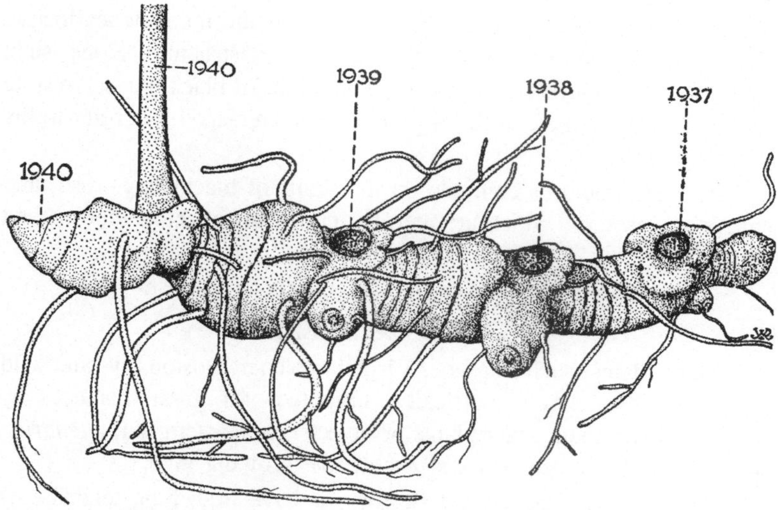

Figure 12.5: Rhizome, roots, and base of an aerial stem of Solomon's seal collected early in July. An erect aerial shoot develops each year from the growing apex of the rhizome. The round scar formed at the end of the season when the aerial stem abscises is the so-called seal. Following the growth of the aerial shoot a new rhizome segment develops annually. The older segments at the opposite end of the rhizome gradually die and decay.

Tuber-like thickening may occur also in aerial stems as in kohlrabi. Some of the so-called short thick roots such as globe radish and turnip, are mostly enlarged hypocotyls.

Another distinctive type of stem resembling the tuber is the *corm,* characteristic of jack-in-the-pulpit, dasheen, and gladiolus. It is a short, upright, thick stem commonly covered by thin membranous scale-like leaves. It bears both lateral and terminal buds.

A *bulb* consists of a short, upright stem bearing thick leaf bases, axillary buds, and a prominent terminal bud. The underground bulbs of hyacinth, tulip, onion, and garlic are familiar to all.

A few bulbs are aerial, such as the sets on the flower stalks of onion and the axillary structures of some lilies. Young bulbs which grow from the axillary buds of the main bulb are sometimes termed *bulblets.*

Failure of the internodes of the stem to elongate may also result in a *head,* as in cabbage; or *a rosette,* as in dandelion, evening primrose, and mullein. Ultimately elongated stems bearing leaves and flowers develop from the terminal bud in the center of the rosette.

Thorns, Spines, and Prickles

Thorns are small, sharp-pointed stems; they may bear buds and leaves. Common examples are the thorns of hawthorn and honey locust. The term *spine* should probably be used for leaf structures alone, such as the spines of barbeiry and the stipular spines of black locust, in spite of the fact that spines and thorns in common language often refer to the same structures.

Pointed structures common on the stems of blackberry, rose, and smilax are *prickles,* which are merely outgrowths of the epidermis and cortex.

CLIMBING AND TWINING STEMS

Many plants, such as grape, Virginia creeper, Boston ivy, and wild cucumber, may extend vertically sometimes for great distances by growing on or about other plants or objects. Some stems have *tendrils'* which encircle the support and anchor the growing vine.

The Virginia creeper and Boston ivy have branching tendrils the ends of which are flattened disks or *hold fasts.* Tiny outgrowths from these holdfasts penetrate the crevices of the surface on which the plants are growing. In this way the vines can "climb" vertical walls.

In the morning glory, the hop, and some beans the stem itself winds about the support and may be called a *twiner.* It is interesting to note that some plants twine clockwise and others counterclockwise, when viewed from above. No explanation of this difference in twining has been established.

Cladodia

This type of stem is found among the cacti and some other desert plants. Leaves are usually absent or ephemeral, and spines often develop on the green stems. Such stems are referred to as *cladodia* (singular *cladodiuin).*

Dormancy in Buds

It is a well-known fact that mature buds of most woody plants, those in the "eyes" of potatoes and in bulbs pass through a dormant period after maturity. During this time there is no external evidence of growth, regardless of the environment in which the buds are placed.

Such dormancy is the result of physiological conditions within the buds, and does not disappear until these inner conditions have changed. In temperate climates it may persist for several months.

It is often commercially important for this dormant period to be shortened as much as possible. Most dormant buds will grow much sooner than usual if they are subjected to various artificial treatments that accelerate certain physiological changes in them. These treatments are referred to as methods of "breaking dormancy."

In temperate climates the internal conditions that cause dormancy in buds disappear under the influence of the low temperature of the winter months. These conditions disappear much more slowly in some species than in others.

As soon as they have disappeared, both flower and leaf buds of many woody plants will grow if the plant or stem cuttings are placed in a warm room and supplied with water. Often root formation occurs at the base of the cuttings.

If the conditions causing dormancy have not disappeared, the plant may slowly die. In recent years the vapor of certain chemical compounds[2] has been used to shorten the period of dormancy in the buds of many plants.

The dormant period of buds of Irish potato has been experimentally shortened from one to four months, depending upon the variety tested. In the latitude of New York some of the common shrubs, such as lilac, flowering plums, crabs, and quinces, if exposed to vapor of ethylene chlorhydrin in December will bloom within a month.

The plants or twigs should be placed within a tight box containing 1 ounce of ethylene chlorhydrin for each 8 cubic feet of space. After two days they should be transferred to a warm room or greenhouse. If these artificial treatments are applied early in autumn the results are unsuccessful.

Treatment with temperatures near freezing for three or four weeks in early autumn before ethylene chlorhydrin is applied shortens the dormant period still more. Methods for breaking dormancy in buds are at present in an experimental stage of development but anyone may try them on some particular plant.

Storage at low and high temperatures, drying, wounding, and treatment with special chemicals have all been used to shorten the dormant period of buds. Diverse results have been obtained with different plants.

In temperate climates dormant buds as well as the latent lateral buds in stems of shrubs and trees survive exposure to low temperatures that would quickly kill actively growing buds. Many dormant buds, however, are killed during unusual winters.

In certain locations wind-blown sand may destroy the buds and all growing regions on the windward side of a tree. This chapter contains a brief account of external similarities in stems and of some of the usual differences in form and habit of growth that may be found. Ordinarily stems may be recognized by the presence of one or more characteristic external features, such as nodes, leaves, and leaf scars.

They may be herbaceous or woody, aerial or underground. They may vary in form from the cylindrical stems of trees, shrubs, herbs, and vines to tendrils, thorns, and the short thick stems characteristic of succulents, tubers, corms, and bulbs.

Most stems bear leaves, flowers, and branches. Under certain conditions roots may also grow as lateral organs on many kinds of stems. The form of the plant and its type of branching are dependent on the relative development of branches from terminal and lateral buds.

Dormancy during summer and autumn is common in buds of most trees and shrubs in temperate climates. The period of this type of dormancy may often be shortened by artificial changes in temperature and by the application of certain chemical compounds. Numerous buds on each plant are kept dormant by apical dominance.

GENERAL REGIONS AND PROCESSES IN STEMS

The facts already learned about processes and structures in cells and tissues of leaves may be applied at once to an understanding of stems. Moreover, we should by this time more fully appreciate and apply four generalizations concerning the relations of structures and processes:

(1) that all structures are the consequences of certain processes;
(2) that these structure-forming processes are conditioned by heredity, and influenced by environmental factors;
(3) that differences in structure, whether they are dependent upon differences in heredity or in environment, were preceded by differences in processes; and
(4) that after the structures are once formed they in turn influence all the processes that continue to occur in them. In the light of these generalizations, reference to any structure as having a "function" leads to a misinterpretation of all plant phenomena.

The more minute differences in stem structure, like those of leaves, are so numerous that one might study them for a lifetime without learning all about them. Much useful and interesting information about processes and structures in stems may be obtained, however, in a short time, and much of it without even a microscope.

All one needs at first is a sharp knife and the stems of several kinds of plants. The familiar trees, shrubs, and herbs of any locality are suitable material. In some of them certain stem structures are more prominent than in others, and there are particular structures that are not present in the stems of all kinds of plants.

A hand lens will be useful in these preliminary observations, and a microscope will be needed to obtain answers to some of the problems that arise.

Woody Stems

If small pieces of woody stems, such as those of apple, ash, and grape, are cut crosswise and split lengthwise, the *bark,* the *wood* (xylem), and the *pith* are at once evident. The relatively greater hardness of the *wood cylinder may* be detected by pressing on each tissue with the edge of the thumb nail.

These three regions are characteristic of all woody stems. If blocks of older and larger woody stems are examined, it is evident that the wood cylinder has increased in diameter, that the bark is somewhat thicker than in younger stems, and that the diameter of the pith has remained unchanged.

Evidently growth in diameter of stems consists of the formation of new xylem and, to a less extent, of new bark tissues. When the older wood in the central part of the stem becomes darker in color it is referred to as *heartwood.*

The younger, lighter-colored wood is called *sapwood.* Almost all the older wood is dead; and when fungi that can digest and oxidize the substances in the cell walls gain entrance into the center of the stem through wounds, they may destroy all but a thin shell of sapwood adjacent to the bark.

Such hollow trees, however, may continue to live and grow for many years. It is evident from the differences in color and texture that the bark is composed of several kinds of tissues and that the cells of the wood cylinder are not all alike.

The annual growth rings (ends of annual cylinders of xylem) may usually be counted in the wood cylinder, though sometimes a hand lens or even a microscope is necessary to distinguish them clearly.

A careful examination of the ends of the xylem tubes (*vessels*), which are visible through a hand lens, will disclose one of the two ways we can distinguish each annual ring of wood. Wood cells must be seen through a microscope for one to discover the second way.

Annual rings are clearly evident in stems of pine and other conifers that have no xylem tubes. Usually radially arranged rays, the *vascular rays,* can be seen in the split surfaces and ends of blocks of wood. The vascular rays in the xylem may be called *xylem rays.*

On the split surfaces they appear as smooth, narrow, thin ribbons of different lengths extending crosswise to the "grain" of the wood. The xylem rays may also be seen on pieces of polished lumber one side of which was cut in a plane parallel to them.

We shall see presently, however, that much of the conspicuous grain of polished wood is dependent upon differences in the wood cells in each annual cylinder of xylem.

Bark Tissues

From the bark of a living woody twig or small branch one may scrape or pick off an outer layer of brownish cork tissue, beneath which there is a layer of parenchyma, which is usually green because many of the cells contain chlorophyll. These two layers of the bark are generally referred to as the *cortex.*

The parenchyma is the *cortical parenchyma,* and any part of it that contains chlorophyll may also be called *cortical chlorenchyma.* The cortex is just within the epidermis, which, being only one cell thick, may be difficult to detect without a microscope.

If one carefully scrapes the cortical chlorenchyma away with the edge of a knife, a number of hard fibers extending lengthwise in the bark become visible. These are *peric ycle fibers.* If the point of the knife is slipped under these fibers, they may be lifted a slight distance from the stem before they break.

Beneath the pericycle fibers is a layer of soft, usually colorless, tissue. When this layer is scraped off, the outer surface of the wood cylinder is visible. This innermost soft tissue of the bark is the *phloem,* containing the food-conducting cells.

In the stems of some species, such as basswood and pawpaw, the phloem also contains fibers, *phloem fibers,* comparable to the pericycle fibers already noted. The term bast fibers is sometimes used commercially to refer to any of the fibers in the bark, whether in the cortex, pericycle, or phloem.

In some twigs the radially arranged vascular rays in the phloem, *phloem rays,* are visible, but they can usually be seen only through a microscope. The phloem and wood cylinder together constitute the vascular cylinder, or *stele,* of the stem. Its outer boundary is the pericycle.

The adjacent innermost layer of cells in the cortex is sometimes referred to as an *endodermis,* but in numerous stems it does not differ in structure from cortical cells immediately external to it.

One may therefore visualize a woody twig as consisting of the *pith,* the *vascular cylinder (stele),* the *cortex,* and the *epidermis* if it is still present. The vascular cylinder in the youngest parts of stems is not completely closed but consists of several separate *vascular bundles* with parenchyma between. Between the bark and the wood cylinder is a cylinder of meristematic cells, the *vascular cambium.*

Since this cambium is but one cell, or at most only a few cells, in thickness, it is too thin to be seen without a microscope. Although in cross section it appears as a ring of very small, thin-walled cells, it should be visualized as a cylinder of meristematic cells immediately surrounding the wood cylinder and lining the innermost layer of the bark.

As the cambium cells divide, new xylem cells develop at the outer surface of the wood cylinder, and new phloem cells develop at the inner surface of the bark. It is the formation of new cells in the cambium that results in the annual increase in diameter of perennial stems. In spring, when the cambium cells are dividing, the bark is easily separated from the wood cylinder.

Those who have made whistles out of twigs or helped peel spruce logs for pulp milling are fully aware of this fact. One should continue to whittle and observe until the relative arrangement of all these general regions is distinctly visualized.

With the exception of the pith, each general region of woody stems should be visualized as a cylinder surrounding other cylinders of the stem. The wood cylinder surrounds the pith, and in turn is surrounded by a cylinder of cambium; the cylinder of bark surrounds both the cambium and the wood cylinder.

Within the bark next to the cambium is a cylinder of phloem, followed in order by cylinders of pericycle, cortical chlorenchyma, cork, and epidermis, provided one is examining a twig or small branch. Within a few years the epidermis, cortex (cortical cork and chlorenchyma), pericycle, and other outer layers of the bark die and slough off.

Consequently, the bark of the trunk of a large tree consists only of the phloem and layers of cork that develop annually from *cork cambiums,* which in turn develop each year from living phloem cells. Most of these features of a woody stem are represented in Figure elsewhere in this chapter.

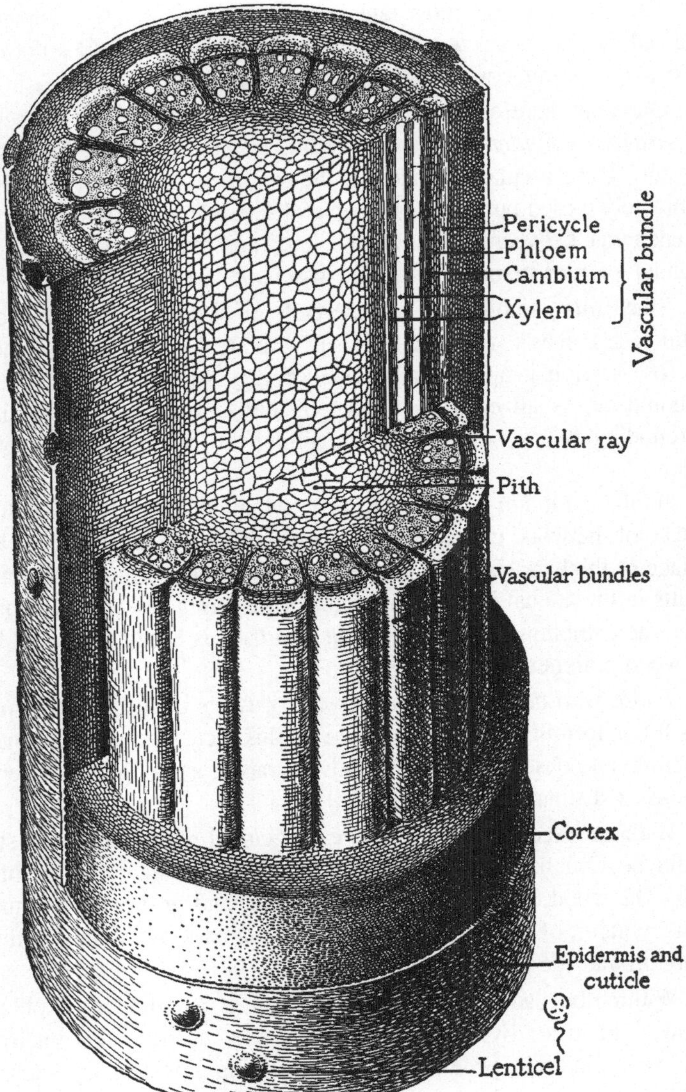

Figure 12.6: Arrangement of general regions and tissues in a stem of moonseed vine.

It is well known that the age of any part of a branch may be ascertained by noting its location in reference to the terminal bud scale scars. Since an annual cylinder of wood is formed each year and the ends of these cylinders seen in cross section appear as distinct rings of wood, the age of the stem may also be ascertained by counting the rings. An annual cylinder of phloem is also formed each year, but the rings of phloem in cross section are not so evident.

They may be seen in the ends of a twig of basswood with the aid of a hand lens. The terminal stem segment contains one cylinder of wood and one of phloem. In the next stem segment below the first terminal bud scale scars there are two cylinders of wood and two of phloem.

The cylinder of wood adjacent to the cambium is the one that extends through both annual stem segments. Likewise, the cylinder of phloem adjacent to the cambium is the one that extends through both stem segments.

In the stem segment below the second terminal bud scale scar there are three cylinders of wood and three of phloem. Only the cylinder of the wood and the cylinder of phloem adjacent to the cambium extend through all three stem segments.

Can you visualize the positions of these cylinders all the way down the branch and trunk of a tree to its base near the soil? If the tree is a century old there should be 100 annual rings of wood at its base. The innermost cylinder of wood adjacent to the pith is as high as the tree was when it was one year old.

The next cylinder is as high as the tree was when it was two years old, and so on to the 100th and youngest cylinder of wood adjacent to the cambium. This cylinder extends all the way from the base of the tree to the tip of the terminal twig.

Each lateral branch also has a similar arrangement of annual cylinders of wood. Likewise, the innermost cylinder of phloem extends all the way from the tip of the terminal twig to the base of the tree. Each branch contains a cylinder of youngest phloem external to the cambium.

The cylinders of xylem and phloem in any stem are continuous with those of the same age in each of its lateral branches. Furthermore, these youngest cylinders of wood and phloem also extend all the way down the root to near its tip.

The older cylinders of wood and phloem in the root, like those in the stem, are successively shorter and shorter until we come to the shortest ones, which were formed during the first season of growth. The pith in the stem, on the other hand, develops from the apical meristem and merely elongates each year and is therefore continuous from the tips of the branches to the base of the trunk.

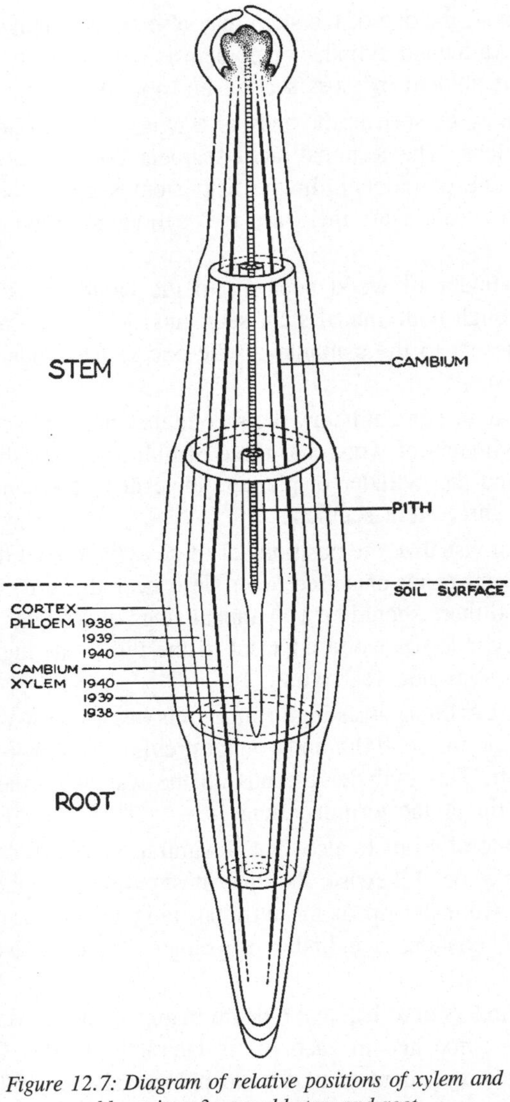

Figure 12.7: Diagram of relative positions of xylem and phloem in a 3-year-old stem and root.

Since annual stem segments bear leaves but once, the youngest cylinder of wood is the only one that is continuous with the xylem in the veins of the leaves of deciduous trees and shrubs.

Likewise, the youngest cylinder of phloem in the stem is the only one that is continuous with the phloem in the veins of these leaves. It is in this youngest cylinder of wood each year that most of the water is pulled up the stem by transpiration. Food translocation occurs mostly in the youngest phloem.

GIRDLING

As the term is used by botanists, girdling consists in completely removing a band of bark and cambium all the way around the stem. If the girdle is made on the trunk of the tree within a few feet of the ground and below all lateral branches, an adequate translocation of sugar from leaves to roots no longer occurs in most species of plants, but movement of water in the xylem from roots to leaves still continues.

In trees the roots and base of the trunk below the girdle may contain enough food to survive for a year or two after the girdle is made. Death and decay of the roots are ultimately followed by the death of the plant above the girdle as a result of desiccation.

In most species of plants apical dominance of the tops is sufficient to inhibit the growth of sprouts from the base of the trunk even in girdled trees. When excessive girdling annuls this apical dominance sprouts may grow from the roots or base of the trunk, as they usually do when a live tree is suddenly cut down.

Likewise, if there are lateral branches below the girdle, or if apical dominance fails to inhibit the growth of sprouts from the base of the tree, the tree may survive for many years. If the bark is not completely removed, or if the girdle is very narrow, new phloem may develop from the cambium before accumulated food in the roots is exhausted, and the tree may survive.

When the girdled area does not become dry and is otherwise protected by grafting wax, a new cambium and phloem may develop across the girdle while the roots are still alive. Advantage is sometimes taken of this fact in horticultural practice. Branches, or even the main trunk, of fruit trees are girdled to bring about internal conditions favorable to the formation of flowers and fruits without killing the tree.

Girdling prevents not only the downward translocation of sugar, but also the upward translocation of the amino acids and proteins made in the roots. Girdling is often incorrectly done in that so much of the younger xylem is cut away with the bark that the movement of water to the leaves is greatly diminished.

In such cases the leaves wilt within a few days, and the top above the girdle dies of desiccation before the roots starve to death. With the death of the top its apical dominance disappears, and sprouts may grow from the roots or from the base of the trunk. Apparent exceptions to these statements of course need further analysis than given here.

HERBACEOUS STEMS

If stems of herbaceous plants, such as those of common weeds, garden plants, and crop plants, are cut and dissected, as directed above for woody stems, soft tissues and vascular bundles are readily discernible, and in some species a hard outer rind is evident.

Here again differences in color and texture are indicative of different kinds of tissues definitely arranged. In stems of dicots the cortex and circle of bundles surround a relatively large pith. Ridges of the pith that extend between the bundles may be visible in cross sections as pith rays.

In old herbaceous stems, as those of sunflower, there may be a conspicuous ring of xylem with narrow xylem rays. Chlorenchyma is usually present in the cortex of herbaceous stems and sometimes in the phloem and pith. In a monocot like corn, the bundles are scattered throughout the stem.

In many species of both monocots and dicots the cells of the pith disintegrate at an early stage of development, with the result that the stem is hollow.

If an herbaceous stem bearing leaves is cut off near the surface of the soil and the cut end of the stem is placed in a weak solution of eosin or other dye that stains the xylem, the dye is pulled up the stem with the water, and the stained bundles in both stems and leaves may be seen more readily.

The stems of most monocots differ from those of dicots also in the absence of a vascular cambium. Hence, stems of most monocot plants, even though they are perennial, do not increase in diameter from year to year.

For example, no slender bamboo stem ever becomes a big bamboo stem, and no big bamboo stem was ever a slender bamboo stem. The diameter of monocot stems usually does not increase from year to year. There are, however, some exceptions.

In the stems of some monocots such as palms and yuccas a temporary cambium develops periodically from cells in the cortex of the stem. The stem thus increases in diameter from time to time.

Place of growth in length. The place of growth in length of the stem may be recognized by both its external and internal appearance. At the top of the stem the leaves are relatively small and young, and several of the internodes are not fully elongated. Internally, parenchyma is the most prominent tissue.

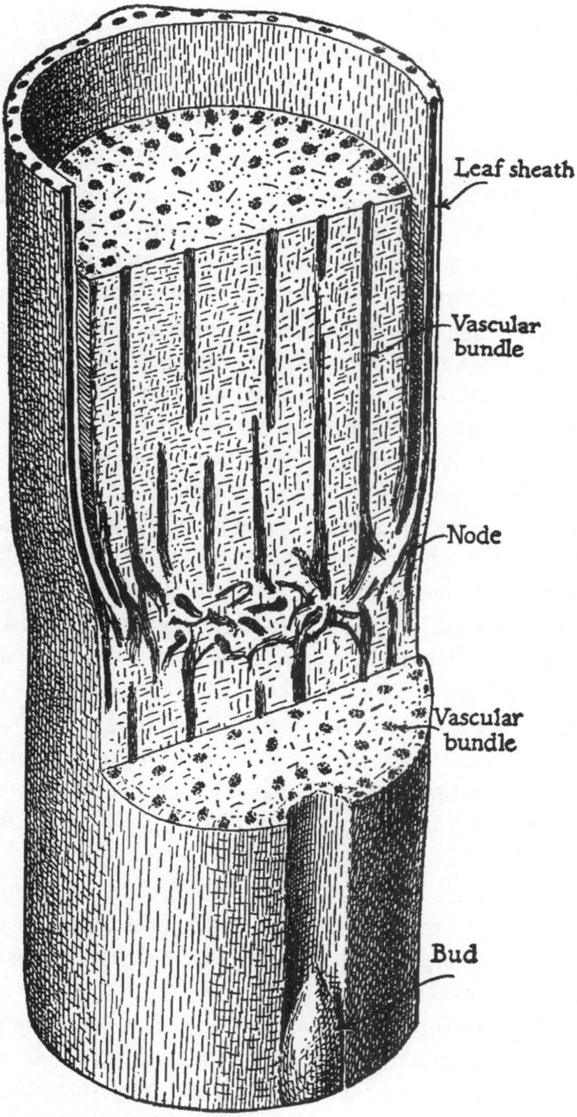

Figure 12.8: Arrangement of tissues in a solid monocot stem (Panicum).

At the extreme tip only parenchyma is present. We have already seen other chatper of this book how such external factors as light and gravity may influence the direction of growth of an elongating stem tip. To see the growing tip of a grass stem one must first carefully remove the ensheathing leaves. Unless the plant is very young the stem tip will be bearing rudimentary flowers entirely hidden within the leaf sheaths. As the grass stem grows, the bases of the internodes are the last parts of the stem to stop elongating and become mature.

SIZE OF STEMS

The forerunner of the whole stem system of a plant is the apical meristem in the bud (plumule) of the embryo. Through the formation and enlargement of cells in this apical meristem the stem elongates and axillary buds develop from cortical and epidermal cells along its sides.

From some of these axillary buds lateral branches develop, each of which also has an apical meristem. Although there are seasonal periods of growth and dormancy, it might appear that the stem of a perennial plant would have unlimited growth in length.

The vascular cambium of woody stems also is perennial, with alternating periods of growth and dormancy. Trees and shrubs, therefore, might be expected to increase in diameter indefinitely. From observation, however, it is evident that there are limits to the age of trees and also to both height and diameter growth of stems.

Furthermore, among the different species there is a wide range in these limits. The smallest species of trees never exceed a few feet in height and a few inches in diameter. Among herbaceous plants there are many species that are even more restricted in age, height, and diameter.

The tallest trees may exceed 300 feet, and the diameter of some trees may become more than 30 feet. Vines in the tropics may become a thousand feet or more in length. Many of us are impressed with the superlative.

Large trees, tall trees, and old trees elicit considerable interest as shown by their frequent mention in the press. Some of the present-day trees are the largest and have attained the greatest age of any plants that ever existed.

What determines the limits of age, size, and height? It would be interesting to consider some of the factors correlated with size limits, but space can be given here only to a few suggestions and to a summary of reports of the largest trees. What world events were in progress when these trees were seedlings?

That the stein may have potentialities of unlimited growth may be demonstrated with plants, such as English ivy, that propagate readily from cuttings. To do this it is necessary only to use repeatedly the upper part of the same stem as a cutting and to keep it in an environment that is favorable to continuous vegetative growth. That is, it must not be placed in an environment in which the terminal vegetative bud will become a flower bud.

Similarly, artificial cultures of root tips, described in other chapter of this book, are evidence that the apical meristem of a root tip has potentialities of unlimited growth if it is repeatedly removed from the remainder of the root system and kept in a suitable environment. What then are the factors that limit the growth in length of stems and roots when they are attached to the whole plant?

Processes in Stems

All the processes characteristic of a vegetative cell occur in the cells of stems. In addition, there are certain processes that occur in some vegetative cells but not in others. Photosynthesis does not occur in all vegetative cells, but such processes as respiration, digestion, and assimilation do.

On the other hand, photosynthesis occurs in any cell of a leaf, or a stem, or a root that contains chlorophyll and is exposed to a suitable environment. But many leaves and stems do not contain chlorophyll. All we can say is that in most ferns and seed plants photosynthesis occurs more abundantly in leaves than in stems and roots.

When all kinds of leaves, stems, and roots are compared, there are very few processes that can be said to be distinctly characteristic of any one of these three types of vegetative organs.

Perhaps there is no process that occurs in all stems that does not occur in some roots or some leaves. There are very few species of plants which have leaves that bear other leaves; roots may never bear leaves, but there are also certain kinds of stems that do not bear leaves.

Flowers do not develop directly from leaves or from roots; neither do they develop on all types of stems. When water and salts move from the soil to the leaves of a dandelion plant, the distance they move through the roots is many times the distance they move through a stem.

There are certain species of plants in which photosynthesis occurs primarily in the stems. There are others in which the absorption of water and inorganic salts occurs primarily in the leaves and stems. The reader may find it both interesting and instructive to add to these examples of similarities among plant organs.

On the basis of what has been learned so far, it should not be difficult for the reader to formulate intelligent answers to questions that may be asked about stem processes. Why may the girdling of a tree result in its death? Why do people girdle trees?

Why may they sometimes fail to obtain the desired results? Why may the leaves soon wilt when the girdle is made deep enough to include a few cylinders of sapwood? If a tree is wounded, will it "bleed to death"? How does healing occur?

What is the gravest danger to which a tree is exposed when it is wounded, and how may it be prevented? How do trunks of trees become hollow? Why may hollow trees live for many years? If a nail is driven in a tree will it continue to remain the same distance from the base of the tree as the tree increases in height from year to year?

Why are there anastomosing longitudinal ridges and crevices in the bark of a tree? What tissue of a tree is used as a source of lumber? Why do plants bearing leaves absorb more water from the soil than they do when leaves are removed?

Why may a young tree have a longer growing period during the summer than an older tree of the same species? Why may the new branches of a pollarded tree grow several feet in length and bear numerous leaves in a single season, while those of an unpollarded tree may grow but a few inches in length and bear relatively few leaves? Can you add other questions, and answer them?

TISSUES AND PROCESSES OF STEMS

Some of the general regions of stems discussed in the preceding chapter are composed of several kinds of tissues. This is particularly true of the cortex, the bark, and the stele. On the other hand, the pith, vascular cambium, endodermis, cork cambium, cork, and the epidermis each consist of a single tissue.

Moreover, some of the tissues of stems are *complex tissues,* being composed of a system of several kinds of cells. This is particularly true of xylem and phloem, if we regard each of these as but one tissue.

Stem tissues that develop from cells in the apical meristem are called *primary tissues*. Those that develop from cells in the vascular cambium, or cork cambium, are called *secondary tissues*. In stems of most monocots, therefore, all the tissues are primary tissues.

In stems of woody plants nearly all the xylem and phloem and the cork are secondary tissues; and the others, together with the first strands of xylem and phloem adjacent to the pith, are primary tissues.

The only primary tissues that may still be present in the trunk of a large tree are the pith and a small amount of primary xylem. On the other hand, stems of herbaceous plants such as coleus consist mostly of primary tissues. Certain microscopic structures in these tissues will be given further attention.

Apical growth and the origin of primary tissues. At the extreme apex of the stem there is a group of small, closely packed, isodiametric, meristematic cells, the apical meristem. Immediately below it is a zone of cells in various stages of enlargement, some of which are also dividing.

In the apical meristem food is being changed into new protoplasm, pectic compounds, and cellulose, as the cells divide and the daughter cells become as large as the mother cells. In the zone characterized by cell enlargement, growth of the cell wall, vacuolation, and the osmotic absorption of water are prominent processes.

Apparently there is a continued synthesis of protoplasm, and the protoplasm that is present is being pushed out against the cell wall by the enlargement of the vacuole formed by the coalescence of many smaller vacuoles accompanying the entrance of water.

In the zone of cell enlargement, and especially toward its lower end, some of the cells are visibly different from others; that is, the results of cell differentiation are becoming evident.

Various types of cell differentiation in stem tips may be noted;

(1) some of the cells soon become the primordia of leaves and axillary buds;

(2) these axillary buds, and sometimes the terminal bud, while still meristematic, may become either vegetative buds or flower buds;

(3) some of the cells may retain their meristematic condition and become the vascular cambium;

(4) many other cells merely enlarge with or without evident change in form and composition, and, because of their position, origin, shape, and differences in cell walls, may be recognized as belonging to the epidermis, cortex, pericycle, phloem, xylem, or pith; and finally

(5) the cross walls of some of the xylem cells partly disintegrate, leaving long tubes, or vessels, the lateral walls of which become thickened and lignified, with spiral thickenings that are particularly conspicuous.

Numbers (1) and (2) above may be considered organ differentiations in meristematic tissue, while numbers (4) and (5) are tissue differentiations in enlarging and maturing cells. All the tissues formed by the differentiation of cells that originated in the apical meristem are primary tissues. The above description applies to both woody and herbaceous stems of dicots.

It applies also to growing stem tips of pines and other conifers, except that xylem vessels do not develop in conifers. Secondary xylem and phloem soon begin to develop from cambial cells.

In stems of monocots, such as grasses, in addition to the apical meristem there is a temporary zone of meristematic cells at the base of each internode. This is the softest and weakest part of a growing grass stem.

In young woody stems a cork cambium develops from cells in the cortex, and a layer of cork may develop on the new stem segment before the close of the first growing season. In some species of plants latent root primordia develop from parenchyma cells in the pericycle.

Just below the apical meristem short internodes, as well as nodes bearing primordia of leaves and axillary buds, are recognizable. Ultimately, flower primordia develop either from the apical meristem or from the meristems of axillary buds.

The cells in the center of the apical meristem are forerunners of pith, which is surrounded by longitudinal strands of primary xylem.

The Pith

Since the pith develops directly from the central cells of the apical meristem, it increases in length as the stem elongates; thus, it is continuous from year to year in perennial stems. In time the cells of the pith usually die, and the protoplasm disintegrates.

All soluble substances may diffuse out, and only the cell walls remain. In stems of some plants (walnut, hackberry, etc.), some of the cell walls also disintegrate or collapse, and the pith becomes chambered. In many species of herbs all the cells of the pith soon disintegrate and the stem becomes hollow.

The stems of all these herbs are solid at the tip where the pith is young and intact. In perennial plants the pith, or certain cells in it, may live from one to many years: one year or less in the European larch, 10 years in Scotch pine, 17 years in horse chestnut, 27 years in gray birch, and more than a century in a columnar cactus of the American desert.

The pith cells in this cactus not only remained alive from 100 to 150 years, but when the pith was wounded some of the cells near the wound divided and formed new tissues.

The Epidermis

The epidermis of the stem is continuous with that of the leaves and is comparable to it in most respects. The outer wall is usually thick and heavily cutinized. Glaucous stems, like glaucous leaves, are covered with wax.

Epidermal hairs are the rule rather than the exception. Stomates are present, though usually not as abundant as in leaves. In many stems they ultimately become ruptured by lenticels that develop from cortical cells beneath them.

The first cork cambium that develops in stems occasionally originates in epidermal cells. The epidermis of a leaf lives as long as the leaf. This is also true of some stems; but in perennial stems that increase in diameter by cambial growth, the epidermis is soon ruptured, except in those plants where it continues to grow for a few years.

The Cortex

When all types of stems are compared, the cortex is found to be a very diversified region. It consists primarily of parenchyma cells. The outer layer of cells just beneath the epidermis is often referred to as *a hypodermis;* the inner layer of cells adjacent to the pericycle is the *endodermis.*

Each of these layers of cells may be parenchyma and differ little if at all from neighboring cells, or they may be easily distinguished by the shape of the cells and thickness of cell walls.

The hypodermis may be composed of ordinary parenchyma cells, sclerenchyma cells, collenchyma cells, or palisade cells similar to those in leaves.

The first cork cambium in a stem frequently develops from the hypodermis. The development of cork from cork cambium is similar, whether it occurs in herbaceous stems, woody stems, roots, or any other plant organ.

Cork cells are short-lived; but the cell walls, which are composed primarily of layers of suberin and lignified cellulose lamellae, last indefinitely because very few kinds of non-green plants can digest them. On stems that increase in diameter by cambial growth, however, the cortex is ruptured and sloughed off.

In herbaceous plants the cortex may live as long as the stem does, but in many woody stems it may die and be sloughed off while the stem is comparatively young.

New cork cambiums periodically develop in deeper-lying tissues.

When cork develops in the pericycle, it prevents the diffusion of water from the xylem to the cortex, which soon dies. In beech the cortex lives and grows as long as the tree is alive.

It is also long-lived in birch and certain other trees. Chlorenchyma is present in the cortex of most young aerial stems. Sclerenchyma and collenchyma are frequently present in the cortex.

In some species of plants there may be many other kinds of cells in the cortex, such as isolated sclerenchyma cells (stone cells or grit cells), groups of stone cells surrounded by a cambium, and isolated cells of groups of cells containing anthocyanins, essential oils, tannins, or calcium oxalate crystals.

Various canals or ducts, such as resin ducts, essential oil ducts, and latex tubes, may also be found in the cortex of some stems. No one of these features, however, is limited to the cortex or eveii to the stem of a plant.

Latex, the milky juice found in many species of plants, is collected in large quantities from a few kinds of plants as a source of rubber. Latex tubes, which originate from cells in the embryo in some species, grow through the parenchyma tissues of the plant as if they were parasites.

In other species they are formed by the disintegration of scattered parenchyma cells. Resin ducts are surrounded by special kinds of cells.

The Pericycle

As noted earlier, the pericycle is the peripheral cylinder of the stele (vascular cylinder) and in cross section appears as a ring of cells. It varies from one to several cells in thickness. When it is composed entirely of parenchyma it may be difficult to recognize.

In fact, in some stems cortical parenchyma appears to extend all the way from the epidermis to the phloem; that is, there is no visible differentiation of either endodermis or pericycle. When sclerenchyma (pericycle fibers) is present, the pericycle is easily recognized.

These fibers may occur as continuous cylinders or as separate strands, and because of their location they often appear to be the outer part of a vascular bundle. Some of the important fibers of commerce are pericycle fibers-for example, flax and hemp.

Those of flax are mainly cellulose, and are less lignified than hemp fibers. The pericycle is important in one other way. It is the region in which the primordia of lateral roots, and frequently those of adventitious stems, develop. It is from the pericycle that roots usually develop on stem cuttings. In some species, such as willow and cottonwood, root primordia develop in twigs on the tree and remain dormant unless the twig is exposed to conditions favorable to their further development.

The Phloem

The phloem is a complex tissue in which several kinds of cells may usually be recognized with the aid of the microscope. The chief food-conducting cells are the *sieve tubes*, which are generally elongate, short-lived, and interconnected through perforated diaphragms called *sieve plates*.

Associated with the sieve tubes, perhaps in all the vascular plants except ferns and gymnosperms, are long-lived, slender parenchyma cells

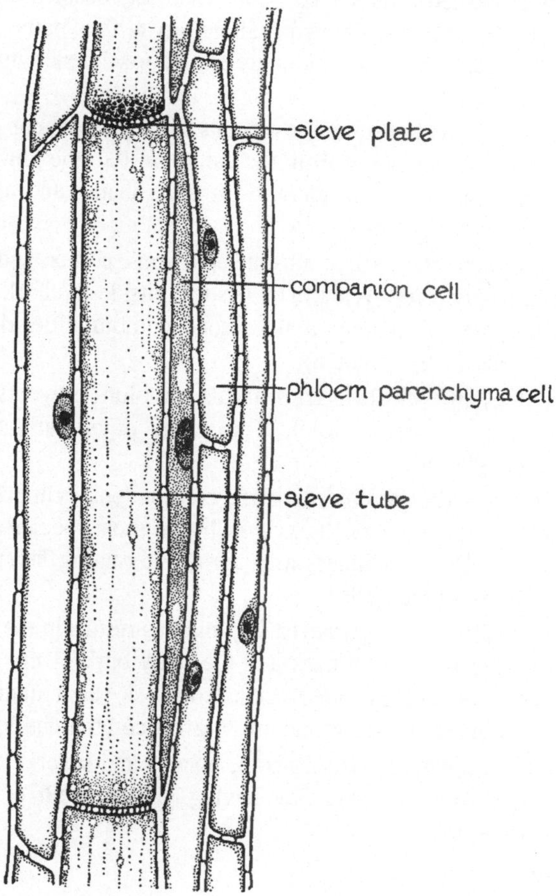

Figure 12.9: Types of cells in the phloem of a gourd stem.

called *companion cells*. Various other parenchyma cells, not associated directly with the sieve tubes, may also be present.

All these cells together constitute the part of the phloem in which conduction of food may take place and in which starch frequently accumulates. In the phloem of many vascular plants, except ferns, some gymnosperms, and most herbs, there are sclerenchyma cells, known as *phloem fibers,* comparable to the fibers of the pericycle.

These fibers may occur in bands, as hollow cylinders surrounding softer tissue, singly, or irregularly. The commercially important fiber, jute, is obtained from the phloem of the jute plant. The individual phloem fiber is a long, tapering cell, usually with lignified walls.

Short thick-walled cells, called *stone cells,* may occur in the phloem either associated with the fibers or alone. In a few plants, such as sycamore and beech, the stone cells are the only sclerenchyma cells in the phloem.

Vascular rays are present in most plants having a vascular cambium. That part of the ray extending from the cambium into the phloem is the *phloem ray,* and it varies considerably in size, shape, and appearance in different species of plants.

In stems of most trees and shrubs the epidermis, cortex, and pericycle are present for only a few years. The tissues outside the cork cambium gradually die, and ultimately a new cork cambium develops from parenchyma cells in the phloem.

The cylinder of cork formed from this cambium prevents diffusion of water to tissues external to it. The whole outer bark soon dies, cracks, and sloughs off.

In the birch and cork oak there are conspicuous cylinders of cork that resemble annual rings of the xylem, but in most species such rings are not evident. These cylinders are due to alternating layers of thin-walled and thick-walled cells.

The thin-walled cells separate easily, and this results in the separation of the papery sheets of birch bark and the scaly bark of the sycamore. External masses of cork in such trees as cork oak accumulate in layers several centimeters in thickness and are of great commercial importance.

Stems of pumpkin, squash, tomato, potato, and several other kinds of plants differ from the usual by having phloem both external and internal to the xylem.

The Xylem

The xylem of a woody dicot is a complex tissue composed chiefly of *vessels,* or *water-conducting tubes; tracheids; wood fibers; xylem parenchyma cells,* and *xylem ray cells.* A vessel may be several millimeters, several feet, or even yards in length.

The length of a vessel depends upon the number of end walls that disintegrate in the row of cells from which it is formed. Old vessels may be closed by tyloses, outgrowths from adjacent xylem parenchyma.

In the xylem of conifers the vessels and sometimes the fibers are absent; the chief cells are tracheids and xylem ray cells. The tracheids are both water-conducting and wood cells. They are thick-walled and spindle-shaped, and have thin areas or *pits* in the walls.

Certain features of the xylem are more easily understood in relation to the growth of the cambium.

The Vascular Cambium

In order to see the cambium of stems clearly, one must have thin sections cut from *growing* stems of dicots or conifers. Between the easily recognized xylem and phloem in cross sections of these stems there is a region composed of several layers of thin-walled cells.

The cells near the middle of this region are very small and thinwalled. These are the cambial cells from which additional xylem and phloem develop by cell division, enlargement, and differentiation and bring about an increase in the diameter of stems.

Adjacent to and on both the phloem and the xylem sides of this cambium there are a few layers of cells which are thin-walled but inceasingly larger at greater distances from the cambium.

One may therefore see from one to several layers of cells in the processes of enlargement and differentiation between the cambium and the mature phloem on the one side and the cambium and the mature xylem on the other.

In the larger stems the cambium is a closed cylindrical sheath between the xylem and the phloem, that is, between the xylem and the bark; but in the younger part of the stem it is present only in the individual vascular bundles, which are separated from one another by broad rays of pith-like parenchyma.

As the young stem increases in age cambium usually develops from the parenchyma cells between the bundles and becomes a complete cylinder in the stem. Since the xylem of woody perennials increases in diameter from year to year, it presses against the encircling bark. Some of the cells of the bark become crushed, and the outer dead parts of the bark are ruptured.

As a result, the outer bark of woody perennials is usually furrowed and irregularly broken. In most parts of the world cambial growth is limited to a few months of each year. In woody perennials of temperate climates it begins in the young twigs about the time the buds begin to open in spring, and somewhat later in the older branches and trunk of the tree.

Two or three months later the cambium becomes dormant in the trunk of the tree and remains in that condition until the following spring. Each season cambial growth may begin first in the twigs or in the larger branches.

Growth of the cambium appears to be dependent upon hormones from the leaves, but the evidence upon which this inference is based is too limited for final conclusions at present.

The xylem cells and vessels that develop in spring are usually larger than those that develop toward the close of the growth period in summer. Consequently the appearance of the inner portion of each annual ring of xylem as seen in cross section is quite different from that of the outer portion of the ring.

Without these differences in *spring wood* and *summer wood* the annual rings of growth would not be evident to the eye. The width of the annual rings in particular species varies with the age of the individual plant and with the fluctuations in environmental factors from year to year.

In certain localities the effects of fluctuations in water supply and humidity are more prominent than those of all other factors combined. Tree rings may therefore be used, along with other data, as an index of periods of drought and of abundant moisture. Such studies have shown that there are rather definite and predictable cycles of periods of drought.

Comparison of annual rings of living trees with those of wooden beams used in dwellings in the southwestern part of the United *States* has made it possible to date quite accurately certain events in the lives of the cliff dwellers and other ancient peoples as far back as a thousand years or more.

Ring-porous, Diffuse-porous, and Non-porous Wood

When the vessels and xylem cells that develop in spring are large and numerous, the annual rings are particularly conspicuous. Such wood is *ringporous*. If the vessels are of about the same size and are scattered uniformly in the annual ring, the wood is said to be *diffuseporous*. In conifer stems, where no vessels occur, the wood is *non-porous*.

These facts are useful in the identification of woods of different species.

GRAIN OF WOOD

When boards are cut from stems and polished, various patterns of wood are often conspicuous. Such patterns are dependent on the relative size of the cells and vessels of spring and summer wood, on the width of the annual rings, and on the plane in which the saw passes through the log with reference to the xylem rays. "Quarter-sawed" boards are cut parallel to these rays.

Tangential or "slab" cuts at various angles to the rays result in a variety of patterns. The summer wood is harder than the spring wood and takes a finer polish; and this difference is the cause of the often attractive grain patterns of furniture, panels, and cabinet work.

In perfect radial sections the grain appears as straight lines crossed by patches of xylem rays. When the cut passes through several annual rings, as in slab-cut boards, the pattern is most striking.

Xylem rays in oaks and some other trees are prominent, and in quarter-sawed boards from such trees the rays appear as the light-colored areas. If the annual rings are narrow, the wood is "fine-grained"; if they are wide, "coarse-grained." Some patterns of wood have special names.

The "silver grain" of quarter-sawed oak refers to the large wood rays. If the patterns are wavy in appearance, as they sometimes are in birch, cherry, and chestnut, the wood is regarded as "curly grain." The best known is the "bird's-eye grain" of certain maples.

This is caused by the presence of numerous partly dormant buds from which minute, embedded lateral stems develop. These small "stems within a stem" are the "eyes" of the wood seen in tangential section.

The Monocot Stem

Since the stems of monocots were discussed with those of dicots and conifers, some of the major facts about them may be summarized. The vascular bundles are scattered throughout the stem.

No cambium, except temporary vestiges, occurs in the bundles, and hence secondary growth, so evident in dicots and conifers, does not occur. The bundles are composed of xylem and phloem surrounded by a bundle sheath of more or less sclerenchyma-like cells.

Growth in length occurs at the apex and also at the bases of several of the uppermost internodes. The epidermis is composed of hard, thick walls and may be subtended by several rows of thick-walled cells, the

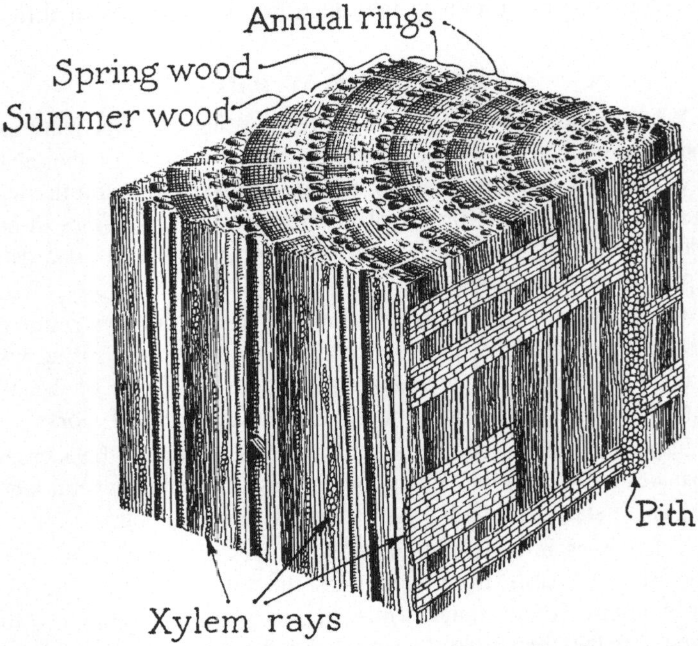

Figure 12.10: Diagram of a block of oak wood, magnified to show the arrangement of tissues which underlies the patterns on polished wood surfaces.

hypodermis. The epidermis, together with the hypodermis, is sometimes called the *rind;* this is evident in the corn stem.

The remainder of the stem consists of parenchyma. It is usually impossible to distinguish pericycle or cortex or pith. In some few monocots the central region is devoid of bundles, and the central parenchyma resembles a pith. Many monocots have hollow stems.

Because of the absence of a cambium, stems of most monocots do not increase in diameter after the cells are mature. The bamboo and corn, for example, grow to considerable heights but remain slender.

Many perennial monocots have underground stems that elongate each year and enlarge the area occupied by the plant. Such aerial stems as those of palms, dragon tree, and yucca have secondary thickening.

Cells in the pericycle or parts of the undifferentiated parenchyma become meristematic, and from them additional parenchyma and new vascular bundles develop.

Healing of Wounds

As a result of the injurious effects of winds, ice, insects, and fungi, areas of living tissue on trees and branches may be killed or completely removed. Girdling a tree is another way of destroying its living tissue. It is perhaps evident by now that "recovery" from such "wounds" is possible only through the activity of the vascular cambium.

Expert "tree surgeons" are able to save valuable trees, apparently ruined by mechanical injury, disease, and decay, by removing the injured areas and covering the exposed tissue with wax, tar, or other substances that reduce water loss and prevent the entrance of destructive organisms.

If the injured area is not too large, the scar may in time be covered completely by tissue that develops from a cambium.

GRAFTING AND BUDDING

The importance of the cambium has long been recognized in grafting and budding. Many cultivated plants, especially fruit trees, do not "come true to seed" and must be propagated vegetatively. Sometimes it is commercially advisable to use vegetative multiplication, instead of seeds, for other reasons.

One common practice used in perpetuating plants without the use of seeds is grafting. In grafting, a twig or stem (the scion) of one plant is attached to the stem or root of another plant (the stock).

If the cambiums of the stock and the scion are in perfect contact and if proper precautions are taken, union of the meristematic tissues takes place rapidly.

There are many types of grafting, and reference to any manual on

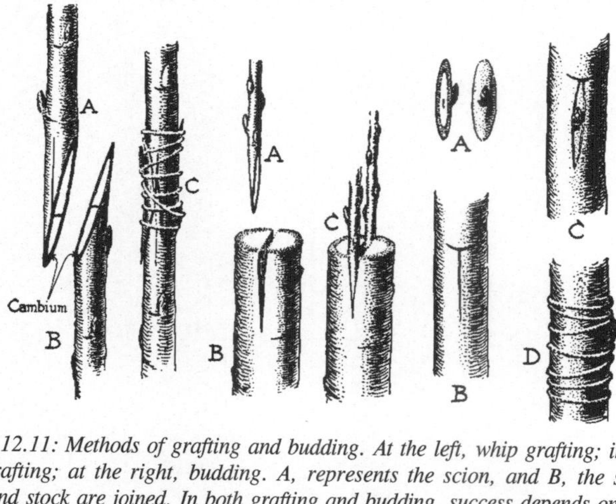

Figure 12.11: Methods of grafting and budding. At the left, whip grafting; in the middle, cleft grafting; at the right, budding. A, represents the scion, and B, the stock. C, the scion and stock are joined. In both grafting and budding, success depends on bringing the cambium of the scion into contact with the cambium of the stock.

horticultural practices will indicate the preferred methods for different kinds of plants.

Budding or bud grafting differs from twig grafting only in the fact that a bud and some additional tissues are inserted in a T-shaped slit in a branch. If the cambiums of the bud tissue and the branch are in contact, the two pieces soon unite.

It is evident that neither twig grafting nor budding is possible in stems without cambiums, as for example in corn, wheat, rye, and many other grasses. A further discussion of grafting is given in other chapter of this book.

INDEX

D

E

Q

R

S

T

U

V